Improving Student Retention in Higher Education

D0217396

Improving Student Retention in Higher Education explores the issue of student retention in higher education and teaching and learning approaches that encourage students to continue with their studies. Underpinned by research indicating that students are more likely to continue if they are engaged in their studies and have developed networks and relationships with their fellow students, *Improving Student Retention in Higher Education* exemplifies best practice of innovative and inclusive teaching and learning approaches, from a range of countries. The book:

- Frames the major aspects of the topic of student retention
- Includes action research-based cases by higher education (HE) teachers globally
- Discusses practical curriculum development strategies that are student responsive, engaging and active
- Features chapters exploring student diversity, alternative teaching and learning approaches and disciplinary study
- Includes reflective reader questions that underpin curriculum development, and thus consider teaching, learning and students

Improving Student Retention in Higher Education appeals to academics, student affairs administrators, policy makers, researchers and support staff in Higher Education.

Glenda Crosling is Senior Lecturer and Education Advisor in the Faculty of Business and Economics at Monash University and works with programs to develop and enhance teaching and learning quality.

Liz Thomas is Professor and Director, Widening Participation Research Centre, Edge Hill University, UK. She is also Senior Advisor for Widening Participation, at the Higher Education Academy, and works for Action on Access, the National Co-ordination Team for Widening Participation.

Margaret Heagney is Co-ordinator of the Student Equity Unit and an Honorary Research Associate in the Faculty of Education at Monash University, Australia.

Improving Student Retention in Higher Education

The role of teaching and learning

Edited by
Glenda Crosling, Liz Thomas and
Margaret Heagney

Routledge
Taylor & Francis Group

LONDON AND NEW YORK

First published 2008
by Routledge
2 Park Square, Milton Park, Abingdon, Oxon OX4 3UD

Simultaneously published in the USA and Canada
By Routledge
270, Madison Avenue, New York, NY, 10016

Routledge is an imprint of the Taylor & Francis Group, an informa business

Typeset in Times New Roman by Keyword Group Ltd
Printed and bound in Great Britain by
TJ International Ltd, Padstow, Cornwall

British Library Cataloguing in Publication Data
A catalogue record for this book is available from the British Library

Library of Congress Cataloging in Publication Data
Crosling, Glenda M. (Glenda Marian), 1950
   Improving student retention in higher education: the role of teaching
   and learning / Glenda Crosling, Liz Thomas, and Margaret Heagney.
   p. cm.
   Includes bibliographical references and index.
   1. College dropouts—Prevention.
   I. Thomas, Liz (Elizabeth) II. Heagney, Margaret. III. Title.
   LC148.15.C76 2007
   378.1'6913—dc22
   2007019054

ISBN 10: 0-415-39920-3 (hbk)
ISBN 10: 0-415-39921-1 (pbk)
ISBN 13: 978-0-415-39920-3 (hbk)
ISBN 13: 978-0-415-39921-0 (pbk)

Preface

Introduction

This book focuses on the significant issue in contemporary higher education of the retention of students in their studies. In the context of student diversity, the book considers teaching and learning approaches that encourage and assist students to engage with their institution and their studies, therefore increasing the likelihood of their academic success and continuation. The aim of discussing such approaches in this book is to encourage our readers to reflect on their teaching and their students' learning, and to shape their teaching in ways that are student-responsive. While there are many factors in contemporary higher education that impact on students' retention, the book makes a valuable contribution to the field in that it focuses on one facet that is within the control of educators – the teaching and learning programme. Thus, we explore in detail ways that the programme can be developed to assist students' engagement and to enrich their learning.

The book discusses the issues surrounding student retention from a scholarly perspective, and also presents a range of practical approaches and strategies, which may also be used as models for future action by teachers in higher education. The lively and engaging cases set in authentic situations provide insight into the ways that higher education staff from across the globe have responded positively and creatively to the challenges posed by the diversity of the student population and the current competitive pressures in higher education. The cases are contextualised by the inclusion in the book of three research-based chapters by the book's authors on the themes of student diversity, alternative modes of teaching and learning, and the disciplines of study. These chapters explore the current thinking in the field on these topics, and pave the way for the cases that follow and elaborate on aspects of the themes.

We have designed the book so that it is suitable for a range of audiences concerned with the quality of teaching and learning in higher education, and the overall student experience. The scholarly content, practical examples and encouragement to reflect on one's own practice are relevant to:

- educational and academic development staff for use in developing ways that teaching and learning and the curriculum can be more responsive to students;

- lecturers and tutors and new teaching staff (including those seeking accreditation) about their teaching and their diverse student profiles; learning and teaching advisors and developers who develop quality educational programs for their faculties and departments;
- equity and widening participation practitioners and retention officers, and staff in higher education concerned with equity and access issues;
- subject specialists, who are concerned to improve retention rates within their disciplinary contexts;
- staff teaching postgraduate courses and supervising research; policy makers in higher education.

The book's content

The introductory chapter sets out the book's main themes, and identifies the background issues linking learning and teaching to the retention of students. By focusing on the formal learning experience, we explore the ways in which student success can be improved through 'curriculum development'. We use the term curriculum broadly to refer to learning, teaching and assessment approaches, as well as course contents. The underpinning tenet of our book is that the learning and teaching context – or curriculum – should be responsive to students; thus we promote a student-centred approach that uses active learning strategies and engages students academically and socially in the learning process.

The book is structured along the three major themes identified previously; these relate to learning and teaching and reflect aspects of contemporary higher education. These sections begin with chapters and are followed by exemplary cases and their discussion:

1 Student diversity: recognises the substantial changes in higher education including reduced governmental funding, global competition for students and increased participation in higher education that has resulted in a diverse student profile;
2 Modes of teaching and learning: emphasises a more holistic, student-rather than teacher-centred approach to teaching and learning and the importance of alternative and innovative learning and teaching approaches to promote student engagement, retention and success;
3 Disciplines of study: recognises the disciplines' particular characteristics and cultures, ways of approaching knowledge, teaching and learning preferences, and emphasises the importance of building students' needs into traditional teaching and learning approaches.

The 15 action research-based cases included in the book are accessible, practical and insightful, and reflect the situations of higher education teachers in countries such as Australia, Indonesia, South Africa, the Netherlands, the United Kingdom and Malaysia. The student-responsive teaching and learning developments discussed in the cases have been implemented to engage students. The cases are structured in an accessible form that, first, sketches the background and the issue(s) that led to the teaching and learning development. The next section explains the actions undertaken in the form of curriculum development, and rationale, while the final section evaluates strengths and weaknesses and future implications.

The conclusion draws together the learning and teaching approaches to engage students in their studies that are presented through the case examples in the book. The cases are discussed in relation to the retention strategies of student-responsive curriculum, academic and social engagement, and active learning that are focused on in this book. Arising from the cases, ways to implement these strategies are identified as the cases are discussed. Finally, we present some questions for our readers' reflection on their teaching and their students' learning.

The book's distinctive features

The teaching and learning context in higher education has changed dramatically in recent times. The importance of students' engagement with their institution and with their studies is made clear in the literature, but the fact is that, compared with previous times, many students no longer engage more broadly with their institution through, for example, support services and extra-curricular activities. The most distinctive feature of the book is that it suggests strategies to encourage and assist this vital aspect of learning that is within the control of academic staff; that is, it explores approaches that are embedded in the teaching and learning program and therefore reach a majority of students.

The book is comprehensive. It includes scholarly content by the book's authors that teases out and contextualises the issue of student retention to larger and global movements in higher education. This includes the importance of students' academic and social engagement, and, indeed, the enrichment of the educational process that follows when student diversity is addressed in educational programs. The cases are self-reflective, fresh and exciting in that they are real-life examples of teachers' responses to changing student circumstances and diversity, and shared generously with readers. As well as 'normalising' the dynamic teaching and learning environment and its inherent tensions, the cases operate as models and suggestions for responses to challenging situations, and, most importantly, encourage positive responses. The final chapter also analyses the cases in detail along the lines of the framework for student retention identified earlier in the book. From the analysis emerges valuable guidance and direction for staff in the context of the student diversity and the dynamic higher education environment.

Acknowledgements

A number of people have assisted us in the development of this book, and we express our gratitude to them. Taylor and Francis staff have been most helpful over the time in which the book was conceived and developed, and in particular, we thank Sarah Burrows, Kirsty Smy and Helen Pritt. In the early stages of the book, the reviewers provided comments which we incorporated in the book, and we are most grateful to Kate Exley and Vincent Tinto for their advice and support for the book. We appreciated the support of our colleagues at our respective institutions as we undertook the authoring and editing tasks: at Monash University in Australia and the Higher Education Academy in the UK. Finally, we thank our families for their continuous love, support and encouragement. In particular, Liz thanks Rob and Lucy Jones.

Glenda Crosling
Liz Thomas
Margaret Heagney
May 2007

Contents

Foreword

Professor Graham Webb
Pro Vice-Chancellor (Quality) Monash University
CEO Monash College Pty Ltd

An old-fashioned and often critiqued way of looking at education is to consider it in terms of content and process. Criticism of this simple notion has come from many directions, including the importance of 'the medium' or process actually comprising 'the message' or content. In *Improving Student Retention in Higher Education: The Role of Teaching and Learning'* content and process go hand-in-hand: each contributes to the other and both are compelling.

The 'content' of the book is structured around the themes of student diversity, modes of teaching and learning, and disciplines of study. These constitute major areas that affect the modern higher education challenge of educating a new, mass and different student population, using new methods and technologies which are appropriate for differing disciplinary contexts. Some of the topics addressed in the content include: retention, success, academic and social engagement, student diversity, internationalisation, curriculum development, and assessment. These provide the reader with a sound framework to understand the impact on student retention of innovative teaching practice.

The 'process' of the book is based on involving the reader in real-life case studies. It follows from the approach taken by Peter Schwartz and myself in *Case Studies on Teaching in Higher Education* in 1993 which led to a later series of six case study books between 2001 and 2003. The case study approach has proven remarkably adjustable and resilient to different 'content' areas and has continued to stimulate interest and provoke readers irrespective of their location around the world; their experience in higher education and their discipline area. *Improving Student Retention in Higher Education: The Role of Teaching and Learning* does what good education always should do – it brings together important and interesting topics of content with an interesting and stimulating approach to engage the learner/reader in the process of education. As education is an essentially social activity for the social good, I hope that *Improving Student Retention in Higher Education: The Role of Teaching and Learning* stimulates you to new and interesting conversations with your students and colleagues, families and friends.

List of Contributors

John Bamber is Lecturer in Community Education in the School of Education at the University of Edinburgh in Scotland. Email: <john.bamber@ed.ac.uk>.

Richard (Bill) Blunt, Director of Faculty Development and Deputy Director of the Department of Educational Services at St George's University in Grenada. Previously, he worked in faculty development at the Nelson Mandela Metropolitan University (formerly the University of Port Elizabeth) and the University of Fort Hare in the Eastern Cape of South Africa. His first university appointment was in the Education Department of Rhodes University, also in the Eastern Cape.

Gavin Brown manages the Access to Medicine Project within the King's College London School of Medicine in the UK. Email: <gavin.p.brown@kcl.ac.uk>.

Veronica Cahyadi is Teaching and Research Fellow in the Physics and Astronomy Department at University of Canterbury in New Zealand. Email: <veronica.cahyadi@canterbury.ac.nz>.

Dr Glenda Crosling is Education Advisor in the Faculty of Business and Economics at Monash University in Australia. Email: <Glenda.Crosling@buseco.monash.edu.au>.

Rob de Crom, MA is Head of Education of the Faculty of Economics and Business at the Vrije Universiteit Amsterdam, the Netherlands. Email: <rcrom@feweb.vu.nl>.

Marlene Drysdale is Associate Professor and Head of the Indigenous Health Unit at Monash University, Department of Rural and Indigenous Health, in Australia. Email: <marlene.drysdale@med.monash.edu.au>.

Isabel Ellender is Lecturer in the Indigenous Health Unit at Monash University, Department of Rural and Indigenous Health, in Australia. Email: <isabel.ellender@med.monash.edu.au>.

Dr Pamela Garlick is the Course Director for the Extended Medical Degree Programme in the King's College London School of Medicine in the UK. Email: <pamela.garlick@kcl.ac.uk>.

Margaret Heagney, MA is Coordinator of the Student Equity Unit at Monash University in Melbourne, Australia. Email: <margaret.heagney@adm.monash.edu.au>.

Christine Keenan is Learning and Teaching Fellow at Bournemouth University in the UK. Email: <ckeenan@bournemouth.ac.uk>.

Kate Kirk is a National Teaching Fellow. She is currently running the Continuing Professional Development Unit at Manchester Metropolitan University in the North West of England. Email: <K.Kirk@mmu.ac.uk>.

Betty Leask is Associate Professor and Dean of Teaching and Learning in the Division of Business at the University of South Australia. Email: <betty.leask@unisa.edu.au>.

Lesley Mcmillan is Lecturer in sociology at the University of Sussex, UK. Email: <Lesley.Mcmillan@Sussex.ac.uk>.

Mark Russell is Principal Lecturer in the School of Aerospace, Automotive and Design Engineering and also a teacher within the Blended Learning Unit (a UK Centre for Excellence in Teaching and Learning). Both posts are based at the University of Hertfordshire, UK.

Dr Janette Ryan is Senior Lecturer in the Faculty of Education at Monash University in Australia. Email: <janette.ryan@education.monash.edu.au>.

Dr Sabine Severiens is Director of the Rotterdam Institute for Socialscience Policy Research, an institute of the Erasmus University Rotterdam in the Netherlands. Her main fields of expertise are inequality and drop-out in higher and vocational education.

Lucy Solomon is Researcher at Kingston University in the UK. Email: <L.Solomon@kingston.ac.uk>.

Judy Tennant is Economics Lecturer in the Faculty of Business and Economics at Monash University in Australia. Email: <Judith.Tennant@buseco.monash.edu.au>.

Teoh Kok-Soo, Senior Lecturer at the School of Engineering, Monash University, Malaysia, was the recipient of the 2006 Carrick Institute Awards for Australian University Teaching – Citations for Outstanding Contributions to Student Learning, and a Monash University Australia Vice-Chancellor's Awards for Distinguished Teaching in 2005. Email: <teoh.kok.soo@eng.monash.edu.my>.

Dr Liz Thomas is Director of the Widening Participation Research Centre at Edge Hill University and Senior Advisor for Widening Participation at the Higher Education Academy in the UK. Email: <Liz.Thomas@HEAcademy. ac.uk>.

Digby Warren is Educational Development Facilitator and Researcher currently working at London Metropolitan University. Email: <d.warren@londonmet. ac.uk>.

Rick Wolff is Researcher at the Institute for Migration and Ethnic Studies (IMES), University of Amsterdam, and is currently working on his PhD-project on students of non-western descent in Dutch higher education. Email: <r.p.wolff@uva.nl>.

Chapter 1

Introduction

Student success and retention

Glenda Crosling, Liz Thomas
and Margaret Heagney

Introducing retention and success

In recent times, a significant concern in higher education (HE) is the retention of students in their studies. Institutions worldwide are under pressure to reduce the rates of students 'dropping out', and develop new and innovative means that encourage students to continue (Thomas and Quinn 2003). For instance, in all parts of the UK, institutions' progression and completion rates are measured via two performance indicators by the Higher Education Funding Council, and institutions are penalized financially for low rates of student retention. Similarly, in Australia, student retention is one of seven institutional indicators of quality teaching and learning utilized by the federal government for the allocation of teaching and learning performance funding. It is also one of four indicators used to assess institutions' equity performance, to which special funding for the institution's equity activities is tied.

This pressure for retention emanates from the recent, momentous changes in higher education worldwide which have resulted in the movement from an elite system of HE educating a small and limited number of the society, to a 'massified' (Trow 1973) one where large numbers of students attend higher education. This has been accompanied by an expansion in the number of students from previously under-represented groups who now attend higher education. These changes have impacted on the HE system in interrelated ways (Radford 1997). A major impact is the dramatic transformation of the composition of the student body because of economic imperatives for a more skilled workforce in the competitive global world. At the same time, governments are now concerned with the quality of the education provided in HE and have put in place quality assurance measures. The increasingly competitive HE global market also means that the institution's reputation is reflected in the quality of the graduates. In this setting, student drop out from study has become an issue of concern because of the implications for the quality of the programme and the graduates, including the degree that programs can cater for students from diverse groups (Crosling & Webb 2002).

The now diverse student population includes students from different ethnic groups and non-English-speaking backgrounds, international, lower socio-economic backgrounds, mature aged students, students with disabilities, as well as those for whom higher education is the first family experience. Higher education can be an alienating experience for such students in that their backgrounds, previous educational experiences and needs may result in gaps, or even chasms, between the students' educational expectations, and those of their institutions and teachers. While discontinuation rates for students from diverse backgrounds can be high, it cannot be assumed that discontinuation occurs because of the students' lack of ability or motivation. For instance, Given and Smailes (2005: 4), in their study at the Northumbria University in the UK, found that students who were of mature age and the first of their family to attend higher education had the 'academic abilities and motivations that are required to study successfully at HE level'.

Defining retention and rates of retention

There are differing definitions of retention and rates of retention across countries. For instance, in the USA, *retention* refers to the proportion of students who enroll and remain at a particular institution, while *persistence* rates refer to the proportion of students enrolled at one institution who transfer and remain enrolled in another college. USA studies show that 51 per cent of students who begin university study in the United States complete their degree within six years within their first institution, and another 8–12 per cent will eventually earn their university degrees via transfer to another institution (Tinto 2002:1). Similarly in Australia, it has been estimated that approximately 20 per cent of students do not complete their courses. However, a new study of students who began a Bachelor's Degree at Australian universities in first semester 2004 counted students who transferred to other institutions not as drop-outs, but as retained in the system. It suggested that the actual drop-out figure could be close to 10 per cent, depending on the proportion of students who follow through their intention to re-enroll later (Long, Ferrier & Heagney 2006). In Sweden five years' study is seen as completion, rather than a focus on graduation.

Students who change universities, or drop out temporarily, are not included in UK studies. It is estimated that one student in six leaves without completing (House of Commons Select Committee on Education and Employment 6th Report, in Thomas *et al.* 2003: 87). Retention of students in higher education is estimated to be 20 per cent in the Netherlands, 26 per cent in Sweden, while in Canada 25 per cent of full-time students and 59 per cent of part-timers do not complete their courses (Thomas & Quinn: 2003).

Variation in completion times impacts on the determination of retention rates. Although completion legitimately takes a long time (McInnis et al, 2000: 6), there is far less flexibility in the determination of completion in England and Wales, where students who do not complete their studies in four years are classified as 'non completers'. In Germany, the standard university degree course is nine semesters long, but most students take more than twelve semesters to complete a degree (Schnitzer & Heublein 2003: 2). While there is this cross-country variation, it is important to identify the factors which affect students' completion times, such as adequacy and specificity of student support.

Students and retention

Factors have been identified that impact on retention and thus encourage students to continue with their studies, rather than dropping out. The rate of drop-out is thus affected by the absence of these factors. One vital aspect for students' continuation is their experience of university, and this refers to their engagement and productive learning (Scott 2005: xiii). While student engagement has academic and social dimensions, academic engagement is reflected in students' attending classes, their active and interactive involvement with staff and fellow students, and with learning resources (Tinto 1975; Scott 2005). Students also need to experience their learning as challenging, and communication with staff needs to be formative for their learning. Teaching and learning approaches that assist students to interact with their classmates and staff providing them with feedback on themselves as students and on their approaches to their study create a climate where students feel 'legitimated' and supported (Coates 2005; cited in Scott 2005: 5), and encouraged to continue. While there are certainly students who discontinue their studies because of a mismatch between their aspirations and interests and those offered by their course, a climate that involves students and provides feedback on their study efforts means that they are more likely to study successfully, and the experience of success in study cannot be ignored as a significant element in students' continuation.

Another influence on students' academic engagement and continuation is the characteristics of current 'school-leaver' students, who are, for instance, accustomed to computers as an integral part of their lives, and electronic communication. Thus, students most likely will have expectations of their educational experience that differ from those of previous generations. Traditional teaching forms, perhaps more teacher-and information transmission-focused, may not 'connect' as effectively with current day students, for whom life is permeated with images, computers and more constant and perhaps instantaneous communication.

old vs. New technology

Social engagement occurs through students developing networks and relationships with fellow students (Tinto 1975; Toohey 1999). In previous times, these  may have developed merely by the fact that students experienced a sense of belonging in that their backgrounds and experiences were like those of their fellow students. As, in general, students in higher education had middle-class backgrounds and family experience of HE, they would also be more likely to have understandings of higher education that corresponded with those of the institution (Bourdieu 1988). Formerly, students may have established friendships and networks through membership of cultural and interest clubs and societies on campus. However, as they bear more of their education costs and their income supports remain low, students are spending longer hours in paid employment; more than 70 per cent of full-time students in Australia are employed for approximately 15 hours per week (Long & Hayden 2001). The outcome is that students are spending less time on campus, and therefore are less likely through traditional means to engage and develop networks.

If students are to continue with their studies, institutions need to recognize their needs and provide them with a reasonable chance of succeeding in their studies. An example of the importance of this is seen in the work in the US of Osbourne, Gallacher and Crossan (2004). They state that the study performance of minority group students is related to how marginalized they feel within the institution. As we have mentioned earlier, efforts to 'legitimate' and support students are thus linked to study success, and to rates of retention. Boylan (2004: 103) also highlights the benefits that arise not only for the individual students with success in their studies, but also for society in general. Students from diverse backgrounds bring to their studies a range of perspectives and backgrounds that provides a richness not only for the curriculum, but for campus life in general (Edwards, Crosling, Petrovic-Lazarevic, & O'Neill 2003). In Boylan's (2004: 103) words, broadened access means that 'new groups with new voices enter the higher education discussion'. As we prepare our students for the globalized world, it is important to offer a broad experience, and students with differing perspectives and views on issues and topics assist in this process.

Curriculum development and retention

The curriculum in one form or another is experienced by all students. Despite different modes of delivery and forms across disciplines, it provides a forum where approaches and strategies that engage students in their university experience and their learning can be implemented. The cases presented in this book exemplify ways that the curriculum has been developed to enhance the teaching and learning experience for students.

While the term 'curriculum' is open to interpretation in higher education circles (Fraser & Bosanquet 2006), our underpinning tenet in this book is that it involves a responsiveness to students in their learning, and thus a student-centred approach, assisting students to engage academically and socially. We concur with Boud (2004: 59), who perceives that responding to students includes recognizing the diversity of needs of different student populations, and 'not simply offering courses in combinations of modes: face to face, weekly, in intensive blocks, by distance learning, using the internet and so on'.

Our interpretation of curriculum is thus broad, where teaching and learning is perceived as an active and interactive process between the teacher and students (Fraser & Bosanquet 2006: 272). It includes Scott's (2005: 6) findings from students' qualitative comments on the Course Experience Questionnaire in Australia, that students need to be 'immersed in learning situations that engage them in action, that are authentic, reflective and collaborative'. Rather than a 'product delivered for students', education is seen as a 'process that enabled student learning' (Fraser & Bosanquet 2006: 274). This suggests a dynamic approach where the curriculum is constantly monitored *vis-à-vis* the student cohort for its ability to engage the students, and adapted or changed to refresh its suitability. In sum, included in our view of curriculum is curricular content, delivery and structure, action and interaction between the teacher and students, and assessment, which needs to be linked to learning and teaching (Fraser & Bosanquet, 2006). Reinforcing responsiveness and interaction between students and teachers, the importance of assessment of a formative nature is emphasized.

Responsiveness to students and their engagement, however, is not devoid of rigour, as it is always driven by the educational objectives of higher education. But a responsive approach acknowledges the developmental nature of student learning, and includes the notion of accepting and beginning action from where students are in their thinking and learning and what they 'say they want', but also leading them into areas that they could never have envisaged (Boud 2004: 59).

Research points out that the teacher's approach is related to the quality of their students' learning (Prosser & Trigwell 2002; Lindblom-Ylanne *et al.* 2006), Thus, according to Lindblom-Ylanne *et al.* (2006: 295), 'one way of improving student learning is to support teachers in developing more student-centred approaches to teaching'. This is a feasible and achievable objective because, as Lindblom-Ylanne *et al.* (2006) also point out, teachers' approaches are not fixed, and vary according to the situations in which they find themselves. The outcome of this perspective is that a different context means that a teacher adopts a different teaching approach (Lindblom-Ylanne *et al.* 2006). In the diverse student population, the idea of flexibility in teaching augurs well for the development and implementation of inclusive curriculum approaches. Furthermore, it underscores the need for student-centred teaching approaches.

The characteristics of the diverse and current student profile, including backgrounds, teaching and learning experiences, and preferences and expectations, present a different context when compared with the traditional student profile. The diversity provides a new setting, prompting teachers to develop and broaden their teaching practices. Furthermore, stressing the need for teachers to keep on developing in their approaches to teaching, Boud (2004: 62) points out that teaching staff may need to change existing work patterns in order to equip students so that they are able to deal with the knowledge demands that are typical of the contemporary world, rather than knowledge that is transmitted to them through a teacher-centred approach. The cases included in this book exemplify a range of ways that teachers have responded to students through curriculum development.

The book

Our aim is to stimulate our readers' thinking about their students and their learning in the current higher education setting, and to present a range of approaches and strategies as food for thought, and as models for the way forward. We have brought together in the cases curriculum-based strategies and approaches that have been developed and implemented by higher education teachers across the world.

These respond to and address the needs of students, facilitating their engagement and thus their success and retention in higher education.

The readership for the book

The book will be of use to the following groups of people who work in higher education settings worldwide:

- Educational development staff in training and development, exploring ways that teaching and learning and the curriculum can be developed to be more responsive to students.
- Lecturers and tutors (including those seeking accreditation), who are concerned with their teaching and their diverse student profiles.
- New teaching staff, especially those undertaking training and accreditation.
- Education staff in higher education who act as learning and teaching advisors and developers, and who are responsible for developing quality educational programmes for their faculties and departments.
- Equity and widening participation practitioners and retention officers, and staff in higher education concerned with equity and access issues.
- Subject specialists, who are concerned to improve retention rates within their disciplinary contexts.
- Staff teaching postgraduate courses and supervising research.
- Policy makers in higher education.

The structure of the book

The book is structured along three major themes. Each of the three thematic sections in the book begins with a chapter authored by one of the editors, which is followed by a series of cases exemplifying various aspects of the theme. The themes reflect salient aspects of contemporary higher education. These are:

- student diversity;
- modes of teaching and learning;
- disciplines of study.

Student diversity

The theme of 'Student diversity' is included in the book as recognition of the mammoth changes that have occurred in recent times in higher education. As universities receive less government funding and are increasingly reliant on finding their own resources, global competition for students means that the student profile is diverse. The need for educated societies to keep pace with the rapid change occurring in contemporary times, as well as governmental access and equity objectives, has also led to a greater proportion of the society participating in higher education, as well as students from previously un- or under-represented groups.

The theme recognizes that there may be common experiences and even characteristics across groups of students, which impact on their response to their studies. At the same time, we emphasize that stereotyping students according to preconceived ideas is risky and even unfair to the students as individuals within groups, who are evolving and developing in their identities. Our purpose in highlighting student diversity through this theme in the book is to provide guidelines that may be useful for teachers as they reflect on and respond to their students and their orientations towards their learning and their university experience. They are in no way meant to be used in a prescriptive mode.

Modes of learning and teaching

The theme of 'Modes of learning and teaching' is included in the book in recognition of the importance of alternative learning and teaching approaches in promoting student engagement, retention and success. It embraces a more holistic approach, where the teacher's approach is seen to impact on students' experiences of higher education and the way students undertake their studies. As the focus has moved from a teacher to a student-centred approach, responding to students, the development of new, innovative and interactive modes of teaching and learning has become increasingly important.

The 'Modes of learning and teaching' theme recognizes the ways in which curricular contents and alternative learning, teaching and assessment approaches can improve student engagement and thus impact on student retention and success. Our purpose with this theme is to acknowledge a range of approaches that may resonate with and engage students in their learning. This is primarily being undertaken by moving from more teacher-centred approaches to learning and teaching, to more student-centred approaches. In particular, induction and the development of academic skills, active, experiential learning and formative assessment are strategies that can be used to promote greater student engagement in the curriculum, and improve student retention and success.

Disciplines of study

It is not feasible to take a 'blanket' or 'one-size–fits-all' approach to the development of a curriculum that is responsive to students and therefore more likely to engage them in their learning and university experience. The disciplines possess their own characteristics and cultures (Becher 1989). These include, for instance, preferences for ways of dealing with knowledge, reporting it, and inquiry methods. They reflect characteristic teaching and learning approaches, such as a preference for large lectures or for small group teaching. Regardless of the discipline, it is important that the teaching and learning approaches are responsive to students, and therefore student- rather than teacher-focused.

The theme of 'Disciplines of study' has been included in the book because the disciplines are integral to study in higher education. Our approach discussed in Chapter 4 is that the disciplines and their traditional and characteristic teaching and learning approaches can be developed in responsive and interactive ways. The traditional approaches can also be expanded to include new modes in order to cater for a diverse range of students.

The cases in the book

The cases follow in general form the structure developed in the Kogan Page series, *Case Studies of Teaching in Higher Education* (Schwartz & Webb 1993; Edwards, Smith & Webb 2001; Murphy, Walker & Webb 2001; Schwartz, Mennin & Webb 2001; Crosling & Webb 2002; Edwards, Baume and Webb 2003).

This format affords a lively and engaging way to make 'real' the responses of teachers in higher education to their students, and to their learning. We are grateful to the Kogan Page series editors for endorsing our use of this format.

The book includes fifteen cases from higher education in several countries, including Australia, Indonesia, South Africa, the Netherlands, the United Kingdom and Malaysia. The cases under the book's three major themes consider ways that the curriculum has been developed to cater for student diversity, and to provide an engaging experience. While the cases are categorized under the themes, there is overlap across themes, and, for instance, a case in the discipline-specific section may raise issues of student diversity, or modes of teaching and learning. We thus encourage readers to take a flexible approach as they engage with the cases.

The cases organized under the themes are mainly based on action research. They relate the efforts of the case authors to enhance their teaching and their students' learning. Action research as seen in the cases in this book uses observation, planning, action and evaluation (McTaggart 1993) in a spiralling form. It leads the reader through the exploration of the situation in which a teaching and learning issue is embedded. It recognizes the possibility of acting differently on the basis of learning progressively from experience (McTaggart 1993), planning and implementing action, and evaluating it. While Scott (2004) states that action research may be seen as eclectic in its use of concepts and methodologies and therefore vulnerable, he also points out that it is responsible for the 'remorseless accumulation of good practice' (Scott 2004: 27). It provides for the dissemination of good teaching and learning practice, and informed policy development, and these are the reasons for the presentation of the cases in this book.

Along the lines of action research, the cases are structured as follows:

*   Section 1. **The situation**; outlines the background and the issue/s. This includes the higher education situation to which the curriculum development was a response.
*   Section 2. **The approaches implemented**; explains the actions undertaken in the form of the curriculum development, and the rationale.

• Section 3. **Discussion**; evaluates the action, considering, for instance, strengths and weaknesses and future implications.

As with the cases in the Kogan Page series, we emphasize the importance for readers of reading the first section of the case, reflecting on the issues and relating them to the reader's particular setting, and considering responses before reading Section 2 of the case. Again, a reflective approach following Section 2 should lead into Section 3, where the reader's responses may be evaluated against those put forward by the case author.

The sections and chapters in the book

Following our introduction to the book's approach and structure in this chapter, the book is organized into the three thematically-based sections as follows:

Section 1 presents Chapter 2, 'Student success and student diversity'. It provides an overview of research undertaken into understandings, assumptions and expectations of higher education studies from the perspective of different groups of students. The case examples are:

• Bill Blunt discusses the challenges of teaching a diverse student body in post-apartheid South Africa;
• Marlene Drysdale gives insights into the ways a cultural awareness program, delivered in 'immersion' style, can help to integrate understandings of Australian Indigenous cultures into Medicine and Nursing curricula;
• Rick Wolff, Sabine Severiens and Rob de Crom explore the way interactive elements in programme design relate to high completion rates and student satisfaction in a diverse population;
• John Bamber provides a case which outlines the positive results that flowed from introducing more participative methods of teaching part-time students who have work responsibilities; and
• Teoh Kok Soo demonstrates the ways embedding language support and cross-cultural awareness-raising exercises in an Engineering curriculum assists culturally diverse students from non-English-speaking-backgrounds to succeed in their studies.

Section 2 begins with Chapter 3, 'Learning and teaching strategies to promote student retention and success', which considers the impact of mass higher education and increasing student diversity on student persistence and withdrawal. Drawing on recent research evidence, it illustrates how students can struggle to adjust to learning in the higher education environment, and the ways in which the curriculum can be changed to promote student engagement.

The cases included in this section explore how the curriculum (contents and learning, teaching and assessment strategies) have been changed to support student retention and success. In particular, the authors have developed more active learning strategies, made the curriculum contents more relevant to students' experiences while seeking to expand their knowledge and skills, and made the teaching and assessment practices transparent to facilitate students' understanding of the learning processes. The cases are:

- Christine Keenan discusses how a pre- and post-entry extended induction process has been introduced at the University of Bournemouth to promote early engagement by students in their disciplinary learning and to make explicit and transparent the skills and expectations of HE learning.
- Digby Warren discusses the redesign of an introductory module to broaden students' notion of what history is, and to develop their academic skills through an integrated curriculum approach.
- Betty Leask describes how, at the University of South Australia, simple ICT tools are being used to facilitate meaningful and engaging intercultural learning for all students.
- Lesley McMillan and Lucy Solomon discuss how they altered their approach to teaching quantitative research methods to overcome students' fears of maths and statistics, enabling them to understand the concepts without worrying about the numbers.
- Mark Russell presents a case from the University of Hertfordshire in the UK which demonstrates how a blended teaching, learning and assessment strategy has improved the engagement and academic success of students studying thermodynamics.

Section 3 presents Chapter 4, 'Facilitating student success. Disciplines and curriculum development'. The natures of the higher education disciplines are overviewed, identifying characteristics, discourses, and typical teaching and learning approaches. The discussion centres on the way that the typical approaches can be utilized, along with further development, to engage and include students, and the way that new, innovative approaches can be embedded in the more traditional forms.

The case examples demonstrate how the characteristics of some disciplines have been utilized to assist students to engage, and to develop relationships with their fellow students and with their teachers. The curricula have been changed and extended to provide opportunities for the students to be included and more active in their learning so that they are legitimated and supported as they undergo academic transformation and come to perceive the world through the lens of the particular disciplines. Often, the curricular changes actually place the students in the discipline's discourse, so that they 'enact' it as they go about their learning task. Their initiation into the disciplines is thus tacit and subtle. These cases are:

- Veronica Cahyadi relates her experiences in teaching physics in an engineering course in a university in Indonesia, where the traditional lecture format was changed to include activities and interaction, both student-to-student and student-to-teacher.

- Janette Ryan investigates curricular changes in a small rural university in Australia for education students. The community-based projects discussed in the case enacted the discourse as they required the students to function in ways compatible with the teacher as a facilitator, compared with the more traditional, didactic teacher mode.
- Pamela Garlick and Gavin Brown explain the development of the curriculum in the course of a medicine degree at King's College in London in the UK. The module to develop students' written and spoken communication skills meant that the students developed personal confidence as they learnt to communicate as medical professionals, as well as being provided with study support.
- Kate Kirk discusses inclusive and participatory approaches for non-traditional students at Manchester Metropolitan University in the UK in Social Work and Youth Studies. By including the students' views in the development of academic support resources, the students and their situations and needs were legitimated. The development and presentation of the resources that responded to the students' comments empowered students. In this way, the disciplinary discourse was enacted with the students participating in it.
- Judith Tennant discusses curriculum development on a rural campus of an Australian university in economics, as part of a business degree. The excursion to a local business provided the students with the opportunity to get to know other students and their teacher. It also allowed the students to see the integration of the range of their subjects that they study in the operations of a business, making their studies more relevant to real-life activities.

Section 4, the final section of the book, concludes in Chapter 5. This chapter draws together the curricular approaches and strategies to engage students in their studies that are presented through the case examples in the book. The cases are discussed in relation to the retention strategies focused on in this book of student-responsive curriculum, academic and social engagement, and active learning. Arising from the cases, ways to implement these strategies are identified as the cases are discussed. Finally, we present some questions for our readers' reflection on their teaching and their students' learning.

In conclusion, we hope that the chapters and cases in this book are useful for you as you go about your teaching and learning activities. We thank the case authors for sharing their thoughts, reflections and practices with us in this book. Finally, we hope that they will encourage you to think in new ways about your teaching as you respond to your students and their learning.

References

Becher, T. (1989) *Academic Tribes and Territories*. Milton Keynes: The Society for Research into Higher Education and Open University Press.

Boud, D. (2004) 'Discourses of access: Changing views in a changing world', in M. Osbourne, J. Gallacher, and B. Crossan (eds.), *Researching Widening Access to Lifelong Learning: Issues and Approaches in International Research*. London: Routledge Falmer.

Bourdieu, P. (1988) *Homo Academicus* (trans.) Cambridge: Peter Collier, Polity Press.

Boylan, H. (2004) 'Access as more: Issues of student performance, retention, and institutional change', in M. Osbourne, J. Gallacher and B. Crossan (eds.), *Researching Widening Access to Lifelong Learning. Issues and Approaches in International Research*. London: Routledge Falmer.

Coates, H. (2005) 'The value of student engagement for higher education quality assurance', *Quality in Higher Education*, 11(1): 25–36.

Crosling, G. and Webb, G. (eds.) (2002) *Supporting Student Learning. Case Studies, Experience, and Practice from Higher Education*. London: Kogan Page.

Edwards, H., Baume, D. and Webb, G. (eds.) (2003) *Staff and Educational Development: Case Studies, Experience and Practice*. London and Philadelphia: Kogan Page

Edwards, R., Crosling, G., Petrovic-Lazarevic, S., and O'Neill, P. (2003) 'Internationalisation of business education: Meaning and implication', *Higher Education Research and Development*, 22(2): 184–192.

Edwards, H., Smith, H. and Webb, G. (eds.) (2001) *Lecturing: Case Studies, Experience and Practice*. London: Kogan Page.

Fraser, S. and Bosanquet, A. (2006) 'The curriculum? That's just a unit outline, isn't it?', *Studies in Higher Education*, 31(3): 269–284.

Given, J. and Smailes, J. (2005) *Pedagogical Needs of Non-traditional Students*. Northumbria University, Newcastle, Red Guide Series 7, Number 5.

Lindblom-Ylanne, S., Trigwell, K., Nevgi, A. and Ashwin, P. (2006) 'How approaches to teaching are affected by discipline and teaching context', *Studies in Higher Education*, 31 (3): 285–298.

Long, M., Ferrier, F. and Heagney, M. (2006) *Stay, Play or Give it Away? Students Continuing, Changing or Leaving University Study in First Year*. Canberra: Department of Education, Science and Training.

Long, M. and Hayden, M. (2001) *Paying their Way: A Survey of Australian Undergraduate University Student Finances, 2000*. Canberra: Australian Vice-Chancellors' Committee (AVCC).

McTaggart, R. (1993) 'Action research: Issues in theory and practice', *Annual Review of Health Social Sciences*, 3: 19–45.

McInnis, C., Hartley, R., Polesel, J. and Teese, R. (2000) *Non-completion in Vocational Education and Training and Higher Education: A Literature Review*, Commissioned by the Department of Education Training and Youth Affairs. Canberra: Commonwealth of Australia.

Murphy, D., Walker, R and Webb, G. (eds.) (2001) *Online Learning and Teaching with Technology. Case Studies, Experience, Practice*. London: Kogan Page.

Osbourne, M., Gallacher, J. and Crossan, B. (2004) *Researching Widening Access to Lifelong Learning. Issues and Approaches in International Research*. Abingdon: Routledge Falmer.

Prosser, M. and Trigwell, K. (2002) *Understanding Learning and Teaching: The Experience in Higher Education*. Buckingham: The Society for Research into Higher Education.

Radford, P. (1997) 'The changing purposes of higher education', in J. Radford, K. Raaheim, R. Williams and P. de Vries (eds.), *Quantity and Quality in Higher Education*. London: Jessica Kingsley Publishers.

Schnitzer, K. and Ulbein, U. (2003) *Under-represented Groups in Tertiary Education, German Report*. Stoke-on-Trent Institute of Access Studies, Staffordshire University. Online. Available www.staffs.ac.uk/institutes/access/research/res16htm.

Schwartz, P., Mennin, S., and Webb, G. (eds.) (2001) *Problem-Based Learning: Case Studies, Experience, Practice*. London: Kogan Page.

Schwartz, P. and Webb, G. (1993) *Case Studies in Teaching in Higher Education*. London: Kogan Page.

Scott, G. (2005) *Accessing the Student Voice*, Higher Education Innovation Program and the Collaboration and Structural Reform Fund, Department of Education, Science and Training, Canberra: Commonwealth of Australia.

Scott, P. (2004) 'Researching widening access: An overview', in M. Osbourne, J. Gallacher and B. Crossan (eds.), *Researching Widening Access to Lifelong Learning. Issues and Approaches in International Research*. Abingdon: Routledge Falmer.

Thomas, L. and Quinn, J. *(2003) International Insights into Widening Participation: Supporting the Success of Under-represented Groups in Tertiary Education*. Stoke-on-Trent: The Institute for Access Studies, Staffordshire University.

Thomas, L., Cooper, M. and Quinn, J. (eds.) (2003) *Improving Completion Rates among Disadvantaged Students*. Stoke-on-Trent: Trentham Books.

Tinto, V. (2002) *Establishing Conditions for Student Success*, Paper presented at the 11th Annual Conference of the European Access Network, Monash University, Prato, Italy, 20 June.

Tinto, V. (1975) 'Dropout from higher education: A theoretical synthesis of recent research', *Review of Educational Research*, 45 (10): 89–125.

Toohey, S. (1999) *Designing Courses for Higher Education*. Buckingham: The Society for Research into Higher Education and Open University Press.

Trow, M. (1973) *Problems in the Transition from Elite to Mass Higher Education*. New York: Carnegie Commission on Higher Education.

Section One

Student diversity

Chapter 2

Student success and student diversity

Margaret Heagney

Background

One of the results of the massification of higher education has been the demise of homogenous student populations in higher education institutions. Students entering universities come from a multitude of backgrounds; they bring a plethora of life experiences and expectations when they enroll. Optimal outcomes for universities include the participation and, finally, the graduation of these students. Retaining students to completion of their courses is an imperative for students and their universities in terms of financial cost and cost to reputation; both of these take on an added significance in these times of higher education markets. Because student populations are very diverse, lecturers cannot assume that all students have the same background knowledge. Learning has to be structured to incorporate the interests and experience of all students.

The link between retention, success and curriculum is demonstrated most succinctly by Vincent Tinto when he argues that 'the more students learn, the more value they find in their learning, the more likely they are to stay and graduate. In the final analysis, student learning drives student retention' (Tinto 2002: 4).

Universities invest considerable resources and effort for little or no return when students leave without completing their courses. The cost of attrition is high for students too. In countries such as England, the United States, Australia and New Zealand, students have to pay tuition fees either up front or through student loans systems. The loans which students take out to pay tuition fees continue to have an impact on their lives well beyond their university days. A 2003 New Zealand study showed that the average loan repayment time for women graduates was 28 years and for males 15 years (Benseman, J., Anderson, P. & Nicholl, J., cited in Thomas, Cooper & Quinn 2003: 118). In addition, the money students and their families spend on items such as books, computers, transport and childcare is wasted if students do not complete their courses.

Not all the costs associated with student withdrawal are financial. Many students who leave without gaining a qualification suffer loss of confidence and experience a sense of failure. Institutions too can suffer a loss of reputation when students leave or transfer. While there is agreement that student retention is of vital importance to universities and to students, surveys of retention literature

(Thomas & Quinn 2003; McInnis, Hartley, Polesel & Teese 2000) reveal a diversity of definitions and measures of retention (outlined in Chapter 1) along with a diversity of institutional responses to the issue.

Reasons for non completion and attrition

The reasons students withdraw from university courses are varied and complex. Factors leading to withdrawal interweave to produce intricate patterns. More often than not, students withdraw from university for a combination of reasons. Student withdrawal is often a very individualized process involving the interplay of institutional, social and personal factors (McInnis *et al* 2000:1). Sometimes one problem such as marriage breakdown can create a domino effect, triggering a series of consequences – financial, employment and health – that can be fatal to successful study.

Students' reasons for withdrawing vary with their age as 'the mix of reasons that come into effect largely relates to the students' stage of life, with different reasons more important for younger and for older students' (Long, Ferrier & Heagney 2006: 168). For example, younger students in one UK study cited choosing the wrong course, stress, dissatisfaction with their student experience and finance as reasons for dropping out (Yorke 1999: 30). These findings were replicated in a recent Australian study which showed that as well as the reasons listed above, younger students tend to use their first-year enrolment as a stepping stone to a more prestigious course or university. In fact, it is not uncommon for students to move strategically through the system to get the course they want. Movement between institutions and courses comes at a cost, both for government and for students, if their previous study is not credited towards their new course (Long *et al* 2006: v).

On the other hand, older students appeared to be more focused (Krause, Hartley, James & McInnis 2005: 72). They tended to stay in their courses and universities because they were clear about what they wanted to study and which university they wished to attend. For these students, withdrawing from their course of study was more likely to be influenced by difficulties in balancing their work and family commitments with the demands of their studies (Long *et al* 2006; Yorke 1999: 22).

Some factors that cause students to discontinue their courses such as academic preparation, choice of course, personal, financial and employment issues, are common to all students. These reasons vary in importance for different groups of non-traditional students (Heagney 2004:5).

Who are the non-traditional students?

Shaped by varying local contexts, different groups of students are the focus of equity activity in different countries. However, the following groups are usually included in international access and retention studies:

- Low income or economic status groups
- People with disabilities

- Students who are first in their family to participate in higher education
- Mature age students
- People from minority groups and refugees.

Other groups designated as disadvantaged in their specific national contexts include children of servicemen and the diaspora in Croatia, part-time students in Canada, travellers in Ireland and people from non English speaking backgrounds such as migrant populations and international students in Australia. Indigenous groups such as New Zealand's Maori people and Australian Aboriginal and Torres Strait Islander peoples are also the focus of equity activity in their respective countries.

Identification of retention issues affecting students from non-traditional backgrounds is complicated by a considerable overlap in equity group membership. This overlap in equity group membership is noted in several studies which show that the problems and barriers experienced by individuals (and groups) who are members of more than one category 'compound' – producing extreme disadvantage (Ferrier & Heagney 2001: 87, Clarke, Zimmer and Main 1999: 42; Dobson, Sharma and Ramsay 1998; Thomas & Quinn 2003: 11).

Australian Indigenous students provide a good example of multiple group membership. Unlike their non-Indigenous colleagues, many Indigenous people are young parents when they enroll in higher education, so they are members of two more under-represented groups, that is, students with family responsibilities and students who are first in the family to attend university. In addition, English is a second language for some of these students.

Equity group overlap is also supported by statistical evidence from the USA which suggests that Black and Hispanic students who have poor higher education outcomes are mostly drawn from low income backgrounds, have parents with no experience of higher education and are less likely to have attended schools with a high standard curriculum (Upshaw 2003: 17).

These layers of overlapping equity categories contribute to the wide range of formal and informal experiences which commencing students bring to higher education. Current higher education students do not have the same background knowledge. This presents a challenge to lecturers in terms of structuring the learning environment so that it includes the interests and experience of all students, including those from non-traditional backgrounds.

Equity students and retention issues

People from minority groups and refugees, students from non-English-speaking backgrounds

People from minority groups and refugees are defined in different ways in different countries. In the main, definitions of 'ethnicity' centre on three aspects – place of birth, language and racial or ethnic group. Some European countries call students born in the country in which they are studying *first generation* or *immigrants* and distinguish them from those born of parents who have migrated to that country, calling these students *2nd generation* in the Netherlands and Sweden and *descendants* in Norway (Thomas & Quinn 2003: 126–7). In Norway the ethnicity category is broken down into students of Western and non-Western cultural heritage and in the Netherlands, the level of parental education is a further marker of educational disadvantage.

Language is a key determinant of educational disadvantage in Australia (Thomas & Quinn 2003: 128). Students who have been in the country for fewer than ten years and who speak a language other than English at home are identified as *students from non-English-speaking-backgrounds*. This gives them equity group status, making them a focus of equity activity by governments and institutions. The non-English-speaking-backgrounds category is quite broad and includes both domestic and international students, as well as Indigenous students in North America, Australia and New Zealand.

Language issues flow into teaching and learning practices in classrooms, laboratories and tutorial rooms. For instance language, or more specifically, lecturers' use of colloquial language can isolate students from non-English-speaking-backgrounds. Similarly, when lecturers use examples which draw on local knowledge such as a reference to the local football team instead of an example drawn from global or international contexts, students from non-English-speaking-backgrounds struggle to understand the lecturer's message and feel left out of the 'information loop'.

Cultural background as well as cultural approaches and philosophies of education also impact on students' learning experience. For instance, students' expectations of lecturers' responsibilities differ across cultures, as do notions of the value of independent learning on the part of the student. Even at the point of referencing and referencing systems, many students from non-English-speaking-backgrounds (especially international students) have different understandings of this issue drawn from the school environment they experienced in their homeland.

At an individual level, the parents and relatives of many students from non-English-speaking-backgrounds have made enormous financial sacrifices to enable these students to attend university in a foreign country. This in turn puts a great deal of pressure on the students to achieve, and their interpretations of success will vary widely. For example, passing a course may get them into the profession or job that they want, but is it considered a satisfactory mark by those at home? Will it get them into an honours course?

Some international students arrive in a foreign country to commence their courses with only their fees paid and expect to get a part-time job to pay their living costs. Many work long hours in lowly paid jobs and jeopardize their academic success because they do not spend enough time at their studies – a phenomenon shared with local students from low socio-economic backgrounds discussed below.

Students from low-income backgrounds

These students also face particular barriers to their success and retention in higher education. Increasingly, large numbers of students work long hours in paid employment to the detriment of their studies. It is important to distinguish between students who work to live and those who work to have a lifestyle or 'extras' such as travel or independence from parents. Three-quarters of 19-year-old Australian students are in the latter category, according to one Australian survey, while 40 per cent of younger students worked to improve their chances of employment after university, and the majority of 20–24-year-olds worked to meet basic needs, to afford extras and to be more financially independent of their parents. Older students worked to support themselves and their families. It is not surprising that students who worked to meet their basic needs tended to be from low socio-economic backgrounds, and that those who worked to improve their chances of employment once they left university and to be more independent of their families were from high socio-economic backgrounds (Krause *et al.* 2005: 51).

A national survey of US undergraduates revealed that approximately four-fifths of the student population worked while studying, and one in five full-time students were also working full-time (McInnis 2001: 6). Australian students were also found to be working long hours during their time at university. As mentioned earlier, 70 per cent of full-time students in a 2001 national study reported they worked nearly 15 hours per week (Long & Hayden 2001). Students who were working long hours off campus had less time to devote to lectures and tutorials and to meet with their teachers and fellow students. Consequently, they were less likely to achieve the academic and social integration necessary for persistence and graduation – something Tinto describes as his third condition for retention. Students who have less time for reading and studying, be it in groups or on their own, also have fewer opportunities for learning – another important condition for retention (Tinto 2002: 4).

Cultural values and curricula

Matching students' own cultural values with those embedded in the curriculum is important for engaging and retaining students, particularly those from low income backgrounds and minority cultural groups. Clarke *et al.* (1999: 52) discuss the importance of 'addressing cultural disadvantage' and helping non-traditional students to cope with a 'higher education culture that may be unfamiliar or even hostile to them'.

This is particularly relevant to teaching, learning and retention of students from ethnic minorities (especially Indigenous peoples) and the ways stories of conquest, colonization and conflict are dealt with in the curriculum. During the apartheid period in South Africa, only the experiences of 'white' settlers made their way into the history syllabus taught in the Bantu education system (as explained by Bill Blunt in his case in this book), and in Australian schools, students were taught that

Australia was 'discovered' by 'white' explorers in the eighteenth century. Findings such as these put extra pressure on academics' learning and teaching practice and present particular challenges to those engaged in curriculum design.

Indigenous students' attrition rates can be affected by a clash of cultural understandings and their participation in higher education complicated by competing loyalties. For instance, is the Indigenous student who succeeds at university being true to their Indigenous heritage? This battle between individual and familial factors can be going on throughout an Indigenous student's candidature:

> ...because of the frustrations caused by cultural mismatch, the alternative for the Aboriginal student is either, resist school to maintain identify or assimilate, whereby Aboriginal children sacrifice their identity to succeed in mainstream society.
>
> (Peacock 1993: 9 in Bourke, Burden & Moore 1996: 9)

This suggests that the education system is failing Aboriginal students by forcing them to make a choice between cultures and by so doing, denying their identity (Bourke *et al.* 1996: 9 in Heagney 2004: 10).

Finances

Finances are listed as a major cause of drop-out in studies conducted in several countries. In the UK, Yorke's research into student withdrawal during the first year of study showed that a lack of financial support was one of the main challenges students faced in continuing with their courses and that some students were so frightened about incurring 'higher education' debt, that they withdrew (Yorke 1999: 34). Another UK study conducted by Universities for the North-East found that both staff and students believed that finance was the prime reason students drop out. Further, financial support was inadequate and accessing it complex (Dodgson R & Bollam H 2002 in Thomas, Quinn, Casey *et al.* 2003:23).

Clearly, the adequacy of student income support impacts on students' decisions to continue with their studies or not. Whether students can actually access student income support is also a retention issue. This factor was a large influence on the decision not to continue with their 2004 studies of 10.6 per cent of students who did not enroll at any university in 2005. For many, inadequacy of financial support along with the demands of work, family and their university course combined to form an insurmountable barrier to staying on at university. As one student explained, she would have continued if:

> I could have afforded it. I could not afford to devote my time to full time study and pay my bills. Austudy and part time work was not sufficient to keep myself and two sons at school and university.
>
> (Long *et al.* 2006: 122)

Mature age students (including part-timers and students with work and family responsibilities)

Many students in this category are also from low income groups, are first in the family to attend university, and are returning to study after a significant period. Frequently, they lack confidence in themselves, believe they have insufficient knowledge of the system, and feel the higher education system is a mystery. They have no one from their family or social group to whom they can put their questions. They lack knowledge about how universities work and also lack confidence in their ability to find out what they need to know to survive. These are the students who need time and specialized support to adjust to the demands of higher education. When these are not forthcoming, students are in danger of dropping out. One non-continuing student describes her experience thus:

> Lack of support from teachers etc., lack of 'how uni works' knowledge i.e. essay writing, WebCT, not knowing what course best suits me as I couldn't find the right person to talk to about it.
>
> (Long *et al*. 2006: 109)

Students with disabilities

There is a great deal of variation in the ways students with disabilities are identified and supported to succeed in higher education. Some countries (Australia, UK, Germany, Croatia and the USA) collect information about the numbers of students with disabilities who apply to and graduate from higher education institutions; others such as Norway, Sweden, Canada and Ireland collect very little data at all. Legislation requires higher education institutions to support students with disabilities in Canada, Australia and the UK and support services for individual students are provided in Croatia, the Netherlands, Australia, the UK and USA. In Sweden, universities are required to give students with a disability the same opportunities as students without a disability (Thomas & Quinn 2003: 167–201).

Many higher education institutions offer supports to individual students, such as alternative arrangements for assessment, note takers for students with hearing impairments, and conversion of texts into Braille for visually impaired students to assist them to complete their courses. In recent times, some universities have begun to approach the issue of supporting students with a disability from an *Inclusive Practices* perspective. In the intellectual environment, inclusive practices can be seen at work when lecturers employ strategies such as:

- speaking slowly and clearly in lectures (to assist students who are hearing-impaired or who come from non-English-speaking-backgrounds),
- providing overheads and power points in large fonts (for the visually impaired), and

- making lecture notes available on line (so that they can be put into alternative formats for visually impaired students).

These adjustments to teaching practice improve the learning experiences and retention rates of students with a disability and those from other under-represented groups such as non-English-speaking-backgrounds students as well. Inclusive adjustments to the intellectual environment work to improve all students' experience of university. This is true of the physical environment also. When institutions install ramps to make their lecture theatres accessible for wheelchair users, those spaces also become accessible for people with mobility problems, and those who use crutches. Ramps also provide easy access to staff who use trolleys to deliver heavy goods and supplies.

The cases

The cases show how retention of students from diverse backgrounds is assisted by innovative curricula and support services which reflect the needs and interests of those students.

Bill Blunt describes the challenges of teaching a diverse student body in post-apartheid South Africa. At a time when academic institutions are under a great deal of pressure to admit large numbers of students from disadvantaged schools, a project was developed to assist these students to succeed in their university studies. This necessitated the preparation of new modules with transparent learning objectives, content and tasks. Other examples discussed in the chapter show how understanding the 'big picture' of a discipline aids students to succeed. In one subject which traditionally had a high failure rate, students reported that they were mystified and did not understand the aims, purpose, scope and techniques of the discipline. To counter this, the Chair took on the teaching of first-year students. At the end of that year, students reported they understood both the discipline itself and lecturers' expectations. In addition, the failure rate was reduced. Other strategies designed to help students from disadvantaged backgrounds succeed at university are explored in this chapter. They include providing lecturers with summaries of students' feedback on their teaching, and helping students with poor language skills by encouraging lecturers to deliver their courses in slow, clear English. Some students are used to regurgitating large sections of material derived from textbooks – a learning method which was prevalent in their secondary schooling. Professor Blunt describes how standardized pre-entry tests in English are used to identify students who need to go into a one-year foundation programme to improve their language skills so they can succeed in their university studies.

Isabel Ellender and Marlene Drysdale explore some of the challenges they faced when conducting a student excursion in remote Australia. The student excursion was part of a cultural awareness exercise offered to students in the health professions at Monash University in Australia. Designed to increase the understandings non-Indigenous students have of Indigenous peoples' health, the cultural awareness programme offered students in medical and nursing courses the chance to meet with Indigenous people and to hear first-hand how their communities work and how their past history impacts on their lives today. The components of the cultural awareness programme included learning about Indigenous rock art, foods and medicines as well as opportunities for the students to discuss and examine their own responses to these learning experiences. In particular, Ellender and Drysdale look at the crisis experienced by one student during the excursion and its impact on the staff and other students. The learning opportunities provided to non-Indigenous students by the support the Indigenous people offered to the student in crisis was of primary importance. It also caused the teachers who were involved in developing and delivering the programme to reflect on some of the values, such as compassion and a sense of fair play which underpin their professional practice.

Rick Wolff, Sabine Severiens and Rob de Crom examine the ways interactive elements in programme design related to high completion rates and student satisfaction in a diverse student population in the Netherlands. Their study of six university course programmes had shown that fewer students from foreign backgrounds gained the maximum number of first-year credits than did 'majority' students, defined as students whose parents were born in the Netherlands. One economics course, in which students from foreign backgrounds had slightly higher progress scores, was the exception. This led the authors to examine the relationship between the course outcomes described above and the characteristics of the course programme and the institution. They found a traditional curriculum which had many lectures for groups of over 500 students (and low completion rates) had been replaced by a new curriculum.

The new system employed an interdisciplinary approach. Subjects were broken down into smaller components and small *Activating Work Groups* of students were formed so that the knowledge students acquired in the plenary lectures could be embedded more deeply in students' minds. These small groups which met frequently also provided a social dimension, helping students to feel comfortable with each other and with their teachers. In addition teachers' performance was evaluated and poor performers withdrawn from the course if their teaching did not improve. Strong student support in the form of three student counsellors was also offered to the students. The case shows how it is possible to offer a curriculum which features structured small learning groups that foster collaboration between students, with improved retention outcomes for students from minority groups.

Part-time and work-based students are the focus of the case provided by John Bamber. All of the students were in a Bachelor of Arts course in Community Education at a UK institution. They had no formal qualifications and all of them were employed for at least ten hours per week in a field of practice associated with the course. Working from the understanding that these students needed to be actively engaged in their learning, a course was designed to encourage them to stop thinking of the lecturer as the fount of all knowledge, to start to discover content for themselves and become critical thinkers. Group discussions on resolving practical issues were an important part of the course design. Students gained experience in working collaboratively – an important skill in the practice of their profession. In discussing the programme's elements the role of key retention strategies such as engaging the students, making the curriculum relevant outside the classroom and social connection via small group work is demonstrated.

The value of learning to work collaboratively, especially in preparation for professional practice, albeit in a very different cultural context, is taken up by Teoh Kok Soo. He presents a case based on his experiences as coordinator of a first-level unit in engineering at an offshore campus of Monash University in Malaysia. The aim of the course is to help students understand the essence of engineering and the environment in which they will work as engineers. The diverse student body includes both local (Malay, Chinese and Indian) and international students from Indonesia, China, Sri Lanka and Iran. English is a second language for all the students and language and learning support is provided by the university. In response to the diverse ethnic and cultural mix of the students and their non-English-speaking-backgrounds status, Teoh Kok Soo included both language development and cross-cultural understandings into the curriculum to promote respect for the different cultures in the student cohort and to build a healthy group dynamic on which to base the teamwork. Working in groups is an important form of learning and of assessment in the course and in engineering practice as well. Feedback on the curriculum has been positive; students have learned to negotiate their way in a very multicultural environment, have more confidence in presenting information (in English) to their peers,and believe they are well prepared for their entry into the engineering profession.

Conclusion

Increasing numbers of non-traditional students, that is, mature-age students with work and family commitments, students from minority groups and non-English-speaking-backgrounds come to university, bringing with them a myriad of life experiences and background knowledge. They also bring a challenge to their teachers and institutions in terms of their retention and how it can be achieved. In this chapter, the importance of adequate financial support, respect for students' life experiences, their cultural values and their work and family commitments is discussed and some of the ways a student-centred curriculum can assist in the retention of students from non-traditional backgrounds are explored. For example, curricula which provide opportunities for students to work in small groups reduce the social isolation often experienced by students from non-English-speaking-backgrounds and mature-age and part-time students. Similarly when language skills are built into a course, students are helped to become active and successful learners who are motivated to complete their courses. While changing the curriculum cannot assist students with issues which have their origins in domains outside the academy such as financial support, the importance of curriculum development in the retention of non-traditional students cannot be underestimated.

> Curriculum is the glue which holds knowledge and the broader student experience together and enables the knowledge to be used effectively by the student.
>
> (McInnes 2001: 11)

References

Benseman, J., Anderson, P. and Nicholl, J., in Thomas, L., Cooper M., and Quinn, J. (eds) (2003) *Improving Completion Rates among Disadvantaged Students*. Stoke-on–Trent: Trentham Books.

Bourke, C., Burden, J. and Moore, S. (1996) *Factors Affecting Performance of Aboriginal and Torres Strait Islander Students at Australian Universities: A Case Study* Canberra: Higher Education Division, Department of Employment, Education, Training and Youth Affairs, Evaluations and Investigations Program.

Clarke, J., Zimmer, B. and Main, R. (1999) 'Review of the under representation in Australian higher education by the socio-economically disadvantaged and the implications for university planning', in *Journal of Institutional Research in Australasia*, 8, 11: 36–54.

Dobson, I., Sharma, R. and Ramsay, E. (1998) *Designated Equity Groups in Australian Universities: Performance of Commencing Undergraduates in Selected Course Types 1996*. Canberra: Australian Vice-Chancellors' Committee.

Ferrier, F. and Heagney, M.(2001) 'Disadvantage is complex: Targeting special groups is not enough', in L. Thomas, M. Cooper and J. Quin (eds), *Access to Higher Education: The Unfinished Business*. Stoke-on-Trent: The Institute for Access Studies, Staffordshire University.

Heagney, M. (2004*) Dropping out in Australia: Young Students from Low Socio-Economic Backgrounds and Non-Completion*, Staffordshire University. Online. Available HTTP *www.staffs.ac.uk/institutes/access/research/res20.htm*.

Krause, K., Hartley, R., James, R., and McInnis, C. (2005) *The First Year Experience in Australian Universities: Findings from a Decade of National Studies Final Report*. Canberra: Department of Education Science and Training.

Long, M., Ferrier, F., and Heagney, M. (2006) *Stay, Play or Give it Away? Students Continuing, Changing or Leaving University Study in First Year*. Canberra: Department of Education, Science and Training, Commonwealth of Australia.

Long, M. and Hayden, M. (2001) *Paying their Way: A Survey of Australian Undergraduate Student Finances 2000*. Canberra: Australian Vice-Chancellors' Committee.

McInnis, C., Hartley, R., Polesel, J. and Teese, R. (2000) *Non-completion in Vocational Education and Training and Higher Education: A Literature Review*, commissioned by the Department of Education Training and Youth Affairs, Canberra: Commonwealth of Australia.

McInnis, C. (2001) *Signs of Disengagement? The Changing Undergraduate Experience in Australian Universities*, University of Melbourne: Inaugural Professorial Lecture Centre for the Study of Higher Education, Faculty of Education.

Thomas, L., Quinn, J., Casey, L., Davidson-Burnet, G., Finlayson, I. and Peters, L. (2003) *International Comparative Research: Under-represented Groups in Tertiary Education, UK National Report*. Stoke-on-Trent: The Institute of Access Studies Staffordshire University. Online. Available www.staffs. ac.uk/institutes/access/research/res16.htm

Thomas, L. and Quinn, J. (2003) *International Insights into Widening Participation: Supporting the Success of Under-represented Groups in Tertiary Education. Final Report*. Stoke-on-Trent: The Institute for Access Studies, Staffordshire University.

Thomas, L., Cooper, M., and Quinn, J. (eds) (2003) *Improving Completion Rates among Disadvantaged Students*. Stoke-on-Trent: Trentham Books.

Tinto, V. (2002) *Establishing Conditions for Student Success*, Paper presented at the 11th Annual Conference of the European Access Network, Monash University, Prato, Italy, 20 June.

Upshaw, W. (2003) *International Comparative Research: Under-represented Groups in Tertiary Education, USA National Report*. Stoke-on-Trent: The Institute of Access Studies Staffordshire University Studies. Online. Available www.staffs.ac.uk/institutes/access/research/res16.htm

Yorke, M. (1999) 'Student withdrawal during the first year of higher education in England', in *Journal of Institutional Research in Australasia*, 8, 1: 17–35.

Turning apartheid around

Richard Blunt

The situation

October 1993: the dawn of the new South Africa. In an interview in the Boardroom on the eighteenth floor of the University of Port Elizabeth, alias UPE, I am being scrutinized by twelve middle-aged Afrikaners. The atmosphere seems informal, but I am not deceived. There are numerous agendas at stake for this institution. 'How do you see this job?', they ask. I have applied for a newly created post: Deputy Director of the Centre for Instructional Development.

Created in the apartheid ('separate development') era and reserved for 'whites', UPE had a reputation for authoritarian management and a council dominated by the Afrikaner Broederbond. In stark contrast, my academic career had begun at Rhodes University, Grahamstown, an English medium institution with a history of anti-apartheid activism. Since 1985, I had been involved in academic development and lecturing in applied linguistics at the University of Fort Hare, *alma mater* to many of Africa's political elite. I was a product of liberal education: discipline-based, rational, discursive and individualist.

The architecture of UPE was impressive: a massive quadrangle of concrete buried in the Eastern Cape bush with a 24-storey colossus rearing from its midst. Built in the 1960s in the *brutalist* tradition, the buildings symbolized apartheid. Nearby was a luxury 'white' suburb at the opposite edge of the city from the African townships. The staff and students were almost entirely 'white'. Students of other racial classifications ('black', 'coloured' or 'Asian') could be admitted only if their courses were not offered by the institutions provided for people of their 'race'.

The language policy was bilingualism. When the idea of a University of Port Elizabeth was first mooted by Afrikaner businessmen, they wanted to establish an institution as a counterpart to Rhodes. However, the 1960s Nationalist Government was eager to unite the 'white group', and financed the institution on condition that it was bilingual – Afrikaans and English. To ensure that neither dominated, the two languages alternated annually. The division was clinical. Professors would stop a student who used the 'wrong' language and tell them to start again.

Language was a critical issue for the new democracy. In the 1970s, Sowetan students had laid down their lives while resisting the imposition of Afrikaans as a compulsory school language. African languages were taught at UPE, but they were recognized as 'official' only in the 'homelands'. Consequently, when admission was opened to students and staff regardless of race, English was the only language that was both acceptable and practical as a medium of instruction. Despite its colonial history, English was an international language and not associated with the apartheid regime. The new UPE language policy that recognized Afrikaans, Xhosa and English as official languages allowed English to dominate as a *lingua franca*. Once the language policy changed, increasing numbers of African students registered for UPE programmes, and within a few years they constituted a majority.

I was encouraged to apply for the post by the new Director of Instructional Development, who had worked with me at Fort Hare. He knew that although UPE had a reputation for being like a high school – imposing strict discipline to ensure that students worked hard and passed – its teaching culture was too rigid to cope with the diverse students who would soon be entering. The model for delivery was lectures delivered as monologues comprising the presentation of information and demonstrations. Practicals were exercises in technical skills, and tutorials were used sparingly, if at all, for marking homework and remediation.

When asked in my interview how I saw the instructional development job, the faces turned towards me were anxiously concerned that my approach should not alienate staff. The professors among them were accomplished scholars, confident of their abilities as teachers and researchers. They were looking for someone who would help staff deal with diversity.

The problem for 'historically white universities' was known as the revolving-door syndrome. Students who had been through the impoverished and alienating 'Bantu Education' system would be admitted to 'historically white' universities, but would fail and drop out. Of the thousands who registered, a mere trickle graduated, particularly in the natural and economic sciences. These students would begin to fail modules, which would prolong their programmes, escalate their costs, and finally they would decide to cut their losses.

The harm of 'Bantu Education' did not lie only in the views it promoted, such as the history syllabus based on the experiences of 'white' settlers. Nor was it only the financial deprivation of schools for Africans. These were headline issues, but the most devastating effects were generated by its system, which pervaded schools for all 'race groups': a plan through which a model society would be created and maintained. To justify it, a phenomenological 'science' called fundamental pedagogics was devised based on the notion of socialization: the adult (parent/teacher) represented society and was responsible for inducting the next generation. Its association with apartheid was self-evident: people of a particular culture could induct children only into their own culture, hence the need to separate people into homogeneous ('race') groups.

This philosophy was obviously neither original nor unique. The themes of Plato's *Republic* ring strongly. Its fallacies lay in the assumptions that culture was a precious heritage, 'transmitted' from adults to children, and that the transmission could be accomplished scientifically. Of course, there was some truth in these assumptions, but missing were the dimensions of individuality, creative reflection and socio-economic development. For example, it explained individuality only as a function of 'input' rather than as a product of the child's independent judgement and assertiveness. The system translated into content- and rule-based education. Rote-learning and regurgitation were rewarded, while critical thinking was ignored. For Africans, the system included the obstacle of learning and expressing themselves through English and/or Afrikaans, neither of which they spoke outside the classroom.

This was the situation in which I found myself when I accepted the job. The major question for 'instructional development' was how we in the universities could respond to the needs of students who had been schooled in this way. How were we to help them develop independent thought and judgement so they could participate in the new democracy? We realized that the question was as relevant for 'white' students as for those from the school systems disadvantaged by apartheid.

The approaches implemented

I threw myself into the job, nervous, but believing that I could 'make a difference'. I was responsible for the induction course, which was compulsory for newly appointed UPE lecturers. I used a three-fold approach.

First, I focused on institutional interests, particularly 'transformation': the university as we knew it had to change fundamentally. We would be responsible for teaching students from disadvantaged schools, and rather than rejecting them as under-prepared, we had to help them succeed. Moreover, all UPE's policies were to be negotiated with our stakeholders in society through a representative 'Broad Negotiating Forum', and the authoritarian hierarchical management culture that had permeated the institution was to become more democratic, participative and empowering.

My second approach was to present modules so that learning objectives, content and tasks were transparent. We needed to discuss our expectations so that students understood and subscribed to them, and we needed strategies to help students develop cognitive perspective: overviews, coherence of ideas, and reflective evaluation. For example, certain subjects such as English literature had a 'traditionally' high failure rate. With the help of the course tutors and supplemental instruction leaders (see below), we realized that the students who struggled were suffering from mystification, rather than from lack of ability. They were unable to see the big picture, particularly the aims, purpose, scope and techniques of the discipline. The chair taught the first years for the whole of the first semester, despite heavy administrative and postgraduate loads. At the end of that year the failure rate was reduced, so that the supplemental instruction support groups were cut back, and became unnecessary by the end of the following year.

Students reported that the chair's overview of the discipline clarified their understanding of the lecturers' expectations, and helped them develop the critical reading abilities that underpinned their success.

Another subject with a 'traditionally' high failure rate was accountancy. We did not believe that the subject was so difficult that so many students should fail. The mathematics was elementary and the systems were logical. However, the teacher avoided teaching models for solving problems, believing that students should – from the outset – realize that there might be more than one way of solving a problem. Rather than giving them a procedure, he tried to get them to understand the nature of the problem and then work out a solution for themselves. The result was another case of mystification. Students unable to perceive the underlying logic of the problem were stuck. The lecturer refused to give them a procedure and they couldn't develop one for themselves. Moreover, the course was so pressured that there was insufficient time to help students who were left behind.

In order to assist the students, I described to the accountancy teacher Kuhn's (1977) research: our understanding of academic disciplines is built around models and exemplars. By the teacher providing models for solving problems in accountancy, the students would gradually gain perspective and work out other ways to solve the same problems. I suggested that the teacher's successful students had probably realized for themselves that they needed to find models. He saw the point immediately, but could not resolve his lack of trust in models. He withdrew from teaching the first-year students and was replaced by a younger lecturer who attended the induction course for new lecturers, where I explained Kuhn's work. The new lecturer used exemplars to show students how to solve problems, and was much more successful. The exemplars served as 'scaffolding' for students to grasp the nature of problem-solving in accountancy.

I believed that lecturers needed a rationale for changing their approach and so I used constructivism: to instill knowledge in the mind of another person, their active participation was required so that they needed to re-create the knowledge in their minds and then practise using it in appropriate ways. This led to my third approach, which was focused on students, with the aim of involving the students in active learning; to show them that the 'empty vessel' teaching methods of their schooling no longer held. If the University was to transform to meet them, they would need to change from being dependent learners – skilled at memorizing and regurgitation – and adopt an enquiry-based approach to learning: discussion, research, discipline and evaluation. Constructivism also implied that learning should be 'scaffolded' – arranged to facilitate learning – a notion that has led to teachers taking closer cognizance of the steps by which learners develop understanding.

For lecturers, tolerance was an issue. They expected high standards of expression, logic and argument. Many of the African students could barely write in English, having depended on rote-learning to gain university entrance. Some were mystified by the expectation of their expressing themselves in their own words. In school, they had been rewarded for regurgitating information verbatim from their notes and textbooks. Conflicts emerged as lecturers penalized students for plagiarism, errors of language and expressing their views without supporting arguments. Many lecturers expressed a sense of helplessness with students who were unable to cope, despite their best efforts.

Innovative approaches often encountered challenges. A law lecturer assigned groups of students to create poster papers and present them to the class. In the plenary, groups discussed each presentation, provided feedback and proposed a grade. During the presentations the lecturer was shocked to discover that her students were organizing themselves into 'race groups' and trading grades.

Some of our well-meant interventions met with resistance. Our unit adopted supplemental instruction (SI, a systematized approach to peer-facilitated learning), providing students with a space to discuss problems, assessments and so forth, with a near-peer senior student. An important advantage was that it was voluntary and did not imply inferiority on the part of those who attended. Consequently, it encouraged students to articulate their difficulties and find solutions together. It was highly successful, but one morning a professor burst into the SI coordinator's office complaining that his students had begun 'interrupting' his lectures with questions. He said he blamed SI for this 'unacceptable' behaviour.

Another strategy I used was to provide lecturers with summaries of students' evaluations of their modules. Although their feedback was mostly positive, there were occasional criticisms, and sometimes lecturers would react defensively. One professor thanked me for my summary and added, 'I chucked it in the bin!' Among my concerns was students' difficulty with English. To counter this, I encouraged lecturers to speak carefully, especially after vacations when many students had not used English for several weeks. One professor applied the advice extremely conscientiously, and spoke so slowly the students complained that he was dictating his lectures!

Despite our various projects, there were serious problems that required radical interventions. My director was concerned that students from disadvantaged schools rarely attained the mathematics grades required for a science degree. There were two obvious solutions. One was to find a way of estimating the mathematical potential of applicants. The second was to provide them with a foundation programme. The director proposed the upgrading of two existing pilot projects and application of all applicants. One was a placement assessment to counsel students on their programme choice,and included tests of their abilities to comprehend and interpret English and numeracy. The second was a foundation programme for students who showed in their placement tests that they were not yet ready for degree studies. Both had a broad reach. The placement assessment included school records, and the foundation programme incorporated the development of language and life skills through small-group facilitation. Instead of repeating the school syllabus, the foundation programme focused on discipline-specific skills. Within three years, these two programmes provided a growing stream of disadvantaged students for the sciences, and steadily reduced the attrition rate.

Simultaneously, the South African Qualifications Authority (SAQA), established in the mid 1990s (see SAQA 1997), gained momentum. With a view to developing a national qualifications framework (NQF), SAQA required universities to register their state-subsidized programmes. To qualify for registration, every programme had to conform to a number of quality criteria; definition of its purpose; specification of how it added value to the student and society; identification of its specific and 'critical cross-field' learning outcomes; statement of how it compared to similar programmes internationally; description of integrated assessment methods to demonstrate achievement of the purpose of the programme; and recognition of prior learning. The main critical cross-field outcomes covered problem-solving, cooperative learning, self-organization, information management, effective communication, critical and effective use of science and technology, and systemic understanding of the field.

The SAQA registration exercise aimed to trigger the transformation of South African higher education; to make programmes more empowering for students. In some cases it succeeded. For the most part, however, academics merely rewrote their existing curricula in SAQA's format. We took a longer-term view. While encouraging the reformulation of programmes, we established a quality assurance unit to build on SAQA's initiative. This unit set up a system for on-going internal self-appraisal against the criteria that programmes had set themselves.

These developments were crucial for improving the standards of higher education because academics were under pressure to accept larger numbers of students from the disadvantaged school systems. The final stage of our educational transformation was the development of a policy to promote learner-centred teaching. We did not want a policy in name only so we generated critical discussion and gradual buy-in. A draft framework was taken through several rounds of discussion with all the faculties and the Academic Planning and Quality Committee comprising the deans and senior administrators. The gradual approach allowed time for academics to take ownership.

Discussion

Our work in creating inclusive approaches for the diverse student population was successful in many respects. However, there were some areas from which we learnt a lot, but, with hindsight, we would have done in different ways.

Clearly, our teaching policy comprised principles that provided a framework for learner-centredness. The policy was linked to quality management, but the focus was 'formative appraisal', to help lecturers develop their teaching. Thus, at the end of each module, students evaluated the teaching, but instead of referring to this process as 'evaluation', we called it 'student feedback'.

Each of the student feedback items was related to a criterion for effective teaching, which we identified from the literature and summarised in our teaching policy. Unlike expansive approaches (some universities have literally hundreds of items in a 'bank' from which lecturers made a selection), we reduced the criteria to 21 under the themes: communication, content and methods, attitude to teaching, and assessment. Students responded to a number of positive statements using a five-point Likert Scale: Agree Strongly, Agree, Undecided, Disagree, and Disagree Strongly. For communication, we had the items: the teacher: communicates his/her expectations; plans modules clearly; provides clear module guides; communicates criteria for assessing learning outcomes; communicates the relevance of learning activities; and communicates high expectations of students' performance. For content and methods, we included: provides learning activities appropriate for achieving the intended outcomes; provides for diverse student needs, interests and abilities; provides supportive learning materials; presents learning materials interestingly; and provides a realistic workload. For the lecturer's attitude to teaching we chose: demonstrates interest in helping students learn; presents him/herself as approachable; encourages dialogue with students; encourages clear articulation of ideas in appropriate academic discourse; encourages students to cooperate in their learning; and wins the cooperation of the class. For assessment we had: assesses learning outcomes appropriately; varies methods of assessment to cater for different learning styles; provides helpful feedback on students' assignments; and guides students to evaluate their own learning.

I presented these criteria and items in faculty meetings throughout the university, emphasising that the emphasis was on facilitating learning, rather than on content. I also stressed that the criteria needed to be generic to accommodate lecturers who used resource-based learning as much as those who gave traditional lectures. This was accepted, and when introduced as university policy, the impact was immediate. Most noticeably, every lecturer prepared a course guide with learning outcomes, as described in the policy. It also impacted on styles of teaching and assessment. Lecturers began planning the questions they would ask during lectures, and consulted students about the kinds of learning activities they would find interesting. They provided greater diversity and choice. Many choices were popular with both students and lecturers. For example, group-work sometimes gave rise to conflict, but many students liked it. After the policy was enacted, lecturers could make the decision to work in groups optional, and when not forced into it, students began working cooperatively out of choice.

Providing a course guide enabled students to understand what was expected of them, and when. They had a constant resource to support them, and scaffold their learning so as to demystify the discipline. In the early days, they sometimes caused confusion because lecturers were unsure how to articulate their intentions, but they became clearer when discussed in class.

The policy provided models for planning modules and programmes, and appendices with formats for a teaching portfolio, a module guide, and a questionnaire for student feedback. It outlined the lecturers' responsibilities with respect to: curriculum planning; facilitating learning; valid and reliable assessment of learning; organization and integration of learning activities; monitoring of student attendance and performance; selection and prescription of textbooks and readings; use of the library; provision of module guides; record-keeping; maintenance of academic standards; compliance with quality assurance; budgeting of modules and programmes; and development of a teaching portfolio. To encourage lecturers to develop teaching portfolios, the university instituted teaching awards. Applicants submitted their portfolios, describing and providing evidence of how they met their teaching responsibilities. Numerous applications for awards were received, initiating a new level of recognition for good teaching. To signal their status to lecturers, the teaching awards were presented by the vice chancellor at the same ceremony as the research awards. Teaching portfolios thereafter played a role in quality audits, enabling lecturers to demonstrate their individual contributions to teaching and learning.

In the post-apartheid era, South African universities were under pressure to perform. It was not enough for them to show academic quality; they needed to demonstrate their commitment to creating an equitable society. Students were admitted to the university who would normally have been considered unprepared, and lecturers had to try to meet their needs, while accommodating larger classes and new methods. In more normal circumstances, the changes we made in a few years would have been introduced more gradually, enabling staff and students to assimilate them step by step. For example, by modularizing all courses, students were shocked by the sudden burden of continuous assessment and the need to plan their curriculum constantly. It would have been better to pilot some courses first until students were accustomed to the new model.

Language was a problem for universities because they were under political pressure to admit disadvantaged students from rural schools. While the official instruction medium was English, teachers often used the vernacular to explain. Most of these students were accustomed to memorizing large 'chunks' of discourse, which they imported piecemeal into their matriculation examinations. Predictably, many of these students failed their first year of university, incurring a heavy financial debt and losing the only opportunity of gaining a tertiary education. Subsequently, when we introduced standardized pre-entry placement tests of English and numeracy, students who needed further development in English were required to register for the one-year foundation programme.

Lecturers were under pressure from one side to accommodate under-prepared students, from another side to modularize, and from a third side to develop the quality of their programmes. In many cases, lecturers simply broke up their courses into sections, thereby fragmenting the learning process and increasing the information load. They needed to re-plan their modules holistically and include capstone modules and assignments to help students integrate their learning. Lecturers in small departments had no one with whom to discuss the structure of their discipline and felt isolated. Our university was not alone in this. Across the country, the debate raged about whether modularizing was wise. Indeed, more recently, there has been a return to courses lasting a full year. Had the process been introduced more rationally, it might have met with more success.

Our classes are so diverse that unless we return to apartheid ('separate development') and treat different 'cultural groups' differently – which we do not want to do – our teaching approach needs to be intrinsically diverse, incorporating a range of teaching-learning and assessment methods designed to optimize students' performance. Although the state retains the 'racial' classifications of apartheid in order to monitor transformation, most South Africans want to be just that – South Africans. We want to put behind us the era of separateness and prejudice and move forward to a unitary society that values, respects and takes into consideration diversity. That was our goal at UPE.

References

Kuhn, T. S. (1977) *The Essential Tension. Selected Studies in Scientific Tradition and Change*. Chicago: University of Chicago Press.

Plato, *The Republic*. Trans. T. Griffith and G. R. F. Ferrari. Cambridge: Cambridge University Press.

SAQA (1997) *SAQA Bulletin*, Vol. 1, No. 1. May/June. Available (as of 13 March 2007). Online. Available http://hagar.up.ac.za/catts/learner/1999/kreeft_c/rmxtwee/bulletin97-1.html.

Websites

South African Qualifications Authority. www.saqa.org.za.

Supplemental Instruction. www.umkc.edu/cad/si.

Case 2

How much is enuff rope?

Isabel Ellender and Marlene Drysdale

The situation

No matter how well you plan a student excursion in a remote location in Australia, something's bound to catch you by surprise! You've done it all before, students are there because they've chosen to be, you've packed in lots of brilliant experiences, and everyone's well prepared and enthusiastic. Then, something happens that threatens to undermine the whole immersion programme as well as your resolve and skills as teachers and leaders. Thank goodness a suicide attempt by a student is a rare event!

But this is what confronted us on one such excursion.

Schools of nursing and medicine across Australia now recognise the need to apprise students of the critical state of Indigenous health and ways in which, as health professionals, they will be able to make a difference. The Indigenous Health Unit at Monash University is charged with responding to the recommendations of a report endorsed by all the medical school deans across Australia. The need is for Indigenous health to be part of the experience and understanding of all medical students. The Unit's intention is to extend this instruction to nursing and health sciences at Monash University.

The focus on Indigenous health is well justified since Australia's Indigenous people have the worst health statistics in our country, with a life expectancy that is 22 years less than non-Indigenous Australians. They suffer from the worst of developed and developing world health. Rates for diabetes, renal failure, and heart disease are much higher for Indigenous people, and social diseases such as alcohol and drug abuse, domestic violence, high unemployment and poor housing continue to plague our communities. This situation has arisen from a 200-year legacy of neglect, racism, paternalistic government, as well as the lack of health care services in rural and remote locations, or they are so poorly regarded by Indigenous people that they are not accessed in a timely way.

Government attempts to solve these problems have been knee-jerk reactions rather than strategic interventions. Money alone will not fix the poor living conditions, high unemployment, high crime, substance abuse, and lack of basic services, all of which impact on people's health. There is little incentive to draw and retain medical and nursing personnel to deal with massive health problems. These circumstances prevail out of the sight of most mainstream Australians as well as government.

We understand only too well how health professionals can contribute by making primary health care more sensitive to Indigenous clients, their culture and their needs. The 200-year colonial legacy inherited by Indigenous Australians is generally poorly understood by non-Indigenous Australians, who therefore tend not to realise how Indigenous people are side-lined by what they perceive as a technology-focused, uncaring, and untrustworthy system. It's not that the many non-Indigenous professionals who frequently run the health clinics are uncaring, but that their Western medical doctrines leave no room for traditional remedies, adequate time to explain treatments and medications, or accommodate cultural sensitivities such as different consent processes, and language differences.

We worked from the premise that perceptions could be corrected if health professionals displayed some recognition and accommodation of cultural values, protocols and needs that are different from their own, but are just as important. This is well addressed by having Indigenous people themselves explain their culture and their concerns to students, rather than students learning from readings and lectures. This direct way leads students towards valuing cultural difference because they will understand it better, and in turn, this should be reflected later in their practice.

With this in mind, and in the context of our student body that comprises mainly highly educated, sophisticated young people, many of whom have never met an Indigenous Australian, we have developed a cultural awareness programme. It provides medical and nursing students with an opportunity to meet Indigenous people, perhaps for the first time, and for those people to describe in their own ways how their communities work, and the lived history and memories which underpin who they are today. Thus, we pass the teaching to those who know first-hand: that is, Aboriginal people. The learning becomes a process begun in an immersion programme with an Indigenous community, and is continued by means of reflection and practice on the part of the learners. The experience aims to integrate into the medical and nursing curricula a better understanding of Indigenous culture and the complexities of contemporary Indigenous societies.

The immersion programme, conducted in a remote Indigenous community far from the usual metropolitan conveniences, throws all participants together and requires them to hone up ways of working to mutual advantage. This was the situation in which we became aware of Gladys, and how her neediness provided an opportunity for a deep and holistic experience of working for mutual advantage for all staff and students involved.

The approaches implemented

So it was that forty international and domestic medical and nursing students settled into a fascinating programme in which they learned of the significance of rock art and country, women's sites and places of significance. They heard the stories and the concerns of the community which aimed to give them insights into social, environmental, historical and economic impacts on Indigenous health. They were shown bush foods and medicines, and had explained to them the spiritual signif- icance of places and ceremonies that protect and purify both country and people within that culture. The two Aboriginal leaders wove together the cold hard facts and the community response.

One student was to find out first-hand how this worked. Gladys was a mature- age student on one such immersion programme. She stood out at the beginning as she embraced the opportunity, arriving at the coach armed with several books, a camera, and a thousand questions. However, she often dominated the group with her questions, and because they were not always culturally appropriate or relevant to the learning of the group, they became a dilemma for the leaders. She also cre- ated diversions from the various activities to focus the leaders' attention on her needs. Although she participated in all activities with great gusto, she always seemed to manage to disrupt departure times by disappearing in the opposite direc- tion and used her skills as a photographer to explain her way out of the situation.

One night, Gladys came into the kitchen just as the staff were clearing up after the forty students had had their dinner and she asked casually:
'Excuse me, but does anyone have a piece of rope?'
Tired staff gazed at one another questioningly:
'Jim – have you got anything in the back of your coach?'
'Nah.'
So, with an 'Oh well ...', Gladys stepped out into the darkness of the night.
'Hang on, ...' said one of the leaders, 'why would she need a piece of rope? Oh no!'

Then the alert was on! All the other students were around a campfire under a starlit night taking up opportunities to ask questions or to have something clari- fied for them by the two Aboriginal leaders who had many a tale to tell and pos- itive attitudes around the contentious issues of land rights, stolen generations, deaths in custody, and poor Indigenous health. The discussion was halted and everyone spread out into the unfamiliar dark terrain to find Gladys!

Fortunately, someone found her curled up on her bunk! And fortunately, no one fell down a rocky slope or got lost! It turned out that Gladys had had a bust-up with her lesbian partner and had wanted to end it all. All of a sudden, issues sur- rounding 'duty of care' and indeed how to enforce protocol and safety measures became uppermost in our minds, as the leaders of the excursion. Gladys was an adult and able to make decisions for herself. However, she had signed a consent form prior to leaving by which she agreed to abide by the conditions set for the excursion. And what about our duty of care to the rest of the students?

As luck would have it, we had with us a staff psychiatrist who had come merely to observe! He spoke with Gladys and settled her down.

For us, the leaders, the problems had just begun! How to fulfil our duty of care to both Gladys and the rest of the students needed to be worked out. What about the objectives and viability of the rest of the programme? We considered our options.

We dispensed with the idea of sending her home because we were several hundred kilometres from any bus stop, railway station or airport. To send her alone was fraught with possibilities of a repeat performance or the potential to become a 'missing person'. We also considered it inappropriate to send a student or staff member to accompany her. We felt we had no choice but to continue with the programme and somehow look after Gladys.

Next day, all eyes were on Gladys, making sure she didn't stray out of sight or find some object intended for self-harm. We saw students picking up baler twine from the ground in case she picked it up with bad intentions. That day, Gladys stretched the limits of tolerance and made the task of actively watching her a constant challenge. Then a marvellous solution presented itself.

That next evening, in a manner quite inappropriate in Indigenous society, Gladys approached the two Aboriginal leaders and asked if they would perform a smoking ceremony so that she could be spiritually cleansed and be rid of old demons. The Aboriginal men were unsure how to respond: in Aboriginal society there is a divide between 'men's business' and 'women's business'. It seemed clear to them that this was women's business and not in their domain as Aboriginal men. Gladys, oblivious to Indigenous protocols, pressured the Aboriginal leaders to perform the smoking ceremony. The two men came to us to discuss their issues. Their embarrassment was obvious, and as excursion leaders, we had concerns about what Gladys would make of being alone in the bush at night with two strange, black men: we were getting a sense that Gladys was actually enjoying every moment of this situation. Finally, we agreed that some ceremony would appease Gladys and, at the same time, would be downplayed as a cultural event.

The leaders spoke quietly to Gladys and all three disappeared into the dark of the bush. Half an hour later, Gladys came back announcing that the purification ceremony had made her a new person, born again and cleansed of all her old ways. We heard later from the men that she had told them she had suicidal tendencies and had tried to kill herself about nine times. They had then helped her make a fire, collect and burn some leafy branches to wave the smoke around her head. They stressed to us that this was not any Aboriginal ceremony that they knew of but if it worked .... It worked to the extent that we slept a little easier that night.

Discussion

After returning to university, we had a discussion on the events of the excursion. Had it been worth it? Did it fulfil its original objectives? Could we have done better in our response to Gladys's crisis?

Gladys's crisis highlighted how one unplanned event could have been disastrous and wrecked the entire programme. We could have been dealing with a death, our academic careers could have been under a cloud, and the Aboriginal community would have been seen in a negative light. But instead, we witnessed a heartening team effort in which students came forward with offers to be with her day and night, the community performed a ceremony, and the staff psychiatrist provided an informed approach. On reflection, we considered that we had adequate planning and organisation, and had made the right decisions in dealing with the crisis. The crisis emphasised the need for sufficient supervising staff, a satellite telephone in a remote location, a number of trained first-aiders, and consent forms which reveal as much as possible the likely medical crises that could arise from known medical conditions.

As far as the learning experience had been concerned, in the light of our programme objectives of raising our students' awareness of the history and culture of Aboriginal Australia, the results from the student evaluations of the programme were most positive. Students felt it had made realistic their assumptions about their prior knowledge of Indigenous culture and society. It had contributed significantly to increasing it in ways that many of our students observed could not be learned from books and lectures. Above all, it had provided insights for our students into how historical, economic, environmental, political and social factors, as well as remoteness, can impact on the health of individuals and communities. Our experience with the programme reinforces for us constantly the need to continue to provide a comprehensive prior orientation, and a concluding debrief. These activities make the most of the experience, and help students create the links between what they hear and observe with the many aspects of contemporary Indigenous health.

Another objective of the programme was to encourage teamwork among this group of international and Australian students undergoing nursing and medical courses. This sort of diversity does not lend itself to easy cooperation. The responses to surprise first-aid scenarios revealed the awkward relationship and expectations one group had for another. Certainly, the Gladys crisis had provided a stimulus for pulling the group together and offers of help from students to stay with her, even though Gladys herself had attempted to undermine our authority and the teamwork, and had alienated herself from the group. The full coverage of this task is covered in a forthcoming journal article.

The third objective related to raising student awareness of a culture different from their own and what that might mean in terms of their future perspectives, values and practice as health professionals. For most, it was the first time they had ever been introduced to Australian Indigenous people or their culture. We observed an initial rapt attention which dissolved into a more easy-going but still respectful attitude of most of the students. We suspect that for these students, it is the beginning of a process of reflection and enquiry that may lead some to return to work in rural and remote clinics, or at least return later with family to revisit such a welcoming community. The reflective journal that the students were required to write revealed enthusiasm and included detailed drawings or photographs to remind them later on. For instance, some students wrote about how 'it opened my eyes to things I had never heard about or thought existed in Australia' and 'it was a great way to encourage positive relationships between health professionals'.

The Aboriginal leaders had become not merely unconventional teachers, but also friends. This was evident in the way students interacted with them and showed respect when they were talking. Others have returned to visit outside of university classes and keen horse-people made a trip to go riding with family members. Many students on returning to their studies have become actively involved in 'Wildfire' (a student club that promotes Indigenous health), or have taken up their clinical placements in remote and rural Aboriginal settings.

What had Gladys got out of the programme? Perhaps her life! Above all, she had received a compassionate, holistic Aboriginal response to her agony since the smoking ceremony had done more for her than the admittedly short sessions with the staff psychiatrist! To the very end of the coach journey home, she continued attention-seeking behaviour and delaying tactics. As the coach was about to leave, she could not be found. At stops along the way, she had to retrieve belongings forgotten in various locations. As we approached home, she expected the driver to negotiate his coach of weary people through narrow suburban streets to drop her at her home. It took some effort to locate a friend who would meet her at the allocated bus stop. Finally and thankfully, we helped her find her belongings dotted throughout the coach and gave her up to her friend.

Gladys did us a good turn by drawing our attention to the need to look beyond our own emotional involvement as teachers and to hang on to compassion, a sense of fair play, objectivity, and the right of education to provide chances in life, which are the important values we uphold as teachers.

Educational innovation: an unexpected diversity tool?

Rick Wolff, Sabine Severiens and Rob de Crom

The situation

Over the last few years, the growth of foreign background first-year students in higher education in the Netherlands has been spectacular (Crul & Wolff, 2002).[1] This increase in numbers has raised the important question in the higher education sector in general, and at the level of institutions, of whether foreign background students perform as well as their local counterparts. The first signs are worrying: national data show less study progress and higher drop-out rates (Crul and Wolff, 2002; Hofman and Van den Berg, 2003). Discussions on the poor performance of foreign background students, more specifically of ethnic minority students, tend to stress that these students do not fit equally well into the higher education system.

An alternative approach is to look at the performance of institutions and their separate courses. The relevant question is whether the study progress of foreign background students depends on the learning environment offered by higher education institutions and their course programs. And if so, the question concerns which characteristics of institutions or course programs contribute to better study results among foreign background students (see Figure 3.1).

Our concerns were not based on anecdotal 'hearsay'; a study of six university course programs[2] (Severiens, Wolff and Rezai, 2006) found that the percentage of students who gained the maximum number of first-year credits was much lower among foreign background students than among majority students (Figure 3.1). In some cases, there is even a percentage difference of 20 to almost 30 points between groups. But of particular interest to us was course program 6 (economics) which presented a pleasant surprise: the two groups performed almost as well. In fact, the study progress of the group of foreign background students is even slightly better than the majority group! This result indicates that institutional and course program characteristics *do* matter. It made us very curious about the special features of the course program.[3]

This had not always been the case with this economics course. By the end of the 1990s, it held an exceptional position in the field, but it was on the wrong end of the scale! The curricular design was rather 'old skool', comprising mainly

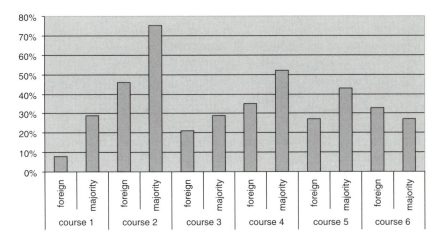

Figure 3.1 Student percentages (cohort 2003/2004) who obtained the maximum number of credits after one year of study (60 ECTS*) by ethnic background.
Source: Severiens, Wolff and Rezai (2006).
Note: * European Credit Transfer System.

lectures for large groups of over 500 students. At the same time, completion rates were low, drop-out rates were high, students were barely motivated and in particular, first-year subjects were evaluated as 'poor' by their teachers. It was no surprise that in national student polls, almost all comparable course programs at other Dutch universities were ranked higher on academic quality. Clearly, changes were needed in order to serve students better, perhaps even to survive. The looming introduction of the Bachelor/Master system in Dutch higher education and a decrease in the influx, down to some 175 first-year students, provided the opportunity to revise the curriculum radically.[4]

The approaches implemented

It was in this context that the new Economics course program was developed. We took a qualitative perspective, with interviews with two policy makers, four teachers, two student counsellors and five students of Moroccan, Turkish or Surinamese descent, who started their program in the academic year 2003/2004.[5] Our investigation revealed that the current situation is a result of general innovative measures, which, by accident, generate positive side-effects for specific groups.

The first step in the curriculum development was that a committee was formed, consisting of some professors, the head of the Educational Bureau and an education expert. It met for the first time some two–and-a-half years before the start of the first cohort of BA/MA-students in 2002/2003. The members agreed wholeheartedly that the new curriculum should be based on a thematic, cross-subject approach in order to show students linkages between separate subjects and to enhance their overall perspective. To this end, the committee decided to assign each teaching period a so-called focal element and then select courses that contributed to this. As such, the period with the focal element of 'Enterprise, entrepreneuring and strategy', which consists of courses in micro-economics, marketing, management and organisation, and statistics, was selected. To make linkages clear between these courses, students are asked to solve a case in which they have to reorganise a bicycle factory that is rapidly losing customers. Micro-economics and marketing each explore relevant consumer behaviour, statistics offers the tools for analysis needed in micro-economics, and the course on management and organisation teaches students avenues through which restructuring of the factory can take place, considering the accounting company strategy and position of the factory in the market.

A second goal was to construct a course program with a minimum of obligations in order to maintain the university character of the program, where students operate as independent learners. However, a minimum of obligations does not equal an uncommitted attitude, or as one program manager explains:

> We give clear guidelines to our students. It is their choice to participate. On the other hand, we care about our students and do everything in our power to offer them the best possible program. In return we expect them to work hard.

Thirdly, the committee stressed the significance of the social component of the new curriculum. Students have to feel at home among their peers, faculty and student support staff in order to feel committed to their course program. Important tools to stimulate the learning process included cooperation in small project groups and discussion among students. In other words, social contacts stimulate the academic development.

The findings of the committee resulted in the current curriculum design. The most striking innovation is the division of the first year into four blocks of eight weeks.[6] Each block consists of four subjects centred around one central theme. Blocks have a 'teaching' period of six weeks and a 'preparation' period of two weeks before the test. In the teaching period, students receive plenary lectures and have the opportunity to deepen and apply their knowledge in what are called the Activating Work Groups (AWV) that meet several times a week. These AWVs comprise some twenty-five students, grouped by student administration. Often, during sessions, the AWVs are subdivided, by the teacher or by students themselves, into groups of three or four students to work on small assignments. Participation in AWVs is on voluntary basis, but the course program stimulates attendance by offering active students a bonus point on top of their final test score. For each new block, student administration groups students into AWVs. Consequently, the course program offers swift rotation, in which students study with different peers in each period. This system is used as a key feature to enhance the social embedding of individual students into the academic setting.

The rationale of an eight-week block structure is three-fold. First, the subjects of the old system are divided into smaller parts, which facilitates the arrangement of different subjects under one central theme. This thematic approach encourages teachers to work together on an interdisciplinary basis, promoting the collaboration between the different sections. Secondly, more than in semester and trimester systems where students have a propensity to postpone learning and to compress the material of a few months into two weeks before the test, students are stimulated to start in time for the 'soon coming' tests. Thirdly, because of this early start, material/knowledge is expected to be sustained for a longer time.

A team of trained teachers and professors educate the students. The quality of teaching is assured through several measures. Poorly performing teachers, evaluated as such by the course program management and by students, are withdrawn from the program if they do not improve their teaching within a certain period of time. Furthermore, it is recommended that new and poorly performing teachers take a one-year teacher-training program in teaching methods, including topics such as activating students, presenting material and structuring lectures. Some 70 per cent of the teachers have undertaken this training program. Teachers who successfully complete the training are financially rewarded. Thirdly, all teachers have graduated, so student-assistants do not teach. Finally, compared to other university courses (as found in the Severiens, Wolff and Rezai study), program management and faculty stress the significance of a balance between teaching and research obligations and are keen to prevent research time from consuming education time.

A final feature of the curriculum is a team of three student counsellors that supports students. The counsellors keep track of the study progress of each student and interview students at three points during the academic year. For the first interview, which takes place in January, all students are invited, including students who perform well. Obviously, study progress is a major issue in these interviews, but student counsellors also try to discover whether students feel comfortable in the course program. Here again, the social component is a fully fledged element of procedures.

The proof of the pudding is in the eating. According to the ethnic minority students we interviewed, the curriculum does what it is supposed to do. The block structure and the AWVs serve several goals at the same time, or as one of the Moroccan students explained:

> The AWVs make me plan my material because you get another chapter every week. The meetings also focus on applying the material, which is what you also have to do at tests.

The curriculum designers stressed the importance of the social aspect of the program. Students also confirm that the measures that have been developed work well. Over a short period, students are introduced to many peers because of the swift rotation system of the AWVs. One student even told us explicitly that the program made him 'more social'. Also, we have noted a linkage between the social component of the program and the academic development of students. This is illustrated by experiences of one of the Turkish students with project groups:

> Working together generates more success. You are confronted with more approaches, you hear more opinions and come up with more answers and solutions.

The social environment of the course (the motto is 'we care about our students') seems to enhance the students' commitment to the program. Strong student involvement is illustrated by the high attendance at non-compulsory course elements such as study groups and interviews with study counsellors.

The model seems to generate effects among students and also teachers. The interdisciplinary meetings, a result of the thematic character of the curriculum, begin the process of breaking down barriers between the different fields of expertise. Before the start of each teaching period, course lecturers are invited to meet and discuss their contribution to the focal element of their period. To elaborate on the previous example, micro-economics and marketing lecturers determine together the relevant elements of consumer behaviour for the theme, which they will present. Similarly, micro-economics first determines which statistical methods students should be able to use, thus helping shape the contents of the statistics course. To achieve this, lecturers need to abandon their traditional course design and adapt their courses to the theme as well as the needs of their fellow lecturers. The same holds for the examinations held at the end of each period; lecturers discuss each other's exam questions, ensuring coherence with concomitant courses and the central theme.

Unlike the previous situation, teachers place subjects into a broader perspective. According to a program manager, these meetings refresh the attitudes of teachers towards their subjects. Some teachers coach each other by attending and evaluating each other's classes.

The teacher training contributes to the skills of faculty to a certain extent. Teachers include more active elements in their classes, and explain material with appealing, concrete examples. One experienced teacher who is also an education expert, has perceived a change in the teaching methods of a number of his colleagues since the introduction of the new curriculum.

The new curriculum does not seem to affect the interactions between students and teachers. Similar to other programs, students report good as well as bad teachers. Good teachers present clarifying material additional to the official test material and encourage their students to be curious and critical in class. They are approachable and take students and their questions seriously. Conversely, bad teachers present boring classes, reproducing the textbook material, and create a sense of distance with their students. Not surprisingly, class forms like the AWVs are the favoured learning settings among both students and teachers. In AWVs, learners and teachers interact directly and have more time to elaborate on the subject material. In other words, AWVs provide more opportunities for contact on a personal basis.

Discussion

It is clear to all that the curriculum innovations have instilled a new set of dynamics in the course and, generally, appear to be an improvement. But how do these new measures work for specific groups such as ethnic minority students?

Considering the even study progress of both ethnic minority and majority students in the economics program which is an exceptional finding compared to other courses, one should expect that special efforts had been put in place in regard to ethnic diversity.[7] Surprisingly, diversity seems not to be an issue. Neither the program management nor faculty, nor even the ethnic minority students, support the development and implementation of a specific ethnic diversity policy. Possible differences between minority and majority students (including situation at home, mastery of language, motivation) are perceived as problematic for only a small number of foreign background students and therefore not suitable for policy development. Ethnic minority students deem such a policy as stigmatizing, especially for students who are doing well.

At one point, however, the ethnic diversity of the student body does seem relevant. Ethnic minority and majority students do not mingle and group with students of the same ethnic background. According to the students themselves, ethnic minority students feel more at ease with each other; they understand each other's background, share the same kind of humour, and so on. However, the students appear to distinguish between formal, within class, and informal, outside class, contacts. In formal settings, students from all ethnic groups work and interact well together, but outside the formal settings, the student body reshapes into separate ethnic groups.

In our opinion, the division between the formal and informal contacts indicates the success of our course. On the one hand, students are free to form their own social networks in informal settings. On the other hand, the organisation of the formal settings, particularly the study groups' system of swift rotation plays an important role in the initial contacts between the ethnic minority and majority students. From an early stage, students learn to study together with unknown fellow students. Thus in a social sense, all students have an equal start and are offered the same opportunities to create academic networks. Furthermore, small-scale teaching is applied throughout the course, with students collaborating in small groups (AWVs, project groups), subjects subdivided into small blocks, and teachers trained for this learning environment. As previously expressed, both students and teachers prefer this small-scale, personal educational setting. Furthermore, the teachers are conscious of the curriculum design and are stimulated to cooperate across disciplines. This contributes to clear guidelines for the operation of the course, and for the students. It also seems that the combination of social and academic factors results in a learning environment where the ethnic minority students perform as well as their majority counterparts.

It may be stated that the course seems strongly directive towards students, and thus contradicts the academic goal of independent learning. However, the program committee is convinced that the curriculum stimulates independent learning within a structured learning environment. Students seem comfortable with the characteristics of the course. As one Turkish student puts it: 'I like the course program because it is so directive. This makes students more involved in the material.'

Possibly, a directive innovative curriculum may even be helpful to certain groups, as the same Turkish student explains:

> The curriculum design connects to the directive needs of ethnic minorities.... You'll find average Dutch student [*sic*] more often at lectures, while ethnic minority students tend to go to AWVs.

This case study is a concrete example of several of Tinto's (1998, 2003) theoretical notions. First, retention is promoted when students are provided with ample opportunities to work together. Secondly, the teaching quality improves if teachers cooperate and attune their own subjects to that of their peer teachers. Such a thematic approach has a positive impact both on students' learning and on teachers' teaching. Thirdly, an important condition in the implementation of effective structural measures is the commitment of policy makers, faculty and staff. In other words, there needs to be preparedness to invest in retention. This facilitates a learning environment in which faculty have high expectations of *all* students. Ultimately, this will enhance students' involvement and enhance the study progress of both minority and majority students.

Our research findings are both surprising and promising: the case study indicates that, under certain conditions, it is possible to develop a curriculum that promotes equal opportunities for students from all ethnic backgrounds, as well as for majority students. However, some important discussion points linger. First, we stressed that the learning environment for ethnic minority students can be improved by educational innovations and that small-scale teaching and learning is beneficial to all students, regardless of their background. However, the question remains as to whether these students will perform even better within an inclusive, diversity-oriented learning environment. At this point, we cannot answer this question, because none of the course programs we examined has a diversity policy. Furthermore, to our knowledge, there is no such course in Dutch universities.[8] Secondly, we have gathered information from a limited number of respondents for this qualitative case study, which raises the question of the extent to which the results represent the situation for the entire first year of the course. However, we can say that representation was not the main purpose of the research. Rather, the purpose was to explore the relevant aspects of the learning environment in relation to the study progress of ethnic minority students. Having said this, it would be interesting to conduct a larger study involving the complete course program in order to deepen our knowledge and to fine-tune the findings discussed in this case study.

Notes

[1] In the Dutch situation, an individual is seen as having a foreign background when at least one of the parents is born outside the Netherlands, regardless if this person is born in or outside the Netherlands.

[2] Two economics, one law and three psychology course programs.

[3] In this study, we focus on differences of study progress between minority and majority students at the same course program. However, this does not mean that students of course program 6 performed best compared with their counterparts in other course programs. For example, foreign background students of course 2 performed best. However, the percentage difference with their majority peers is exceptionally high.

[4] The decrease of influx partly reflected a national trend, but a more important reason was the faculty had started a new business administration program, which proved more popular to students than the old-fashioned, if thorough, economics program.

[5] Our main focus is on students who are members of target groups of Dutch policies. Since all of our student respondents belong to one of these groups we refer to them as 'ethnic minority students' instead of the broader term 'foreign background students'.

[6] Each block is followed by a practicum period of four weeks in which students form groups and work, accompanied by a teacher, on an assignment related to the central theme of the former block. At the end of the period each group has to deliver a paper and present its work. These practicum groups are also a new element in the curriculum, but the eight-week blocks are considered the core of the course program.

[7] Diversity comprises more than ethnicity. It can also refer to issues such as race, gender, disability and age. However, we confine ourselves to ethnicity since this was the main theme of our research.

[8] Although diversity policy is pursued at the institutional level in several universities in the study of Severiens, Wolff and Rezai, it appears to be invisible at the course program level.

References

Crul, M. and Wolff, R. 2002, *Talent gewonnen. Talent verspild?* Utrecht: ECHO, 2002.

Hofman, A. and Van den Berg, M. (2003) Ethnic-specific Achievement in Dutch Higher Education, *Higher Education in Europe, 28,3:* 371–389.

Severiens, S.,Wolff, R. and Rezai, S. (2006) *Diversiteit in leergemeenschappen: Een onderzoek naar stimulerende factoren in de leeromgeving voor allochtone studenten in het hoger onderwijs.* Utrecht: ECHO.

Tinto, V. (1998) Colleges as communities: Taking research on student persistence seriously, *Review of Higher Education* 21 (2): 167–177.

Tinto, V. (2003) Establishing conditions for student success, in L. Thomas, M. Cooper & J. Quinn (eds), *Improving Completion Rates among Disadvantaged Students.* Stoke-on-Trent: Trentham Books.

My father wants me to study engineering!

Teoh Kok Soo

The situation

The Real Player on my PC had just finished playing Tchaikovsky's 1812 overture when I heard a knock on my door. As I turned towards the door I saw three eager, young and anxious-looking faces. 'Come in', I said while waving my hand to signal them to enter.

These three students, two Malaysian and a Sri Lankan, stepped into my room hurriedly. Han Ming, a Chinese local student, was the first to speak:

> Sir, we want to talk to you about our group member, Mahmood. He is not doing the project work that we had assigned to him. In our previous four group meetings that were held on Friday afternoon, he only turned up twice and then he was late too. During our group meetings, he just sat there and hardly contributed to our discussion.

Prabu, the Sri Lankan international student, added: 'His work in Stage 1 project work was so bad that I had to spend extra four hours just to make the necessary amendments and revision to our group report!' Prathiba, the other Indian local student, also expressed his concerns:

> Yah, there was once I assigned, via MSN Messenger, a very small part of the project to him, and I ended up having to completely redo the whole thing he handed to us. And this is so unfair, we have to do all the work for him but he is getting the same marks as all of us.

I am the unit coordinator of a first-level unit called engineering profession at an offshore campus of an Australian university in Malaysia. The unit is taught to the first-year engineering students, including both local and international students. The local students include three different major ethnic groups, Malay, Chinese and Indian, while the international students come mainly from Indonesia, China, Sri Lanka and Iran. English is a second language to all these students, albeit that it is the language used in teaching and learning in this institution.

The aim of my unit is to introduce the essence of engineering and to provide an understanding of the environment in which engineers work and interact with the community to the new students in the engineering program at the campus in Malaysia. The students must do group projects that last for the whole semester, where the approaches adopted are problem-based learning and teamwork. Students are divided into groups of four to work on a group project that simulates a real industry project. The assessment includes submission of project assignments, reports and oral presentations over the 13-week semester.

Han Mong continued to explain to me: 'Sir, this is already the sixth week into the semester. We don't want to keep doing his share of work and not getting a good mark at the end. Can you change Mahmood to another group?' I could see from Han Ming's body language that he was clearly feeling very frustrated about the poor quality of work of Mahmood. As the other two students nodded their heads in agreement with Han Ming's comments, I realized that this group had reached their limit of tolerance and they were ready to explode. Mahmood, a Muslim student from Iran, did not appear to be able to 'mix' well and interact with his group members.

In the context of the local education environment, throughout their primary and secondary education, students seldom challenge the system, tutors or the authorities, nor do they ask for any changes. They are passive in their approach, and are taught to be obedient and tolerant of others. So when these students approached me, it seemed to me that they had reached the last straw and had come to a decision. They wanted me to take some action to solve their problem, ease their anger and end their frustration with what seemed an unfair system of reward for the work done.

The approaches implemented

I asked Mahmood to see me so I could hear his side of the story. Mahmood expressed his view strongly:

> I did all the work they asked! I don't understand why they complained about me. Rather, they always call the meeting on a Friday afternoon. You know, I need to go to the mosque! I tried running to the meeting twice, but their discussion had nearly ended. I don't understand the assignment and they do not want to teach me. They just don't think about me, nobody does.'

My first reaction was that this was a cultural misunderstanding that has soured the relationship. But I also wondered if there was something else as well. 'You mean, nobody thinks about you?', I asked Mahmood. He responded:

> I never wanted to do engineering. Just because I did well in my physics and mathematics subjects at my pre-university study, my father wanted me to take this up. I'm not sure if this is right for me. Of course I'll do whatever I can to please him.

I was not really surprised by Mahmood's response, because it is a common scenario at our campus. Many students enter a certain discipline not because this is their choice, but because it was their parents' choice. Local culture and, to a certain extent, many Asian cultures expect obedience and accomplishment of what is expected of them and chosen for them by their parents or communities, rather than the students making a choice of their own.

Mahmood told me that he did not know what he wanted to do at the university. As he did well in his pre-university education, he agreed to his father's choice of course for him. On further investigation, he told me that when he started his first year, he found it difficult to adapt as the course is conducted in English. Language is a major issue for him. He found it difficult to speak in the class, as he was afraid that others might laugh at him. And on the rare occasion when he spoke up, all the students would look at him because he took a long time to find the right words to express himself. He told me that he felt embarrassed, even though no one had actually belittled him. He felt inadequate and hence chose to remain silent most of the time in class, unless he was asked to speak.

I thanked him for sharing his situation with me, He said that he was surprised at my response, and at the same time, felt relieved to be able to share his feelings. It was not easy for a male Muslim to disclose matters close to his heart to someone of a different religion. It was even more uncommon for a tutor to thank a student for sharing his personal feelings, something to which they were not accustomed as they were used to a system of hierarchy. In the course of our discussion, I discovered that Mahmood was actually interested in engineering, even though this was not his chosen field at first. I encouraged him to speak up and interact with his peers on the campus and reassured him that English is a second language for most students and tutors alike at the campus in Malaysia, and he should not be afraid to speak up and practise his spoken English, especially in his small four-member group. He had missed the group meetings several times and a sense of group rapport had not been established. Hence, his feelings of unfairness and distrust ensued.

Later, I invited his group to visit me for an open discussion on their respective cultures, traditions, beliefs and religions, and Mahmood explained to the group that Friday lunch-time was not a good time to hold the meetings as Muslims need to perform their prayers. The local group members apologized for overlooking that issue, while this was a new understanding for the Sri Lankan student. I discussed the language issue with the group as a whole, and all of them felt that their language levels were similar. Following a discussion on group work and group dynamics, all members seemed happy to give it another try as a group with a common understanding and some basic ground rules drawn up.

When the time came for the group to do their oral presentation, Mahmood presented his share of the work. He had rehearsed it a few times with his group members, the group had reached an understanding and its members were able to work well together. At the end of the industry project, Mahmood came to me and said he now understood what engineering was about and wanted to be an engineer. His English had improved and it did not deter him from doing well.

Discussion

Despite English being well recognized as a global language, it is a second language in many countries. For international as well as local students in an offshore campus of an Australian university, recognizing the need to strengthen their English-language skills is important in order to facilitate students' learning. A language and learning support service is provided at the university for students who are identified as weak in the English language. It is a tailored program lasting a semester, and students who complete this are awarded bonus marks to encourage them to strengthen their language skills.

At the same time, the teaching and learning program I present builds in language development and cross-cultural understandings. At the first tutorial of the unit, I conduct an ice-breaking exercise where students are first paired up and have to find out about each other. They describe their country of origin, culture, tradition, and way of life in their respective countries, as well as their own interests. They then introduce their partner to the class. This session allows the students to share and understand the cultural diversity among their group. It also stimulates discussion, respect and tolerance for different cultures. Group dynamics are initiated and more often than not, friendships develop between the partners. The oral presentation in this first tutorial is used to help students overcome 'stage fright' in speaking in front of the group as many of these students rarely, if ever, present in class during their primary and secondary education. This is different from a western classroom even in the early primary years where presentation is commonplace.

The sharing of diverse culture, history and tradition is pertinent. Misunderstandings can be avoided if we try to understand each other's culture and religion. It encourages the students to appreciate the beauty of diverse cultures, as well as explore their similarities and differences.

Local students have been used to a very competitive environment throughout their years of education, where achievement equates with marks and grades. Communication and social skills have not been emphasized at all. This situation is also seen in international students studying at the Malaysian campus. Nearly all students at our university are supported by their parents, who have paid the costs themselves, or taken a bank loan to support their children. Such strong financial support may be seen as a legitimate reason for the parents to expect their children to succeed, as their education may be regarded as their investment for their child's future or career. For instance, Han Ming was eager to score well in assessment as this was the way he could demonstrate that he had excelled in his study and met his parents' expectations. Similarly, Prabu needed to make sure that he did well to finish the course within the stated period of time, both to satisfy parental expectation and the financial pressure.

In order to divert the focus solely from academic achievement, we introduce teamwork as a form of learning and assessment. We explain and discuss with the students the criteria for effective group work, such as identifying team members' strengths and weaknesses, establishing relationships, developing communication skills, and learning about leadership. We discuss group formation, group work and group dynamics. In the classroom, tables are rearranged so that students can sit in a circle to facilitate discussion. I sit in on their group discussions to facilitate the problem-based learning approach.

Oral presentation forms part of the assessment process. This encourages the student to learn how to present themselves, to be assertive and to lead. Peer assessment is also utilized to represent individual student's performance. Students perceived this to be a fair system of award for their work.

We also use industry projects that simulate a real industrial project tendering process. This unique project encourages and stimulates interest in the engineering discipline and profession. As a teaching and learning approach, it has been received well by the students and profession alike. It also allows the industries to understand what the students have been taught, and cooperation is established with the industrial partners which helps the students understand about the profession and career development.

Students' attitudes towards the modified teaching method

The students have made positive remarks and given feedback on the curriculum. They enjoy the interactive nature of the classes, something that is different from what they had been exposed to throughout their early years of education. The industrial project allows them to think laterally and critically while, at the same time, needing to be self-directed, learning to collaborate and communicate, as well as understand the team approach. It stimulates their interest and a sense of belonging to the profession.

The limitations of this curriculum lie in the time constraints and resources to carry out all these activities in a 13-week semester. Student counselling takes time. The industrial project is a shock to the students at first as it is seen as a 'mega project' that is difficult to achieve at their level within the specified time. However, all is worthwhile towards the end of this unit as the students indicate clearly in their evaluations that the unit has given them a good exposure and assisted them to become a more rounded person to face future challenges in the engineering field.

One question remains in my mind: is there another way of assessing individual performance in group work in this multicultural environment, apart from the peer assessment that we have introduced? Apart from assessing students' academic achievements, what about interpersonal and communication skills, leadership and the ability to work in a team that are important elements in their future career as engineers? These are also aspects that reflect students' cross-cultural and language development, and will require further reflection and action on my part.

Maximising potential in higher education: a curriculum response to student diversity

John Bamber

The situation

'The lesson is clear', wrote Stuart Hall (1998: 4), 'If all students are to maximise their educational potential, the institutions of higher education have to increase their awareness of, and support for, the growing diversity of students who enter higher education.' The need for change is starkly exemplified in the exponential growth of the student population in the UK. From just over 800,000 students in 1987, there were over two million in 2006. In this context the Dearing Report (DfES, 1997: 101) stated that the expansion, 'must be accompanied by the objective of reducing the disparities in participation in higher education between groups and ensuring that higher education *is responsive* [my emphasis] to the aspirations and distinctive abilities of individuals.'

As a university lecturer, I responded to the diversity of my students at the level of curriculum. In so doing, my focus was on the learning experiences of 22 of my students who were part-time and work-based. These students undertook Work Based Learning 1: Professional Development (WBL1), which is one of nine undergraduate courses in a professionally endorsed BA in Community Education.

Stored on a CD, students download the course on to their computer at home or at work. It is not necessary to be on-line, but if they are, they can make use of hyperlinks to selected websites. The course combines weekly face-to-face meetings over two semesters with distance approaches in a structured learning process, which incorporates an integral resource base of content materials. It is an example of blended or resource-based learning.

The students ranged between the ages of 21 and 50. Employment among the four men and eighteen women was varied, with some in full-time, permanent positions while others worked on a paid part-time basis, or had voluntary commitments. All worked at least ten hours per week in the associated field of practice. Their entrance to the part-time programme placed a high premium on the candidate's relevant experience, who had a variety of qualifications. A few had a Higher National Certificate, or some other evidence of recent study of equivalent status. In addition, an arrangement with the University's Centre for Lifelong Learning meant that a number without formal qualifications could gain entry to the programme by taking accredited courses. Most lacked the standard entry qualifications, however, and even where they had qualifications, these had been obtained many years ago. The students were white British, with most coming from Scottish manual working-class backgrounds.

As teachers, it is important that we understand the experience of such students because they often find conventional teaching and assessment approaches, such as heavy reliance on lectures for delivery and essays and examinations for assessment, difficult to cope with. It is not appropriate to regard these students as inherently problematic; they bring to their studies a range of strengths and qualities such as motivation, commitment and a desire for their learning to be personally meaningful. My experience is that mature students are more likely to want a truly participative experience in Higher Education (HE), where they do not simply receive knowledge, but play their part as active learners, interacting with and 'authoring' knowledge. Conventional teaching and learning approaches have their place but by themselves, they are not enough to facilitate the necessary conditions for full participation. At bottom, the students need to take control of the underlying assumptions and premises upon which their own knowledge is constructed. The need, therefore, is for the curriculum to address powerful beliefs held by some students about the process of teaching, the way students see themselves as learners, as well as their awareness of ways of thinking and practising in a given subject area.

While I had long recognised the issues involved, the opportunity only came for me to design a different kind of teaching and learning experience when timetabling restrictions meant that the part-time students were not able to access two elective courses that were available to their full-time counterparts on the same programme. I had to provide tailor-made courses, and my aim was to create a very different course from the more usual format in my own department.

Curriculum design issues to be addressed

There were several sorts of issues that needed to be addressed in the curriculum design. A major issue was that the students needed to move from a transmissive to a transformative understanding of teaching and learning processes. In other words their views needed to move from a position where knowledge and theories are deemed to be either right or wrong, to one in which finer judgements have to be made about alternative theories, based upon evidence and analysis. Transition, however, is not a quick or easy process for students in this situation, and the stronger the belief, the more difficult it is for the student to change. Short courses on study skills are insufficient because they often fail to address deep-seated convictions that 'the teacher knows best', the flip side of which is the debilitating notion that students know nothing. I knew that I would need to incorporate active engagement, involving students in discovering content for themselves and presenting what has been learnt to others in the class. In this way, I thought they might come to see that the teacher is not the only source of knowledge.

The way that students think about themselves as learners is also a crucial element in the learning process. Many adopt 'surface' approaches to study where they seek only to 'retell' information in order to pass assessment tasks. For others, study is 'deeper' and more personally meaningful, so that students are drawing links and making meaning for themselves. In this regard, non-traditional students often inhabit an ambivalent space where, on the one hand, they see study instrumentally as a means to a qualification, while simultaneously wanting it to be personally meaningful. I needed to develop strategies for encouraging students to seek depth as they studied. The trick, I felt, would not be to give too much support which can give students a false idea about their abilities, but to increase the level of challenge as students proceeded.

Particular disciplines have their own ways of thinking and practising, but students' understanding of these cannot be left to osmosis, especially with non-traditional students for whom HE can seem like an alien environment. My design needed to include appropriate and explicit teaching and learning strategies to encourage the students, for example, to develop their own views and to be critical of established sources. Giving form to such strategies means going beyond typical modes of course delivery. Consequently, I decided to use live projects where students would have to work out for themselves what constituted the important elements of complex situations, and test strategies for dealing with problems. The intention was to connect with their desire for studies to be personally meaningful and to relate concretely to the world outside academe. The process would also use group discussion and collaborative work to provide multiple perspectives on the resolution of practice problems. I knew from experience that creating a trustful atmosphere would also be crucial for students who lacked confidence in their own views and found it difficult to assert their ideas in the classroom setting. Realising these issues was my first step, and the key challenge was to include them in the curriculum design.

The approaches implemented

Work based learning 1: professional development

The design of the course addressed the students' need for the course to be relevant outside the classroom, and for the students to be actively engaged. Work Based Learning 1: Professional Development is thus divided into four sections, each of which covers a major aspect of professional life. As can be seen from Figure 5.1, each section has two parts, and each part addresses one learning outcome through an extended exercise.

The course content as follows indicates an attempt to meet the key challenge that I had set myself:

- **Section 1: professional practice**
  - Assessing competence using a competence framework
  - Preparing learning objectives for the designated placement period

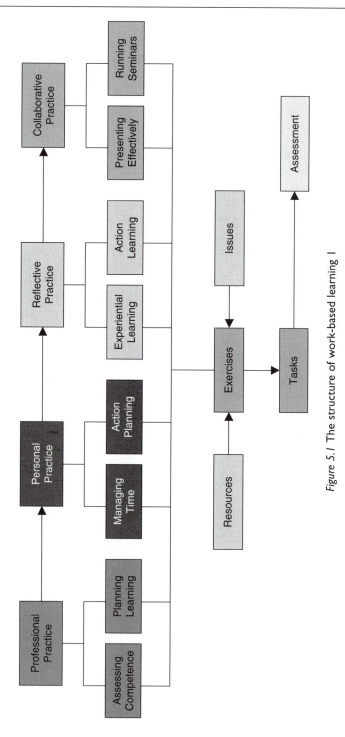

Figure 5.1 The structure of work-based learning 1

- **Section 2: personal practice**
  - Managing time effectively
  - Setting work-related goals and developing action plans
- **Section 3: reflective practice**
  - Learning from experience at work
  - Applying action learning at work
- **Section 4: collaborative practice**
  - Making effective presentations
  - Organising effective seminar activities.

All eight exercises have associated resources such as relevant readings or links to related websites. The need for a scaffolded approach to the students' learning is addressed by the results of one exercise being germane to the next. In this way, the developmental and progressive nature of the course supports cumulative development in a phased and incremental way. The aim was not to undermine student agency. The exercises replace lecture inputs, and two tutors are available to support the groups on their day in university, as well as through email contact. The students are assessed through the completion of the eight exercises and three essays. Importantly, the exercise work is formatively assessed, and quick feedback is given to students on their ideas.

In Section 3, the students are formed into 'learning clusters' with four or five other participants. Each cluster engages in an action learning exercise focusing on complex problems, situations and issues that each member brings to the group from their own work situation. In the action learning exercise, participants challenge and encourage each other to explore feelings as part of the process of uncovering their own approaches to situations and factors that might be holding them back. In the final section, WBL1 culminates in seminars organised by the clusters where the groups demonstrate their learning to one another in relation to the issues they have chosen and researched.

Students' attitudes towards the modified teaching methods

So much for the design, but what did the featured students make of the course? Initially, the students were hostile to and negative about WBL1. They expressed deep concerns about finding the time to engage with the course in and among other, out-of-university commitments. Instead of a sense of 'freedom to work when and where you wanted', I was surprised that the lack of a formal structure (in contrast to attending lectures) resulted in students feeling uncertain, and in some cases panicking, at the 'uncontrollability' of this part of their lives. Examples of students' negative responses are:

- Frustration with technology and high levels of stress
- Dislike of the distance-learning element
- Preference for face-to-face contact and lectures

- Subversion of the technology by printing everything off
- A sense that the exercises were boring.

By the end of the course, however, I was relieved to note that the students' reactions had changed considerably. 'Brenda's' insightful statement below reflects a common student view:

> As stated in my essay, I was very sceptical of WBL1 as I looked at it as open learning and I have never been any good at that! I find it difficult to be motivated and I know a lot of the other students did as well. I think after the initial exercises were completed I realised that I was going to get something out of it and that I was actually learning. More specifically I was learning more about me – both professionally and personally.
>
> (B, female, 30s)

Clearly, Brenda had come a long way in her understanding of the transformative nature of studies in HE.

This led me to consider what the students were learning professionally and personally. My own reflections and observations were validated in some of the students' comments from the course evaluation. A major outcome about which I was delighted was that the students were embracing the nature of learning in higher education. Increasingly, students came to appreciate the importance of the development of critical thinking. In many ways, this was a disconcerting process for them, because critical thinking meant questioning their deeply held assumptions and seeing the bigger picture, for example, in organisational, policy-related, political or ideological terms. The following quote from 'Alice' is representative and indicates the degree to which critical thinking was entwined with students' personal development:

> The main area of learning is developing critical thinking. Engaging with case studies, learning about experiential learning theory and action learning theory, is very important to our professional development and confidence.
>
> (A, female, 20s)

Students also adopted new approaches to learning, including experiential and action learning, further demonstrating the way that the students were changing as their studies progressed. As 'Kaylene' said:

> This exercise [action learning] brought our critical thinking to the group, where we could actively engage in critical dialogue. There was so much learning that took place during the set's meetings, i.e. people, personalities, how people work, etc., what challenges they face in their practice. This was very interesting, and it definitely dulled the feeling of isolation.
>
> (K, female, 20s)

These exercises helped students to appreciate and develop a commitment to collective learning. This was a most important aspect, as collective learning counters the isolation that is endemic to part-time study, which was the situation that was confounded for some students by the introduction of the unfamiliar technology associated with WBL1.

Students reported significant learning after the time management and action planning exercises. They expressed a greater awareness of how they had previously operated in what may be seen as an unthinking way, and merely reacting to immediate demands. For the students, this realisation was profound and brought forth commitments from them for more focused activity in the context of their own priorities in terms of work, personal lives and study. As 'Lee' commented in relation to work, 'Before doing this course I had little control in my work but I had just accepted this without realising it' (L, female, 40s). Students came to appreciate that 'busy-ness' and lack of organisation meant that they were not concentrating efforts on their priorities. Because they had not been asked to think about the wider organisational and policy context of their work in the past, they had not considered it! They were now more likely to allocate time to develop forward plans and to identify and stick to priorities linked to the wider objectives of their organisation. Students also explained how they applied the time management principles in their personal lives. For example, domestic arrangements had changed for some so that household tasks were more equally shared with children and partners.

The group exercises, which began in Section 3, were demanding in their own ways and also had repercussions in terms of authority and control over learning. As 'Cathy' explained:

> I initially enjoyed working in a group for exercises five, six, seven and eight. However it began to feel a bit too much by the end of the seminar, although this was probably my steepest learning of the whole eighteen months ... and made me realise that I must take more responsibility for my own learning.
>
> (C, female, 30s)

Students generally acknowledged that the course gave workplace discussions with line managers and colleagues a new legitimacy and urgency. However, they also realised that critical questions created tensions with colleagues in the workplace when 'taken-for-granted' practices were suddenly scrutinised and challenged. In some instances, this led to changing relationships with colleagues who were threatened by the student's attitude. It was noted, for example, that line managers could take issues personally where these appeared to involve the line manager themselves. I had to acknowledge therefore that there was a potential for the learning from the exercises to lead to conflict if it was not sensitively handled. To counteract this, I included an important focus as part of this behavioural learning on students' developing an appreciation of the need to challenge in ways that did not gratuitously offend colleagues or unnecessarily trigger defensive and aggressive reactions.

Discussion

A defining feature of WBL1 is the focus on real and live problems or issues of interest to and relevance to the students. Obviously, many disciplines cannot draw from life or work situations. However, educators in any discipline have the opportunity to relate studies to the actual interests of the students. In my case, the students could focus on the specifics of their work, providing them with the opportunity to test developing ideas in real situations and, in turn, to bring the results of action back into the learning process. I was delighted to note that among the students, there was evidence of deeper learning concerning what learners do in new contexts in which there are no immediate or straightforward answers, and how they apply their ideas.

A significant achievement of the course was that the students learned ways of thinking and practising that are characteristic of the particular subject area. WBL1 is located within a vocational degree in which students are challenged to develop a creative relationship between theory and practice. There is an explicit expectation that theory underpins activity, and, crucially, the results of activity feed back into the theorising process. This is because no one theory fits every given eventuality and practitioners have to interpret the possibilities suggested in broad concepts and frameworks in new and unpredictable situations. One important implication here is that educators need to be aware of ways of thinking and practising in their own areas. If they are not, the possibilities for inducting and socialising students into particular cultures, at least in conscious and deliberate ways, are undermined. I have learned that understanding and insight about such matters can develop in a staff team that is prepared to discuss and debate 'how' as well as 'what' to teach.

Thinking of new and innovative ways to teach can present difficulties on a number of levels. WBL1 was time consuming to construct, for example, and initially involved more work than putting together a more conventional teaching programme. I have already noted how the students found it difficult to begin with. The upside, however, is that it forced me to consider the principles underpinning my teaching so that, for instance, I thought much more carefully about how each of the parts related to the whole. Having constructed one course along such lines made it easier, and quicker, to design others. The experience has taught me to place more emphasis on initial instructions and clarification when beginning a new venture with students, and to respond quickly to any indications of problems or frustrations. Finally, the course has now been run with successive groups of students with little modification required. There can be a good return, therefore, on what appears to be a heavy initial investment.

WBL1 involved a significant element of e-learning in its use of the CD and in the use made of email for communication and feedback purposes. Some educators may be put off by anecdotal accounts of technical difficulties associated with e-learning, while others may be sceptical because of the notion that it lacks the important face-to-face opportunities for collective and collaborative learning when students are together in groups. It is true that there are technical challenges for educators who are new to e-learning, but these difficulties can be exaggerated. It is important to know that there is now a growing literature about e-learning to support academics. Salmon (2004), for example, has provided an accessible five-stage developmental model for e-learning which weaves together technical and pedagogical issues. Among other useful suggestions and insights, the model shows how to construct effective collaborative experiences. Groupwork was a central feature of WBL1, reinforced by the focus on action learning in Section 3 where students helped each other to learn from dealing with their own live problems and issues in the workplace.

The experience of the students involved in the intervention points to and illuminates the true meaning of participation where they do not simply receive knowledge, but play their part as active learners, interacting with and 'authoring' knowledge. Participation in this more exacting sense is diminished when they only choose, or have the capacity, to engage superficially with the teaching and learning processes on offer. True participation is more likely to occur when the curriculum has been carefully designed and structured so that the students' active participation is integral to the learning tasks. It nurtures deeper learning approaches in that students are required to discuss their growing understandings with other students and to face challenges and questions as differing views and understandings are negotiated in the groupwork. The clear implication for educators here is to think seriously about incorporating a transformative approach into their teaching. Making such a recommendation is not meant to dismiss transmissive approaches which have their place in properly planned teaching and learning environments catering for different learning styles and capacities. It is to recognise that transmissive approaches need to be supplemented with more participative methods in order to stimulate deeper forms of learning. While it is not easy to change established ways of teaching and of student learning, the outcomes and rewards in terms of the quality of students' learning more than justifies the effort.

References

DfES (1997) *Higher Education in the Learning Society: The Report of the National Committee of Inquiry into Higher Education.* London: HMSO.

Hall, S. (1998) *It was a Worthwhile Slog! Scottish Access Students in Higher Education.* Spotlight 68, Edinburgh Scottish Council for Research in Education.

Salmon, G (2004) *Etivities: The Key to Online Learning* (London: Routledge Falmer).

Modes of teaching and learning

Chapter 3

Learning and teaching strategies to promote student retention and success

Liz Thomas

Implications of mass higher education for learning, teaching and assessment and student retention and success

In many countries the state of 'mass higher education' has been reached. This occurs when the majority of the population from the relevant age-group participate in higher education (HE) (Trow 1974). For example, in the US, Japan and Scotland more than 50 per cent of young people enter HE. In other countries, including Australia, England, Ireland, the Netherlands and Sweden, national policy is striving towards an expanded HE system (Thomas & Quinn 2003). Mass, or almost mass, higher education systems frequently exhibit a decrease in units of resources as well as worsening staff: student ratios as HE finance does not keep pace with the expansion in student numbers. This tends to result in greater reliance on large lectures, ICT and independent learning, larger seminar groups and the abandonment of traditional personal tutoring systems (Thomas & Hixenbaugh 2006). These responses have reduced the contact between staff and students, providing students with fewer opportunities for clarification, interaction and feedback about their academic studies. These and related reasons (for example, greater reliance on paid employment to finance HE study) may also make it more difficult for students to engage in their higher education experience.

A further consequence of mass higher education is greater student diversity: students coming from a wider range of educational, social and cultural backgrounds (as discussed in Chapter 2). This has been accompanied by concerns about student retention, progression and completion (House of Commons Select Committee 2001; National Audit Office 2002; McInnis & James 2004; Long, Ferrier & Heagney 2006). Reputational and financial penalties for institutions with comparatively high rates of student non-completion (Yorke & Longden 2004) have prompted some institutions to reflect on their learning, teaching, assessment and support strategies, especially in institutions that have successfully widened participation (Action on Access 2003; Thomas, May, Harrop *et al.* 2005). With growing pressure in many countries on all institutions to expand the diversity of their student population, the issues of student retention and success are of great importance to individual universities and colleges, and the HE sector as a whole (Yorke & Longden 2004).

Student withdrawal and the impact of the curriculum

Recent research in the UK with young, working-class students who have withdrawn from higher education identified a wide range of reasons why students leave early (Quinn *et al.* 2005). What is striking, however, is the significance of the learning experience for students' decisions to withdraw. This finding is supported by other UK research, which concludes that learning and teaching environments are highly influential on students' success (for example, Laing & Robinson 2003; Davies 1999), and by international evidence which was presented to the research team at an international colloquium (Quinn *et al.* 2005). For example, Davies argues that issues relating to pedagogy, practical organisation and student support have the most pronounced impact on retention rates. In the Australian context research on students' experiences has focused on the first year (McInnis & James 1995; McInnis, James and Hartley 2000), and issues about retention and withdrawal are extrapolated from the responses of those students who have considered leaving during this period. As with UK studies, these surveys reveal the complexity underlying students' feelings about participating in higher education and leaving early, but overall, academic rather than personal or financial reasons predominate (McInnis & James 2004).

In the UK qualitative study, some students experienced what has been described as 'academic culture shock' (Quinn *et al.* 2005). Students felt that they were not prepared for the transition from school or college to university. Key factors that made this transition difficult were large class size, the combination of increased work load and more freedom/less structure and not knowing how to adjust to this new learning environment. This was frequently experienced as an increasing sense of loss of control. For example, one student in the study explained in the following dialogue:

> *Q:* What sort of things led up to you leaving, what sort of triggered it off?
> *A:* No support, too much of a heavy workload, thinking that I was losing control in everything that I was studying.

Students expected the higher education learning and teaching experience to be different from school or college, but they were not adequately prepared to cope with the transition. For example, some students did not know how to utilise lectures effectively, how to plan and manage their workload or how to structure and write their assignments:

> They just talk. That's about it, it's a lecture, you listen and take notes. When you take notes you forget what they are saying. When you go back to your

notes you wonder what you have written down. You don't know whether to take notes or listen.

The majority of students were not aware of specific advice and guidance available to help them to develop their study skills, and feedback from teaching staff did not indicate why low grades were being awarded and how students could improve:

> There was some work that I felt I was doing enough in but I wasn't really getting the marks for it. Most of the class agreed they weren't getting a clear indication as to what was required for it.

Lack of feedback represents a significant change from school and college environments, where work is continually assessed, and there may even be opportunities for students to revise submissions following feedback from staff. In addition, the large size of many first-year lectures inhibits students from asking for feedback and support, and the teaching staff seem to be unapproachable:

> There were lots of people in the lectures. It was hard to speak to the lecturers. If I had any problems it was hard to get them sorted. The classes were just so big.

Furthermore, many of these students did not want to draw attention to the fact that they were struggling; for example, one student said he 'didn't want to feel like an idiot'.

Classroom practices therefore have a significant impact on students' experiences of higher education, and can be highly influential in students' decisions to leave HE early. Moreover, if students do not adapt and prosper in the HE academic environment they are liable to fail, and thus be forced to withdraw.

Many students seem to find learning most effective when they are able to interact with staff and other students (Astin 1984; Thomas 2002; Tinto 1997). Worsening staff–student ratios are a threat to interaction – for example, within lectures, seminars and personal tutorials. Alternative learning and teaching strategies can be utilised, however, to enable students to have greater interaction with each other, and to improve their understanding of and engagement in the learning process.

Teacher-centred and student-centred approaches to learning

Many efforts to improve student retention and success via learning, teaching and assessment approaches focus on promoting greater student engagement in the classroom. This is primarily being undertaken by moving from more teacher-centred approaches to more student-centred ones. In summary, teacher-centred approaches view students as 'empty vessels' and lecturers as owners of epistemological knowledge, directing the learning process and controlling students' access to information. Learning is viewed as an additive process; instruction is geared for the 'average' student and everyone is forced to progress at the same rate. In contrast, student-centred approaches acknowledge the knowledge, experience and ways of understanding that students bring with them, and thus they are not perceived as empty vessels (Erickson 1984). The different ways in which students learn (Briggs-Myers 1980) are also recognised. Learning is therefore conceptualised as an active, dynamic process in which connections are constantly changing and their structure is continually reformatted (Cross 1991). Students construct their own meaning by talking, listening, writing, reading, and reflecting on content, ideas, issues and concerns (Meyers & Jones 1993).

Teacher-centred and student-centred approaches to learning and teaching place teachers and students in radically different roles, which in turn influence the choice of teaching methods employed. Ellington and Earl (1996) categorise teaching methods into three groups: mass instruction, individualised learning and group learning. Mass instruction, which includes lectures, film and video presentations and mass practical work, positions lecturers in a traditional role, controlling the contents and learning process; students are largely passive and dependent on what they are taught. Individualised learning includes directed study of texts and materials, use of multimedia, assignments and projects. The role of the teacher is thus to produce the learning resources and guide and support students through their use. Students therefore have much greater control over their learning and are largely able to determine the timing, pace and depth of learning. Group learning includes buzz sessions, class discussions, seminars, group tutorials, games, simulations and group projects. These require the lecturer to be the organiser and facilitator of learning. Students have greater responsibility for their learning and must work collaboratively with their peers.

It is in group learning contexts that students are most able to engage with the learning process. Active group learning strategies promote engagement with peers and provide opportunities to check understanding and clarify meaning. Furthermore, classroom interaction can be extended into the social sphere with additional benefits for the learning experience and integration into higher education more generally. Research indicates that both academic and social integration have a positive impact on student retention and success (Tinto 1998, 2000; Thomas 2002).

One approach to developing learning environments that encourage engagement and the development of higher-order learning skills is the creation of 'powerful learning environments' (Entwistle 2003). In brief, these are conceived of as drawing on students' experiences, using active or problem-based learning approaches, viewing knowledge as constructed and encouraging students to reflect on and take responsibility for aspects of the learning process. De Corte (2000) (in the context of Belgian schooling) identified the following features of a powerful learning environment. It should:

- include group discussions of both the content and the process of learning and studying;

- provide authentic tasks and realistic problems that have personal meaning and future use;
- initiate and support active and constructive learning processes (conceptual understanding); and
- enhance students' awareness of their own cognitive processes and their ability to control their motives and feelings (cognitive and volitional self-regulation).

Three ways in which the curriculum can support students to engage and reflect on the learning process are: extended induction and the development of academic skills; learning and teaching strategies which draw on the philosophy of experiential learning; and formative assessment. These issues are discussed below, before a summary of the cases in this section of the book, which address these aspects of learning and teaching, is presented.

Induction

Traditionally HEIs have offered new students a 'Welcome' or 'Freshers' week on arrival. Using teacher-centred methods of communication, the emphasis has been on conveying the status of the institution and overloading students with information. More recently, there has been greater cognition of the need to induct students into the wider HE environment via more student-centred strategies to enable students to learn about and understand the expectations and culture of HE (Yorke & Thomas 2003).

In short, induction programmes should provide clarity about what is expected of students at university, build confidence and motivation and allow students to integrate into their new environment (both academically and socially). This is most effective if it is a longer process, starting before enrolment, and extending through the first semester – as this is when the majority of students who withdraw do so – or beyond. Early engagement could include the provision of timetables, course handbooks and reading lists, summer schools, or materials accessed via a virtual learning environment. In some circumstances involving parents by providing them with information can be appropriate and useful. Early engagement can benefit students by preparing them for their course, demonstrating what will be expected of them, and assisting them to feel a part of the institution.

An inclusive approach to induction, including all students and staff, and other groups from across the institution (such as the Students' Union, Student Services, etc.), helps students and staff to get to know each other. It also signals the importance of the induction process to both staff and students, and allows staff to have a greater understanding of the diversity of students entering their courses. Further aspects of inclusivity include the provision of relevant and appropriate activities and timetabling them to enable all students to participate.

Participatory approaches, drawing on the students' previous experiences and their existing knowledge and skills, can help to build relations between students, as well as promoting a deeper understanding of the issues. For example, peer learning and teaching about study skills and IT can be used to ensure the cohort has comparable skill levels, and forms social alliances.

Integration of the induction process into the subject-specific curriculum helps students to learn in the context of their discipline. For example, some institutions have an accredited first semester induction module, which is discipline based, and involves group-work to explore aspects of the transition process. This can be assessed using transparent and formative approaches to allow students to develop the skills and understanding of learning in HE, while also developing their subject-based knowledge.

Such approaches to induction enable students to adjust their expectations of learning, teaching and assessment, and encourage staff to use learning and teaching strategies that enable students to engage and feel included in their studies. This requires a responsiveness to students, and a student- rather than a teacher-centred approach to the learning process.

Active learning

Student-centred learning conceives of students as playing a more active role in their learning processes. Active learning is often associated with experiential, problem-based and project-based learning, and other forms of collaborative learning, and less reliance on the large lecture format. Kolb's (1984) work on the theoretical foundations of experiential learning can be seen to underlie all of these approaches to learning (Tight 2002: 106). Broadly, experiential learning relates to the knowledge and skills gained through life and work experience, but different interpretations have extended the notion of experiential learning to 'meaningful discovery' learning (Boydell 1976). This has given rise to approaches such as problem-based and project-based learning, which are educational approaches that make use of the learning strategies suggested by the theories of experiential learning within the classroom context. These forms of teaching promote collaboration among students to solve problems, and, by using realistic problems or situations for learning, a deeper understanding of the relationship between theory and practice can be developed and understood by students (Tight 2002: 108). Boud and Feletti (1997:2) identify the key features of a problem-based learning approach as:

- Using stimulus material to help students discuss an important problem, question or issue;
- Presenting the problem as a simulation of professional practice or a real-life situation;
- Appropriately guiding students' critical thinking and providing limited resources to help them learn from defining and attempting to resolve a given problem;
- Having students work cooperatively as a group, exploring information in and out of class, with access to a tutor who knows the problem well and can facilitate the group's learning process;

- Getting students to identify their own learning needs and appropriate use of available resources;
- Reapplying this knowledge to the original problem and evaluating their learning processes.

It is the development and utilisation of such learning and teaching strategies that promote a more active, student-centred approach to learning, which draws on students' previous experiences and interests, that helps to enhance student engagement, course commitment and retention on the programme. ICT can offer teaching staff new ways to develop problem-based and project-based learning activities.

Formative assessment

Many students struggle to make the transition from a more structured learning experience in schools and colleges to the greater autonomy in higher education. Pedagogical research, especially with non-traditional students, reports that formative assessment offers an integrated and structured approach to equipping all students with the information and skills they need to make a successful transition into higher education and to continue to succeed academically. For example, George, Cowan, Hewitt and Cannell (2004) found that the nature of assessment used was significant for students' experience and engagement with the course. They suggest that the incorporation of both summative and formative assessment helps to build confidence, a positive attitude towards learning and successful engagement with the cognitive demands of the programme. Similarly, Bamber and Tett (1999) found that non-traditional students, and particularly mature learners, benefited from formative feedback. For example, formative assessment can offer students:

- space to explore, try out different approaches and develop their own ideas;
- an opportunity to become aware of their own progress and find out about themselves as learners;
- an opportunity to negotiate with tutors and/or peers on matters of assessment including the allocation of marks. (Povey & Angier, 2004)

Formative feedback is integrated into the learning experience, and so does not detract from discipline-focused teaching and it reaches all students, not just those who have the knowledge and confidence to seek support. Furthermore, formative feedback provides a vehicle for interaction between students and staff, thus helping to develop student familiarity and confidence to approach staff for additional clarification and guidance if necessary. Feedback information can also be used by staff to realign their teaching in response to learners' needs.

Juwah et al. (2004) present a feedback cycle, which involves feed-forward as well as feedback. The cycle consists of the following stages: task, interpretation, preparation, performance, assessment, feedback, interpretation, learning and informed (improved) performance. The task must be set, and then it needs to be interpreted to understand what is required. Students then need to be prepared to undertake the task, which they then undertake. The performance is assessed and feedback is provided. Again this needs to be interpreted and understood by students, who then learn from this and improve their performance. Students occupy a central role in this process, and so their capacity to interpret and use feedback needs to be developed. In order to facilitate good feedback Juwah *et al.* (2004) discuss seven principles of good feedback, summarised below. Good feedback:

- facilitates the development of self-assessment (reflection) in learning;
- encourages teacher and peer dialogue around learning;
- helps clarify what good performance is (goals, criteria, standards expected);
- provides opportunities to close the gap between current and desired performance;
- delivers high-quality information to students about their learning;
- encourages positive motivational beliefs and self-esteem; and
- provides information for teachers that can be used to help shape teaching.

Formative feedback offers an integrated approach to providing students with clarity about what is expected of them, and a way of engaging with peers and teaching staff to discuss academic issues in a safe environment so that they develop the skills, understanding and integration they need to succeed. Furthermore, formative assessment can be used to promote an active approach to learning, as students are encouraged to reflect on the learning process, rather than just the outcomes.

The cases

Research about student withdrawal indicates that learning, teaching and assessment strategies are crucial to student retention and success. In particular, extended induction, active learning and formative feedback can be used to promote understanding of, and engagement in, the learning process. As discussed, this requires staff to develop and utilise more student-centred, as opposed to teacher-centred, learning approaches, for which they may require motivation, inspiration and support. The cases presented in this section of the book should offer some ideas for ways in which learning, teaching and assessment could be developed to improve student retention and success.

The cases that follow all explore how the curriculum (contents and learning, teaching and assessment strategies) have been changed to support student retention and success. In particular, the authors have developed more active learning strategies, made the curricular contents more relevant to students' experiences while seeking to expand their knowledge and skills, and made the teaching and assessment practices transparent to facilitate students' understanding of the learning processes.

Christine Keenan considers how 'Stepping Stones 2HE' has been developed and implemented to improve the retention of students during the critical first few weeks of the course. Students often do not know what to expect from their course and they can have difficulty making friends and settling in. Stepping Stones 2HE provides students with information, course reading and tasks and a learning self-profiling questionnaire before they arrive at the university. Students are informed about support services, skills audits and information about their course. Students are also given discipline-based activities to work on before they arrive. These are linked with group-work during induction week when students are given time, resources and rooms to come together in groups to share the knowledge and information they have brought with them and to develop a specific output such as a poster or presentation. In addition students complete the self-profiling questionnaire, which encourages them to report and reflect on their previous learning experiences and their expectations about studying at university. Students are able to ask questions and extend their knowledge if necessary. Not only does this encourage reflection and understanding prior to entry, but it also allows staff to identify students who are especially anxious either to provide them with support or to monitor them when they arrive. Stepping Stones 2HE is designed to help students manage their transition into Higher Education and extends induction beyond the traditional boundaries. Staff value students engaging with discipline material before they arrive, and students are enjoying the learning experience, and developing academically and integrating socially. The success of the initiative has led to a university-wide policy to implement Stepping Stones 2HE.

Digby Warren discusses the opportunity he had to redesign an introductory history course for level one undergraduates, who came from a diversity of backgrounds. The aim was to use this module to broaden students' notion of what history is, and to develop their academic skills through an integrated approach. In other words, the aim was for students to develop the skills they need to study history (such as critical thinking, reading and writing) through the teaching and learning of the discipline. In addition to lectures, Digby introduced task-oriented seminars, a small-group project, an essay-writing workshop and 'feed-forward' tutorials – all of which were situated within the study of history. The seminars encouraged students to work on tasks to explore epistemological questions through concrete examples. Group projects and presentations were used to enable students to research and discuss aspects of historical practice; this was supported by an individual reflective report on the process. Students were required to write essays during the course, but this was supported by an embedded essay-writing workshop, which provided practical information and explicit marking criteria. Students were invited to discuss essay plans and academic writing with staff, providing an opportunity for 'feeding forward' to support the assessment process. Thus, through this module students experienced a range of learning and teaching strategies and developed their academic skills, while also expanding their understanding of the history discipline.

Betty Leask describes how, at the University of South Australia, simple ICT tools (e.g. email, internet and discussion fora) are being used to facilitate meaningful intercultural learning for all students. She presents examples from two discipline areas – physiotherapy and international studies. In each case students are required to use email and the internet to research and develop their understanding of a specific issue from the perspective of people from other countries and cultures. In addition discussion boards can be used to share information between groups of students and enable them to work together. What is striking in these examples is how the learning utilises independent and group project-based activities that require students to research issues relevant to their discipline area. This enables them to develop a wide range of knowledge and skills in an authentic and meaningful way. Students acquire both discipline-specific knowledge and skills, and the ability to operate in the global environment – there is, however, a need to develop innovative assessment practices which capture learning via these activities. Furthermore, all students can benefit from this learning experience, not just those who have the opportunity to study abroad, or those who interact with visiting international students. This model of internationalising the curriculum is being explored and implemented in other discipline areas across the university.

Lesley McMillan and Lucy Solomon discuss how they altered their approach to teaching quantitative research methods to level two sociology students. The sociology programme attracts students from a diversity of backgrounds, including a significant number of mature students. Many of the students lack numerically oriented qualifications and have a fear of maths and statistics; some also have limited experience of using computers (especially for statistical analysis). The aim of the curricular intervention is to enable students to understand the concepts without worrying about the numbers; thus, culinary analogies are used to explain them, and research design is compared to the process of planning and cooking a meal. For example, the need to collect data at the highest level because categories can be collapsed but not disaggregated is demonstrated by cutting up apples in different ways and considering the limitations this poses for cooking some recipes (e.g. those that require a whole apple). Group formative assessment is integrated into the course, and the culinary analogies are extended into this too. The use of non-threatening language supports the students to talk about the research process, and to give each other feedback. Using familiar language and processes offers students a way of both understanding the concepts and being able to talk about the issues with less fear. This is particularly valuable in relation to peer formative feedback. Furthermore, prior to this intervention students were achieving lower grades than for their other sociology modules, but now this trend has reversed.

Mark Russell presents a case from the University of Hertfordshire in the UK which demonstrates how a blended teaching, learning and assessment strategy has improved the engagement and academic success of students studying thermodynamics. ICT has been used to create bespoke weekly assignments for each student. These are numerical, problem-solving tasks, which encourage student discussion, but which make answer-sharing impossible (as each student has a slightly different problem). The aim of the weekly assessments is to promote greater student engagement with the course, and distribute student activity across the semester rather than focusing solely on the exam at the end of the module. The use of ICT not only enables students to be set different problems, but facilitates the provision of fast, individualised feedback, and the identification of students who are struggling during the course rather than when they fail the final assessment. Of particular significance in this example is the relationship between the ICT-based assessments and the weekly face-to-face lectures and group tutorials. The score data shows cohort trends, such as topics that all students are struggling with. This data is supported by the responses to open questions that require students to provide written answers. The open questions about the learning process enable students to enter into a dialogue with staff. Taken together, cohort trends and student feedback are used by the teaching staff to inform the contents and level of subsequent lectures and tutorials. The improvement in exam results over the last few years demonstrates the effectiveness of this strategy.

Conclusion

In this chapter I have argued that learning, teaching and assessment strategies play a key role in improving student retention and academic success. This requires the use of integrated student-centred learning approaches. Examples include extended induction, experiential or active learning methods which make learning relevant to students and engage them in the process rather than just the outcomes (or facts) and formative assessment. These types of integrated curriculum approaches to improving student retention and success offer ways of reaching all students (rather than just those that elect to participate), and are more likely to be sustainable than some other retention initiatives as they are not reliant on project funding. Furthermore, pedagogic research indicates that learning and teaching developments that benefit students from underrepresented groups, such as first-generation entrants or disabled students, are of benefit to all students enabling each to fulfil his or her academic potential (see, for example, Preece & Godfrey 2004, Tinklin *et al.* 2004 and Avramidis & Skidmore 2004).

References

Action on Access (2003) *Student Success in Higher Education.* Bradford: Action on Access Online. Available (www.actiononaccess.org/resource/aoadocs/ssintro.doc (accessed 15 June 2005).

Astin, A,W. (1984) *Preventing Students from Dropping Out.* San Francisco, CA: Jossey-Bass.

Avramidis, E. and Skidmore, D. (2004) 'Reappraising learning support in Higher Education', *Research into Post-Compulsory Education*, 9, 1: 63–82.

Bamber, J. and Tett, L. (1999) 'Opening the doors of higher education to working class adults: a case study', *International Journal of Lifelong Education*, 18, 6: 465–475.

Boud, D. and Feletti, G. (eds) (1997) *The Challenge of Problem-based Learning*, 2nd edn. London: Kogan Page.

Boydell, T. (1976) *Experiential Learning.* Manchester: University of Manchester Department of Adult Education.

Briggs-Myers, I. (1980) *Gifts Differing*. Palo Alto, CA: Consulting Psychologists Press.

Cross, K. P. (1991) *College Teaching: What Do We Know about It?* Louise McBee Lecture Series. Athens, GA: Institute of Higher Education, University of Georgia.

Davies, P. (1999) *Student Retention in Further Education: A Problem of Quality or of Student Finance?* Paper presented at British Educational Research Association Conference, University of Sussex, 2–5 September. Available from: www.leeds.ac.uk/educol/documents/00001257.doc.

De Corte, E. (2000) 'Marrying theory building and the improvement of school practice', *Learning and Instruction*, 10: 249–266.

Ellington, H. and Earl, S. (1996) 'Selecting appropriate teaching/learning methods'. Aberdeen: Robert Gordon University Online. Available http://apu.gcal.ac.uk/ciced/Ch04.html (accessed 26 October 2006).

Entwistle, N. (March 2003) 'Concepts and conceptual frameworks underpinning the ETL project'. Online. Available www.ed.ac.uk/etl/docs/ETLreport3.pdf (accessed 26 October 2006).

Erickson, S.C. (1984) *The Essence of Good Teaching: Helping Students Learn and Remember what they Learn*. San Francisco, CA: Jossey-Bass.

George, J., Cowan, J., Hewitt, L. and Cannell, P. (2004) 'Failure dances to the tune of insecurity: Affective issues in the assessment and evaluation of access learning', *Journal of Access Policy and Practice*, 1, 2: 119–133.

House of Commons Select Committee on Education and Employment (2001) Sixth report. *Higher Education: Student Retention*. Online. Available www.publications.parliament.uk.

Juwah, C., Macfarlane-Dick, D., Matthew, B., Nicol, D., Ross, D. and Smith, B. (2004) *Enhancing Student Learning through Effective Formative Feedback*. York: Higher Education Academy www.heacademy.ac.uk/senlef.htm.

Kolb, D. (1984) *Experiential Learning: Experience as the Source of Learning and Development*. Englewood Cliffs, NJ: Prentice Hall.

Laing, C. and Robinson, A. (2003) 'The withdrawal of non-traditional students: Developing an explanatory model', *Journal of Further and Higher Education*, 27, 2: 175–185.

Long, M., Ferrier, F., and Heagney, M. (2006) *Stay, Play or Give it Away? Students Continuing, Changing or Leaving University Study in First Year*. Canberra: Department of Education, Science and Training.

Meyers, C. and Jones, T.B. (1993) *Promoting Active Learning: Strategies for the College Classroom*. San Francisco, CA: Jossey-Bass.

McInnis, C. and James, R. (1995) *First Year on Campus: Diversity in the Initial Experiences of Australian Undergraduates*. Canberra: AGPS.

McInnis, C., James, R. and Hartley, R. (2000) *Trends in the First Year Experience in Australian Universities*. Canberra: AGPS.

McInnis, C. and James, R. (2004) 'Access and retention in Australian higher education', in M. Yorke and B. Longden, *Retention and Student Success in Higher Education*. Buckingham: Open University Press.

National Audit Office (2002) *Improving Student Achievement in English Higher Education*. Report by the Comptroller and Auditor General. London: The Stationery Office.

Povey, H. and Angier, C. (2004) '"I can do it, but it'll be a battle": Finding her place as an undergraduate mathematician'. Sheffield: Sheffield Hallam University.

Preece, S. and Godfrey, J. (2004) 'Academic literacy practices and widening participation: First year undergraduates on an academic writing programme', *Journal of Widening Participation and Lifelong Learning*, 6, 1: 6–14.

Quinn, J., Thomas, L., Slack, K., Casey, L., Thexton, W. and Noble, J. (2005) *From Life Disaster to Lifelong Learning: Reframing Working Class 'Drop Out'*. York: Joseph Rowntree Foundation.

Thomas, L. (2002) 'Student retention in higher education: The role of institutional habitus', *Journal of Education Policy*, 17, 4: 423–442.

Thomas, L. and Hixenbaugh, P. (2006) *Personal Tutoring in Higher Education*. Stoke-on-Trent: Trentham Books.

Thomas, L. and Quinn, J. (2003) *International Insights into Widening Participation: Supporting the Success of Under-Represented Groups in Tertiary Education. Final Report*. Stoke-on-Trent: Institute for Access Studies, Staffordshire University.

Thomas, L., May, H., Harrop, H., Houston, M., Knox, H. Lee, M. F., Osborne, M., Pudner, H. and Trotman, C. (2005) *From the Margins to the Mainstream: Embedding Widening Participation in Higher Education*. London: University of London.

Tight, M. (2002) *Key Concepts in Adult Education and Training*, 2nd edn. London: Routledge Falmer.

Tinklin, T., Riddell, S and Wilson, A. (2004) 'Policy and provision for disabled students in higher education: The current state of play', *Studies in Higher Education*, 29, 5: 637–659.

Tinto, V. (1997) 'Classrooms as communities: Exploring the educational character of student persistence', *Journal of Higher Education*, 68, 6: 599–623.

Tinto, V. (1998) Learning Communities and the Reconstruction of Remedial Education in Higher Education, *Replacing Remediation in Higher Education Conference*. Stamford University, Bangladesh, 26–27 January.

Tinto, V. (2000) 'Reconstructing the first year of college', in *Student Support Services Model Retention Strategies for Two-Year Colleges*. Washington, DC: Council for Opportunity in Education.

Trow, M. (1974) *Problems in the Transition from Elite to Mass Higher Education in Policies for Higher Education*. Paris: OECD.

Yorke, M. and Longden, B. (2004) *Retention and Student Success in Higher Education*. Buckingham: Open University Press.

Yorke, M. and Thomas, L. (2003) 'Improving the retention of students from lower socio-economic groups', *Journal of Higher Education Policy and Management*, 25, 1: 63–75.

Students getting down to work before they start at university: a model for improving retention

Christine Keenan

The situation

Why do students drop out in the first few weeks of term, and what can we do to improve retention during the first few critical weeks at university?

Recruitment to engineering courses has been on the decline across the UK Higher Education sector for a number of years. On top of this, over a similar period of time, we have been concerned that students were leaving our Engineering Department in large numbers during the first few weeks of term. This was an issue in financial terms for the institution, but also a concern for us to understand what was going wrong. When I spoke to students who had made the decision to leave, they often referred to problems encountered in settling in. Some had found it difficult to form social friendship groups and others expressed concerns that the course wasn't what they had expected. Often, students said that induction week had been overwhelming because they had suffered from information overload, and frustrating because they had wanted to get going with their studies after the long summer break. The students on most of our engineering courses were predominantly male and predominantly eighteen years old, but students coming to our electronics courses in particular were often students from more diverse backgrounds. These included mature-aged students coming from Access courses, and many were also international students.

From my discussions with students, I realised that the way we approached induction was turning students off university. They were often not settling in socially or academically as quickly as they had expected. We therefore developed and introduced the 'Stepping Stones 2HE' programme. This is a novel approach to transition and induction, and it has been a focus for developing a fully integrated approach to the first-year experience at our university for five years now. Over this time, we have witnessed an improvement in student retention rates, particularly during the first term. The majority of our students are first-generation university entrants, who may be seen as lacking the 'cultural capital' of other students who are more prepared for university life by family tradition. Stepping Stones 2HE is designed to provide an introduction to university life that is accessible, meaningful and relevant to all students, whatever their background. It is offered in accessible language, and is designed to increase confidence by helping students develop an understanding of, and a relationship with, the course they are coming to study, and also with the wider university community.

The approaches implemented

It seemed to me that when students arrive at university, they are particularly interested in making friends and getting down to work. This had been my instinctive understanding, and was confirmed in interviews I carried out with students. There is little or no point in delivering induction information to students during their first week at university. It is the wrong time, and the information simply goes right over their heads. You know the routine, we bring in vice chancellors, librarians and others, and place them in front of a hundred or more students whose only real concern at this time is checking out their peers, first of all to make sure they feel they will fit in, and secondly, trying to work out who they will be making friends with. Any information or instruction given to students at this time in these large groups is de-contextualised, de-personalised and de-pressing! As an outcome of the investigation of students' responses, I discussed with colleagues the possibility of delivering induction information to students at home prior to their arriving at the university. It was from these discussions that Stepping Stones 2HE was developed, first of all in our engineering department, and now more fully across other disciplines within the university, including our Health and Community Studies department.

The approach we adopted was to work with students in a way that values them as individuals in the educational process. We wanted to develop an approach that works with the individual and allows them to absorb information in their own space, in their own time, and at their own pace.

Stepping Stones 2HE therefore provides information to students before they join us. We let our new students know about support services, skills audits, and information about the programme of study to which they are coming. We also give students discipline-based activities to work on before they arrive. That is, we ask them to start work. Our course teams have designed activities for new students such as some research or reading, some thinking, and bringing their work with them when they arrive at university. These activities are carefully linked with group work during induction week, when students are given time, resources and rooms to come together in their smaller groups, share the knowledge and information they have brought with them, and develop some output. The output can be in the shape of a poster, a presentation, or whatever means chosen by the course team and students.

Imagine the scene: your students learning from each other in the first week before you've had chance to start your lecture programme. Just think of the potential! Our Operating Department nursing students came together in induction week and taught each other about medical advancements throughout the ages. Computing students pooled their knowledge and gave presentations about computing pioneers, setting some context to the area of their study. Multimedia students critiqued huge websites in terms of their interactivity and multimedia characteristics. In this way, all students' voices are heard, all students contribute, and course cohesion is engendered in a fun, practical and highly interactive way.

We are finding that students really enjoy this approach. It excites their curiosity and the learning that is taking place from each other is remarkable, particularly given that at this point they have had no formal teaching input. This approach also encourages both academic and social integration. The process of students working together in this more meaningful, contextualised and purposeful way has been shown to improve course cohesion and lay the foundation in terms of our expectations of them. It is also introducing students to a more positive and engaging social learning experience at university.

Another significant feature of this approach is to encourage students to complete and return an online self-profiling questionnaire. This questionnaire asks students to report on their previous learning experiences and to reflect on them. We ask the students how they feel about coming to university, and to provide us with some examples of what they have enjoyed doing at school, and how they like to learn. It seems logical that we can only 'manage' student expectations if we know what they are. So, for the past five years I have been asking students what their expectations are, not only of the university, but also of themselves. This encourages students to stop and think about their next steps, why they are coming to university, why they chose this course, rather than just stepping thoughtlessly on the next rung of the education ladder. Also, I had thought that students may be leaving early because of our lack of understanding of their starting-points, so we also ask students to tell us about the content of their entry qualifications. This helps us to ensure that we start off at points with which students are comfortable.

The self-profiling has another purpose as well. Where most students express excitement, nervousness and curiosity about coming to university, some will disclose more unusual levels of anxiety. Students have the opportunity to ask us questions (great for developing a rapport between tutor and student) and sometimes in this way, we get an indication that a student may have some more significant concerns about starting at university. These students can immediately be flagged. In some cases, course managers have contacted particularly anxious students by phone prior to induction week to chat with them. Others monitor the attendance of these students during induction week to ensure that they are, first of all, attending, but also that they are integrating socially. One outstanding example of this was a mature-aged student who expressed concerns about fitting in. Although we contacted her by email to try to reassure her, she didn't arrive on the first morning. Her personal tutor contacted her by phone during the morning to find that she had indeed arrived, but had turned round and gone home again. In the past, she would have been registered as a 'didn't show up', but with this process in place, we managed to retrieve the situation and she came back that afternoon and joined the course. It was important to encourage this student to continue because she was a student from a non-traditional background, in this case, a mature returner to education taking a brave leap into a world she did not know, and she had many doubts about her own ability to fit in. We were, through this process, able to work with her, help her settle in and get her working with her peers.

Another example is a mature-aged student I spoke to prior to her starting on her nursing course. The qualities she described of a university student were someone who is: motivated, enthusiastic, mature, dedicated, conscientious, and who can set targets. Yet she described herself as having felt: overwhelmed, inadequate, least-able, and scared. She said, though, that Stepping Stones 2HE had helped her to understand what university life would be like and had helped reduce many of her anxieties. This approach therefore benefits all students, not just our traditional 18-year-old entrants. It also impacts on widening participation students, that is, those students from backgrounds that have, typically, been disadvantaged in their access to HE in the past. This approach is also of benefit to international students, and our international office is building it into their contacts with overseas students.

Discussion

Stepping Stones 2HE is designed to help students manage their transition into higher education. It is now widely adopted across my university and will become policy across all courses soon. However, it is one part of a process, and not just a discrete intervention.

In designing this approach, I felt confident that 'lifting out' some information to give to students prior to arrival would help make the transition more manageable and informative for students. Also, other information could be lifted out and provided to students in a more useful way. For example, it seems pointless to me to provide students with a detailed library induction during induction week. Such a de-contextualised activity has no relevance at this time. As a response, we now phase induction across the whole first-year experience from the pre-induction period covered by Stepping Stones 2HE up to the end–of-year exams, and progression on to the next level of study. Library induction now takes place when first assignments are set. Our support systems are also fully integrated. Students have access to Stepping Stones 2HE for about a month prior to starting at university and, when their courses begin, other support systems take over. For example, Peer Assisted Learning, personal tutoring and personal development planning programmes are then put into operation. This ensures that students engage in a fully integrated and coherent first-year experience which meets their social and academic aspirations.

What do staff and students think of the Stepping Stones 2HE programme?

The following are typical comments from our evaluations this year:

> We all thought that the students engaged with their activities and the end result has been the production of some excellent pieces of work.

There was a general feeling that Steps had been fun, enabled group bonding at an early stage, and that the students had been keen to participate and create an end product.

All academics were impressed at the standard of work that had been completed in such a short space of time and the vast amount of knowledge that students had gained. In one programme the students demonstrated their work to second year students who were amazed at what the first years had produced. There was a genuine 'buzz' around the School.

The pleasure that was engendered by the programme for both the students and staff is evident in the following comments:

For us, the commitment shown to working together having only been recently introduced to each other was a delight.

We had a great time today and they did good work and presentations. We worked from ten until one o'clock and the students put together a complex concept with little to no background from us.

Students' comments from the evaluations also attested to the programme's value:

I have to say that the Stepping Stones idea is really good, it really made me feel part of the University before I had even arrived and was a nice introduction into studying again for me.

Steps, fantastic. But could have done with it earlier, a month was just not enough!

Useful and enjoyable for the start of a new course.

Finally ...

The challenge for us in HE is to help students move from feeling overwhelmed, inadequate or scared as quickly as possible. Stepping Stones 2HE provides a framework that helps build confidence, reduce anxiety and help students feel more settled in a personalised way. It is *not* about hand-holding, or spoon-feeding. It is *not* looking at students as deficient in some way, and it is *not* about making judgements of prior learning experiences. Rather, it is a relationship-building, active, interactive way of developing confident, self-directed learners who develop bonds with each other, with the course teams and with their subject, from the very first day of their studies.

There is plenty to think about for the future. I want to extend this approach to our partnership colleges. I want to involve students in the design of the resources and to make contributions to the website. For example, one final-year student is currently building some interactive, personal development planning materials that can then form the basis of an e-portfolio. As an institution, we are moving towards ensuring that all commencing first-year students have the opportunity to engage in this approach to transition and induction. It will clearly involve resource issues, but these are not particularly expensive in financial terms given the massive impact on student perseverance with their study, particularly in the difficult first few weeks at university.

Thinking and writing history: an integrated approach to learning development

Digby Warren

The situation

At the heart of successful study at university is the ability to work with disciplinary knowledge. With widening participation, however, many entrant students are unfamiliar with academic modes of thinking and communicating. To assist first-year students in my course, a number of whom have 'non-traditional' backgrounds, to develop that ability I redesigned a core introductory history module/course (that is, a semester-long component of a degree programme). I was excited by this project as it presented an inviting chance for me to meld 'know-how' accrued as an educational development facilitator with my former experience as a history lecturer. Refreshing my acquaintance with my original home discipline after some year's absence made the curriculum journey as engrossing for me as I hoped it would be for the students.

Initially, students commonly think that history is 'a static story of dates and events', or 'just a collection of facts that are undisputed and have to be learned by rote'. Comments that they wrote in their reflective reports indicate this perception. It also echoes popular conceptions of history as narrative about dynasties, wars, constitutions and the deeds of 'great men', which are often sustained by school, newspapers, best-sellers, television, cinema and the 'heritage' industry. Despite this, over the last century this traditional 'political' kind of history has been rivalled by a wealth of new approaches to viewing the past. Through the influence of social and cultural theory, postcolonialism and postmodernism, historical writing has branched out in new directions. It now encompasses issues such as class, gender, race and ethnicity, the impact of imperialism and its aftermath on colonised peoples, or the role of discourse in shaping a society's values, actions and cultural practices. The field of history abounds in conflicting interpretations, and students of history have to be able to engage critically with them, at the conceptual and empirical levels of argument.

Coming from a range of backgrounds, my students taking the 'Uses of History' introductory course had differing prior historical knowledge and proficiency in academic writing and analysis. The heterogeneous cohort of middle- and working-class students, full-time and part-time, has typically included black and white British students of various ethnicities – African-Caribbean, Asian, Indian, Pakistani, Irish – as well as a small group of (usually white) American students visiting on a 'Study Abroad' programme. Mature-age students (over 25 years) and those from 'ethnic minority' backgrounds have always constituted significant contingents (about 40–50 per cent). The gender mix has been reasonably balanced.

For me, the course redesign involved a double challenge: to expand students' understanding of the discipline of history, and, at the same time, to incorporate academic skills development in a way that made it integral to studying the subject. In addition, the content and intellectual level of the course had to be accessible and absorbing for all students in the class, which was characterised by diversity of background and aptitude.

The approaches implemented

The course redesign

My first step was to acknowledge that some features of the old course provided sturdy foundations on which to build. In terms of content, it was academically robust and apposite, the topics and reading lists having been originally compiled by a recognised authority on historiography and historical method, Professor John Tosh. At a later stage, group presentations had been introduced to add a more student-centred dimension to the course. However, the delivery was basically through the traditional formula of formal lectures followed by seminar discussions of recommended texts. The assumption was that students would obtain the texts from the library and read them in advance of the seminar. It was also a second-year course, pitched at a fairly high level. This posed something of a challenge when, as part of curriculum reorganisation, the course was shifted to the first year as a core 'theory and method' unit, with the purpose of introducing students to the discipline.

To fulfil that purpose and to enhance the academic literacy of our diverse group of students, I adopted an integrated approach to learning development. In a nutshell, this entails embedding the requisite skills for analysing, constructing and communicating knowledge into the teaching and learning of the subject. The integrated approach differs from the prevalent 'study skills' approach in that it moves beyond generic guidance about how to read an article or write an essay, for instance, to link such skills directly to an exploration of the nature of knowledge in the discipline. Pedagogical researchers in higher education emphasise that understanding how subject knowledge is created and contested (technically termed 'epistemic cognition') is crucial for accessing academic texts and tasks. This was the goal behind the redesigned 'Uses of History' course: to introduce such epistemic knowledge as a means for developing students' critical thinking, reading and writing in the discipline.

Since I had to work within a prescribed syllabus, the main scope for redesign applied to seminar activities and assessment tasks. These became the main vehicles for integrating academic skills with learning the subject. Lectures continued to serve the more conventional function of presenting the main themes and concepts, but were recast for a first-year audience. However, in the case of the evening course for part-time students, I was able to employ a workshop mode of delivery, in which inputs on 'theory' could be interspersed more organically at relevant points among the student activities.

In weekly seminars that built on preceding lectures, the students worked on tasks. The purpose of these was to explore epistemological questions through concrete examples. These tasks mainly involved analysis and discussion of extracts from secondary sources which illuminated issues in the practice of history. For instance, the problem of explanation in historical writing was explored by looking at the 'intentionalist' *versus* 'structuralist' debate over the origins of the Holocaust. The influence of theory on historical interpretations was examined using short accounts representative of 'History from Below', such as the role of the crowd in the French Revolution, women's history and postcolonialism. The use and abuse of historical knowledge was illustrated by looking at the representation of empire and colonised peoples in history textbooks used in schools during the height of imperialism. One seminar focused on a set of primary sources of various types related to a common topic (for example, the Vietnam war). Here, the learning objectives included ways to analyse verbal and visual texts and statistical data, developing students' awareness of problems in using historical sources (such as relevance, context, reliability and bias) and of appreciating how accounts of the past are constructed from historical evidence.

An advantage of basing seminars on tasks and extracts is that it fostered students' active participation and resolved the problem of their lack of prior preparation. Because of the variety of sources and examples used, all students could find something to say, and this helped to create an ambience for more equitable participation. Indeed, I considered cultural inclusivity carefully when I selected the material, in consultation with my colleagues. In addition, I included regular, close analysis of shorter passages as an effective way to build up, or reinforce, skills in reading critically. At the same time, the course ensured educational balance by requiring wider and deeper reading for the course assignments.

Another significant feature of the redesigned course was the coursework, which provided an opportunity to investigate key issues in more depth, and for interactive learning. It included, first, a small-group presentation with about five students per group, in which students were required to elaborate and debate on an aspect of historical practice. An example of a topic is E. H. Carr's (1961) famous dictum that history is a 'dialogue between the present and the past'. For their talks, students could decide on the empirical content they would use to examine the given quotation about history. This strategy captivated their interest and therefore worked well, as the students tended to choose topics about which they were passionate, and which resonated with their own lives. This process also facilitated cultural exchange among students, making them feel that they had something valuable to contribute from their different backgrounds. Moreover, it made the presentations fresh and interesting for me and other tutors!

Secondly, students had to produce an essay on a broad theme such as 'the problems in using history for political ends'. For this they could again select the specific example(s) that would serve to analyse the theme. Some students opted for topics inspired by other courses or their life experiences; some turned it into an opportunity to explore something new, or to interrogate versions of the past instilled in them at school or as members of particular communities or nations.

In the revised course, to give disciplinary substance to the challenge of essay-writing, a lecture and seminar session was devoted to a workshop during which students conducted a detailed, critical analysis of a short exemplar of academic writing. This was used to model argument construction in the subject. I deliberately chose a piece that could illustrate less successful as well as good practices, such as sweeping, emotive generalisations *versus* conclusions backed by sound evidence. Frameworks for devising an essay plan were also presented, and guidelines on referencing and ways to avoid plagiarism were handed out and briefly discussed. An assessment sheet containing explicit criteria was distributed and later used to provide formative feedback on the structure and content of the students' essays. It doubled as an optional self-assessment form to be submitted with the final work.

In the interim, students were invited to prepare one-page essay plans for subsequent discussion with their tutors on an individual basis, prior to producing their final essay responses. This afforded another opportunity for talking about academic writing and clarifying expectations, and this can be especially helpful for new students who are trying to find their academic voices. The approach taken corresponds with the notion of 'feeding forward' into assessment tasks, rather than just 'feeding back' to students, as practitioners in higher education have been advocating.

The third assignment students had to complete was an individual reflective report on their presentations, where they were required to comment on their experiences of the group task and on insights they had gained from doing the module about the nature of history. In these reports, students have made numerous observations – often reassuringly and touchingly candid – that have endorsed the value of the approach of the redesigned course. Drawing on student feedback in these reports and in module evaluation questionnaires, plus my own reflections on the learning process and analysis of outcomes evinced in the students' academic work, I turn now to an appraisal of the revisions made to the design and delivery of the history course.

Discussion: the redesign in retrospect

The essence of the redesign was the integration of academic skills development with subject content via the mechanisms of the task-oriented seminars, a small-group project, an essay-writing workshop and 'feed-forward' tutorials. Students were highly positive about the seminar programme. They felt that the seminars had been very helpful for clarifying issues raised in lectures, as well as enjoyable, thought-provoking and conducive to their participation. Representative comments from evaluation forms are:

> The seminar sessions were very useful. They provided a safe environment that enabled everyone to contribute and all contributions were valued. It [*sic*] also utilised the knowledge, experience and opinions of all the students and I gained confidence in making contributions. They also provided me opportunities for rehearsing study skills, for example speed-reading, analysis and group work.

> [Seminar] discussions were good and I was able to participate throughout all the sessions. There were always handouts that covered a range of examples that gave a lot of help for me to understand issues.

> The seminars were excellent, mainly because it was a small group compared to the lectures. During the seminars debates were held which gave me an insight into some of the topics and ... the opportunity to listen to other people's point of view.

Many students also reported that the groupwork exercise was very beneficial to their growth of understanding and confidence, particularly through being exposed to different ideas as 'different individuals from different cultures as well' (as one student put it); for example:

> As a group we worked democratically, sharing and expanding ideas. I felt more comfortable expressing my views within a small group environment. Over the course of our preparation work I feel we all grew in confidence.

> I did find the group project of particular benefit because it made me look at causes much more objectively and to question their validity. It was also a challenge to work as a team and to listen to other interpretations and views.

> One of the things I enjoyed most about the group presentation was the discussions we had [when preparing] ... The points that were raised were very thought provoking and working in a group is an interesting experience because of this differing of opinions [and] backgrounds.

From my perspective as a tutor, the presentations on the whole showed that the students had a good grasp of the issues of historical practice with which the course was concerned, with teams often bringing in lively examples. However, the quality of delivery in the presentations varied. Although the assessment criteria included the more technical aspects of presentation and had been explicitly negotiated with the class, there was no input on presentational skills as such. This is because the primary purpose of the exercise was to promote collaborative learning of course content, and in that respect it was generally successful. In a course that already had an ambitious agenda of introducing students to the discipline and developing their academic skills, it was difficult to find space to include training in presentation techniques. However, this dilemma has since been partly addressed by an institutional scheme that requires each undergraduate curriculum to offer a compulsory first-year component aimed at providing students with a grounding in study and academic skills. These components, known as 'higher education orientation' courses, typically include teamwork and presentations among the suite of skills.

In their reflective reports where they identified insights acquired through the module, all students demonstrated to varying degrees a more sophisticated understanding of the nature of the discipline. As expressed by one of the more articulate students:

> Taking this module has opened my eyes to how History ... is broached in terms of the interpretation and re-interpretation of the past, written or recorded ... Moreover, that [it] is never stagnant [but] an ongoing process constantly open to new evaluations, analysis and therefore a constant arena of debate for historians ... [And] that written history can select, emphasise, highlight and, knowingly or unknowingly distort either [the] significance of this or [that] event, or the impact and motives of this or that personality.

What shines through most of all is the students' recurring claim that 'the course has taught me to read history in a much more critical and objective way', as one student said. Another observed:

> When I pick up a History book or turn to an article in a newspaper or magazine I will no longer be able to accept what the writer has to say at face value. Now I will be looking at it with eyes that have been shown how to analyse and question.

Along with critical thinking and reading, another central goal of the redesigned course was developing the students' abilities to write academically. From running workshops and tutorials and marking student essays, I could certainly suggest anecdotally that the conscious attention placed on essay planning has paid off in terms of a better quality of writing, especially where students engaged seriously with the drafting opportunity that was built into the assessment process. But I feel more confident in suggesting this, because after the first time the course was run,

I analysed a sample of final answers for indications of learning outcomes under three related categories:

1   historical awareness;
2   cogency of argument; and
3   academic language.

My analysis focused on the extent to which the students' papers demonstrated:

1   a grasp of the value and constructed nature of history and issues of bias in historical sources and accounts;
2   some ability to present relevant, properly substantiated and well-structured ideas; and
3   appropriate register (that is, apt use of English in an academic context) and understanding of key disciplinary concepts.

It showed that, among the sample group at least, the majority of students had produced competently argued and capably expressed essays that reflected a good understanding of the discipline.

Students have also confirmed the usefulness of the essay assessment pro forma for helping them to see the strengths and areas for improvement in their writing. Disappointingly though, few students were willing to use the criteria sheet for undertaking a self-assessment before submission of their work, perhaps out of lack of confidence, or time. One way to encourage students to engage with this, I think, would be to introduce a short peer exercise in class during which students could discuss with one another their progress in writing up their essays, using the assessment sheet as a checklist. I have also realised that referencing is an issue that needs to be revisited and treated as an integral aspect of argumentation, not merely as a technique. For instance, in devising tasks to guide students in critical analysis of academic texts, I have now included questions about the acceptability and authority of particular statements or evidence, thereby highlighting the role that referencing plays in endorsing the strength of an argument as well as in enabling researchers to track back to the original sources.

Overall, while initially the course redesign was time-intensive, the task-based, subject-embedded approach to academic skills development used in this redesign offers a framework that can be readily updated and adapted to other courses. The course also clearly gripped the interest of most students and had a transformative effect on their learning in that it widened their perceptions of history, themselves and others, and strengthened their academic skills and confidence. A top-performing, mature-age student acknowledged this in noting that 'the whole module ... has provided a critical framework for understanding and challenging concepts of history, which I am sure will be of great value for my own writing and reading of text further along in my course'.

Internationalisation of the curriculum in an interconnected world

Betty Leask

The situation

Traditionally, in all parts of the world, internationalisation of the curriculum has been linked to globalisation and focussed on student mobility through study abroad, exchange and the recruitment of fee-paying international students. This has had both a limiting and an uncertain impact on the student community. It is limited in that such an approach restricts the benefits of internationalisation to a limited number of students – the sojourners, those students who can afford to be mobile and those students in the host country who interact with them. It is uncertain in that doubt has been cast on the actual learning that results from student mobility for both the hosts and the sojourners. Both the sojourners and the hosts may in fact have their simple stereotypes of cultural others confirmed due to a lack of engagement with each other. The issue is therefore how to internationalise the learning outcomes for all students in a planned and systematic way. This requires a reorientation of the concept of internationalisation of the curriculum – to one that is inclusive of all students, regardless of whether they are mobile or not.

The higher education institution in Southern Australia in which I work has a strong commitment to internationalisation of the curriculum for all students. It has a policy framework that supports through the explication of a set of defined student learning outcomes related to internationalisation of the curriculum. These outcomes focus on connections between the international and the intercultural and between culture, knowledge, teaching and learning in the disciplines.

The policy has been developed in the context of globalisation, which has been a speedy process that has increased the interconnections between nations and peoples of the world. It has put increased pressure on educational institutions to prepare students for life in an increasingly connected and borderless world. One of the main functions of an internationalised curriculum is the 'formation of the skills ... required to operate in the global environment itself' (Marginson 1999: 19). Thus internationalisation of the curriculum is clearly linked to globalisation, and relates to 'those processes by which the peoples of the world are incorporated into a single world society, a global society' (Albrow 1990: 9) usually against their will or at least without their conscious consent. Information and communication technologies (ICTs) are often cited as an agent of globalisation through their contribution to the movement of money, services, goods, images and ideas around the world.

It is in this context that my institution explored information and communication technologies to enable and facilitate intercultural communication, and thus to assist students to better understand and be able to live and work in a globalised world. The approach that the institution was keen to develop is very different from the largely unstructured and unplanned approach to internationalisation of the curriculum which is common across the world and has focussed on student mobility. The possibilities associated with utilising ICTs to assist students to explore cultural diversity, to interact with and enrich each other and to gain fresh cultural insights was taken up in a number of disciplinary areas, as explained in the next section. The approaches taken are rich in that they can be used to achieve similar learning outcomes for students in other institutional contexts.

The approaches implemented

Exploring professional practice in another cultural context

Williams and Blaney (2000) describe their use of the internet in a Health Sciences course to assist Australian students to explore cultural issues in professional practice in physiotherapy, and this is relevant to the situation at hand. Students were required to make contact with and collect information from a physiotherapy educator or student outside of Australia or New Zealand. Each student was allocated a cardiorespiratory patient scenario which contained basic information concerning a patient presentation. Three questions concerning the physiotherapy assessment and management of this patient were posed. Students were required to contact a School of Physiotherapy outside of their home country, to present the questions to the international educator or student in that school and to collect information concerning the assessment and management of the patient scenario. They were encouraged to contact non-Western schools and schools in developing countries. The internet was used to locate possible schools and email contact was the main medium of communication. In this way, students were given the opportunity to develop their understanding and appreciation of the way their profession is practised in a different country and culture, to appreciate the relation between their field of study locally, and professional traditions elsewhere. Two simple online tools, the web and email, were all that was needed. Students were required to write a critical review of the international response including a statement concerning the similarities or differences in terminology, conditions managed, techniques or interpretation of problems between their own and the other country. This assignment contributed to the final grade for the theory component of the course. The initial trial of this approach with a group of forty-three students resulted in student contact with nine different countries, including Thailand, Hong Kong, Ireland, Canada and the USA. Feedback from students and staff was that this assignment assisted in the development of international perspectives among students and staff.

Looking at a problem from a different cultural position

In an international studies course, a web-site and a series of online discussion fora have been used to develop international perspectives among students through assisting them to see a problem through the eyes of someone from a different culture. A scenario based on a fictional international crisis was described in stages on a web-site. Thirteen countries were called to the table and asked to present their respective position statements regarding the crisis (and developments, as they occur), with a view to concluding a draft resolution, based on a majority decision, at the end of the crisis talks. Each student was allocated to a country/group and each group was required to research the background to their country's stance on the international crisis and prepare a position statement. Within each group, students were advised to assign specific tasks to individuals and to select one person to act as the 'head of state' – the individual who would post the country's position statement and negotiate on behalf of the team for the final vote. The scenario incorporated elements of ethnic conflict, nationalism and human rights and involved students in the challenge of credibly shaping and constructing a country's perspective, based on their research.

Students were also required to actively engage with the simulated 'international community' in negotiation and decision making. Every student was required to participate actively in the scenario, which was made deeply interactive through role play and online discussion. Communication and collaboration within a country group occurred online via a discussion forum. This allowed students to share documents in draft form and to participate actively and thoughtfully in the drafting of their country's position statement. This area was 'private' to the country representatives and to the lecturer/moderator. Discussions between country groups also took place online. The larger 'emergency forum' set up by the 'United Nations' to deal with the crisis took the form of a general online discussion group which was used as a forum for country representatives to give their views and, potentially, to negotiate shared positions. The lecturer, acting as moderator, could view all discussion groups and could intervene if and when necessary. The immediacy of the online environment enabled the lecturer to manipulate the simulated international crisis to challenge or assist students in their learning. Participation in the online discussion groups and associated tasks and in an interactive online seminar accounted for 25 per cent of the assessment for the course.

This scenario gave all students the opportunity to use ICT to research and interact and, in so doing, to develop their understanding of other cultural and national perspectives; to display an ability to think globally and to consider issues from a variety of perspectives.

The potential of ICTs for internationalisation

These examples illustrate the potential of ICT to assist all students to achieve a range of internationalisation outcomes by using simple online tools (email, a website, online discussion groups), to interact across national and cultural borders, and to research and represent other national and cultural perspectives.

While using ICTs in these specific examples, we came to appreciate that there are many other ways in which ICTs can be used to enable all students to access information from a variety of cultural perspectives, and to interact and collaborate with other scholars and learners all over the world. These are being explored in various courses and units across the university. Distance, time and money need not be barriers to international exposure and awareness for any student with access to a computer and a modem if technology is used strategically. For example, technology may be used to:

- establish international contacts and networks in the discipline/professional area;
- enable 'virtual' visits by guest lecturers/presenters with an international profile who address specific topics or answer-specific questions online at appropriate times during the programme;
- conduct group and individual projects with a focus on international issues, case studies and/or exemplars;
- develop cross-cultural communication skills through the establishment of working relationships with people from diverse cultural backgrounds in completion of tasks such as group analysis of media reports from international newspapers from different cultural perspectives, 'online' interviews with students from other cultures, and/or professionals who have worked internationally;
- locate, discuss, analyse and evaluate information from a range of online and offline international sources;
- provide opportunities to analyse the issues, methodologies and possible solutions associated with current areas of debate within the discipline from a range of cultural perspectives;
- access online international sources – such as journals, conference proceedings and professional associations;
- facilitate simulations in which students from different cultural backgrounds have the opportunity to participate in and learn from dynamic and complex cross-cultural role-plays in a controlled online environment (Leask 2004: 341).

Discussion

Internationalisation outcomes for all students

Descriptions of generic skills in higher education – also referred to as key skills, graduate attributes, graduate qualities, graduate capabilities, graduate capacities, graduate competencies, professional skills and employability skills – frequently include reference to international or global perspectives. These are variously described and may be focussed very differently in different disciplines. For example, the international perspectives required of a nurse or a pharmacist might focus more on socio-cultural understanding than those of an engineer, where the focus might be more on the understanding of the global and environmental responsibilities of the professional engineer and the need for sustainable development. And while practising nurses, pharmacists and engineers should all be able to recognise intercultural issues relevant to their professional practice and have a broad understanding of social, cultural and global issues affecting their profession, the strategies they will need to use to deal with them will be different in some ways, even though they may be similar in others. Comparable differences exist between the international perspectives required of for example, accountants and teachers. Some common and generic student learning outcomes associated with internationalisation outcomes and a sample of tasks associated with these through the development of students' abilities to function in an intercultural and international environment is listed in Table 8.1.

The uniqueness of the online environment gives the lecturer the capacity to closely monitor, intervene in and control some aspects of the learning environment should this be desired, while simultaneously allowing students to learn independently and autonomously, in groups and across cultural boundaries. It also enables students and staff to learn with and from each other. Planned and strategic use of information and communication technologies to achieve explicit internationalisation learning outcomes through engagement in meaningful and purposeful interaction across cultures is a useful way of preparing graduates to live and work effectively in an increasingly globalised world.

However, if the potential of ICTs for internationalisation of the curriculum is to be fully realised, students will be required to participate in and be rewarded, through the formal assessment system, for their involvement in such activities as:

- synchronous or asynchronous online discussion groups that link students from different cultures to enable them to complete tasks, solve problems, gain international perspectives on issues and to establish international networks within the discipline;
- an online forum (discussion room) where they can (and are required to) discuss cultural and regional differences in values and assumptions affecting the discipline, together with how these might impact on the actions of individuals;
- a range of group projects for assessment that require them to work online or via email with people from another/other cultural group(s) to compare and contrast perspectives on similar professional issues;
- online tutorial 'group tasks' that examine ways in which particular cultural interpretations of social, scientific or technological applications of knowledge may include or exclude, or may advantage or disadvantage people from different cultural groups.

Table 8.1 Internationalisation outcomes and ICTs

Student learning outcome	Online learning tools/tasks/activities to achieve this outcome
Ability to think globally and consider issues from a variety of perspectives	Students participate in an online simulation in which they take the role of someone from another culture they have researched previously
Awareness of their own culture and its perspectives, and other cultures and their perspectives	Students are required to explain their own cultural perspective on an issue in an online discussion group and compare and contrast this with the cultural perspectives of other online group members
Appreciation of the relation between their field of study locally, and professional traditions elsewhere	Web-based research into professional traditions in other cultures Online interviews with students from other countries/cultures studying in the same professional area
Recognition of intercultural issues relevant to their professional practice	Scenarios from professional practice, with obvious intercultural issues embedded within them are presented as problems to be solved by an online tutorial group of mixed cultures
Appreciation of the importance of multicultural diversity to professional practice and citizenship	Online multicultural teams are set problem-solving tasks related to the professional area
Appreciation of the complex and interacting factors that contribute to notions of culture and cultural relationships	Students from different cultural groups interview each other online and post a report to a shared website on key aspects of their own and their partner's culture
Valuing of diversity of language and culture	Undertake a research project into contributions made to the professional area by different cultural groups. Students should then post the results to an online seminar
Demonstration of the capacity to apply international standards and practices within the discipline or professional area	Compare international standards based on collaborative research and analysis undertaken by students from different cultures
Awareness of the implications of local decisions and actions for international communities and of international decisions and actions for local communities	Appropriate case studies related to professional area are included in the programme and then analysed by the students

Note: This table originally appeared in Leask (2004: 343).

Such tasks can quite easily be related to specific 'internationalisation' learning outcomes.

Overall, our experience is that it is important to make internationalisation objectives explicit and to design learning and assessment tasks carefully so that students are rewarded for the efforts required to engage in meaningful intercultural learning.

References

Albrow, M. (1990). Introduction to A. Albrow and E. King, *Globalization, Knowledge and Society* (London: SAGE Publications), 3–13.

Leask, B. (2004). 'Internationalisation Outcomes for all Students Using Information and Communication Technologies (ICTs)', *Journal of Studies in International Education*, 8, 4.

Marginson, S. (1999). 'After globalization: Emerging politics of education', *Journal of Educational Policy*, 14, 1: 19–31.

Williams, M. and Blaney, F. (2000). 'Report on graduate quality exemplar.' Accessed 1 June 2006. Online. Available www.unisanet.unisa.edu.au/gradquals/example/physiov1.doc.

'A spoonful of sugar helps the medicine go down'

Lesley McMillan and Lucy Solomon

The situation

Teaching quantitative social research methods to undergraduate sociology students poses a particular challenge. For a number of reasons these courses are not popular, but students are compelled to take them. Students often fear quantitative methods because it involves numbers and they have a tendency to equate it with mathematics. Even those who are not frightened of the topic are often turned off by it, and it is difficult to engender any enthusiasm for the course.

With the exception of students opting for psychology degrees, most students taking arts and social science degrees do not anticipate they will have to learn quantitative methods and statistics. The majority of arts students also enter university with A levels or non-standard qualifications that rarely include mathematics or other numerical or science-based subjects. As such, when students are faced with a course on quantitative methods, they often feel out of their depth and anxious.

These feelings are reported by many, or perhaps even most, students. We noted, however, that students from widening participation backgrounds, in particular women and mature first-generation students, expressed the greatest anxiety. Discussion with these students revealed their heightened anxiety and subsequent fear that stemmed from their anxiety about numbers and mathematics as it had often been a long time since they had studied any numerical subject. Many of these students also divulged a fear of computers (the course involves learning to use a computer-based statistics package).

Fear is a significant barrier to learning for all students, and increased fear levels experienced by students from widening participation backgrounds may further marginalise them in the learning process. The student feedback and assessment data was reviewed and there was concern about the low level of performance. The majority of students were scoring significantly lower grades compared to their other courses and feedback data indicated students found the course frightening, confusing and boring, and included such comments as 'I'm no good at this, I can't do maths'. When colleagues previously involved with the course mentioned an incident where a mature female student broke down during a class because of her frustration about using computers and 'maths', we were determined to find a way to facilitate all students' learning of quantitative research methods and to address their feelings of fear and dread of the subject, as well as improve assessment methods to facilitate maximum student satisfaction with the course.

The approaches implemented

This case study describes the use of culinary analogies to facilitate students' learning of social research methods and to improve their experience of this course. The case study described was based in a large higher education institution in the South of England. The university in question has a higher-than-average intake of social class 1 and 2 students and as such the needs of widening participation students can be overlooked. Social research methods is a compulsory second-year course for all students studying sociology majors. The course comprises two components: qualitative social research methods and quantitative social research methods. The course is taught over one academic year and involves a range of teaching methods including: lectures; interactive and practical-based workshops; and computer laboratory workshops.

Reducing the fear

The aim was to facilitate students' learning of quantitative methods and, primarily, to think of a way to pull it away from mathematics and numbers – many students claimed to want nothing to do with numbers! It is our belief that quantitative methods are primarily about concepts – the numbers are merely the material the concepts work with. If students could understand the concepts without worrying about the numbers, this could facilitate learning.

Given that significant learning is more likely to take place when it is related to a person's interests or experiences (Rogers 1994) it was decided to find something that all students could relate to. The decision was to use culinary analogies. Everybody eats; most people at some point will have cooked food, even if it is just beans on toast or a boiled egg, therefore it should be something that students could identify with. In particular, given the concern about increased fear levels and potential marginalisation of widening participation students, culinary analogies seemed particularly suitable because eating and the preparation of food is not culturally specific – there are, of course, specific cultural practices and 'norms', but all cultures prepare food and eat it in some form. Mature female students were often those expressing the greatest fear, and the majority of these students were likely to have families and dependants to care for and were therefore very likely to be familiar with the organisation of cooking and recipes and the preparation of food. As such, culinary analogies seemed an everyday comparator that all students, irrespective of background, would be able to relate to.

'Recipe' for success

Before introducing the culinary analogies into the quantitative methods teaching, we decided to 'set the scene' or 'whet their appetite' by encouraging students to see the research process as a 'recipe'. Students attended a lecture which took them through the process of research design and likened the various stages to a recipe. For example, students were told that research design involves a number of decisions, just as a recipe does. A decision has to be made about what course to make (starter, main course, dessert) and in the research process this could be likened to deciding what the topic of the research would be. Similarly, deciding whether or not to cater for vegetarians and who you would invite can be likened to procedures for identifying a population for the research. Selecting ingredients could be likened to selecting a sample of participants. Cooking the meal could be compared to analysing the data – researchers must make a decision as to how to analyse (computer-based, by hand, quantitatively or qualitatively, etc.) just as chefs must decide how to cook a meal (bake, grill, fry, steam, microwave, etc.). Overall, the oral feedback received from students about this technique was very positive indeed. In fact, several weeks later during a workshop session very positive feedback was received when a mature female student, pouring over her computer, was heard saying under her breath as she went to select a method of analysis for her data: 'and now I cook it!'.

Following the initial success of the recipe analogy, it was decided to extend the culinary analogies into all the quantitative method teaching. Students had already been introduced to this way of thinking about research concepts and felt comfortable with the parallels being drawn. It has often proved difficult to get across to students the importance of the level of measurement of data when conducting quantitative research. Essentially, level of measurement refers to the format in which we record the answer to a question (which is determined by how we ask it). For example, if a question was asked in a survey that said 'how old are you in years?', the data this would generate would be what is called *ratio* data. Ratio data are one of the highest levels of measurement because the numbers actually mean something intrinsically – they have an intrinsic numeric value – for example, someone who is 14 is half the age of someone who is 28. Data measured on a ratio scale can be analysed using a very wide range of statistical techniques that are regarded as more powerful statistical tools. If the question was asked slightly differently, like this: what age are you?: 18–25, 26–35, 36–45, or 46 and over, because respondents would have to highlight the category they fitted into, this would generate data with a *categorical* level of measurement. This is a 'lower' level of measurement than ratio data because the numbers we would assign to these categories would have no intrinsic meaning. (SPSS, the statistics package used to analyse data, only recognises numeric data and therefore, to distinguish which box someone has ticked, we would assign '1' to age 18–25, '2' to 26–35, and so on up to '5'). These numbers have been assigned by us and do not mean anything in themselves; therefore we cannot subject them to statistics that use mathematical procedures based on the fact the value has an intrinsic meaning. Therefore, categorical data are a lower level of measurement because we can run fewer statistical tests on this sort of data and the tests are less powerful.

It is important for quantitative methods students to learn that they should always collect their data in the highest level of measurement possible. If respondents are asked for their age in years, this can always be collapsed into categories later if the researchers so wish, but what the research cannot do is disaggregate data such as numbers of people in an age-group back to individual ages if the researchers only asked people to indicate a category they fitted into. This is something many students have had difficulty understanding. This was the area where it was decided that culinary analogies to facilitate learning and understanding would be best used.

After explaining the different levels of measurement to students in class, a slide which had three (abbreviated) recipes that could be made using apples was presented. Then, in order to facilitate interaction to promote deep learning, students were presented with three whole apples, a knife and a chopping board. These were placed at the front of the lecture theatre where all the students could see and one apple was cut in half, one into small pieces, and the remaining apple left whole. Students were then asked to write down how many of the recipes could be made with each of the three apples. One recipe involved a whole apple, one involved halved apples and one involved chopped apples.

Students were asked to shout out the answer to the question for each of the apples as they were pointed at. The students shouted out the answers and thankfully got them correct. The whole apple can be used to make all three recipes because it can be cut or chopped up. The halved apple can be used to make two of the recipes because it can be used as it is or chopped up. The chopped apple can only be used for one recipe because it is already chopped and the other recipes require a halved or a whole apple. The message for students to learn was that data, like apples, can be chopped up but cannot be stuck back together, and like data, the more the apple resembles its highest form (whole) the more recipes (statistical tests) can be made with it.

During the next teaching session students were prompted for feedback on the 'apple session' and the comments were reassuringly positive. They did say they thought it was crazy when the apples began to be chopped up at the front of the lecture but it had facilitated their understanding of the issue and it would be something they would always remember.

The success of these initial developments led to the introduction of culinary analogies throughout the course. These were introduced for elements in the course that students found particularly frightening, confusing or challenging in order to facilitate their learning of the *concept*, rather than the mathematics behind it. These analogies were successful, although some required refining after initial use, and the process of 'doing' through working with food and recipes proved a useful method for engaging students with what can otherwise be a dry topic.

Formative assessment was integrated within the course on a weekly basis by giving students questions based around culinary analogies, for example, how might you 'cook' or analyse the following example? Students were split into small groups, given an amount of time to consider their answers and then presented their answers to the remainder of the class. In doing this they received useful formative feedback from their peers and the class tutor as well as increasing their understanding of the research process. Students also spoke with confidence and little anxiety, and it is possible this is a result of being able to talk using terms and concepts with which they are very familiar – food and cooking – in lieu of concepts that are more alien to them. The use of common concepts also allowed the students to provide more formative feedback for one another as there was less anxiety about using the wrong terms in their responses. Students also exhibited considerable collaborative learning in this formative assessment process as they would spontaneously debate the suitability of some of the analogies they had come up with themselves, and on one occasion had a debate about whether a particular method of analysis was analogous to beating egg whites or folding them in!

Discussion

As previously stated, initial feedback from students as the course progressed indicated students found the use of culinary analogies facilitated their learning and allowed them to engage with an otherwise abstract topic. Final course evaluations from students would provide the opportunity to evaluate the impact and usefulness of this curriculum development from students' perspectives. Another 'test' of the effectiveness of this teaching approach would also come in the form of student assessment performance, as students had historically performed poorly in quantitative methods compared to their other courses. Students' evaluation forms recorded positive scores for the quantitative methods course for the first time and students commented particularly on the novel teaching methods used and 'the apples'.

The students' final assessment scores (the course is assessed through the presentation of a portfolio of work that assesses their ability to both use quantitative methods and understand the concepts behind them) also offered considerable support for the success of the teaching intervention. In fact, the students were considered by the exam board to have performed a little too well at the course! A greater than average number of students scored grades in the first-class range and no students failed the course, whereas previously a high proportion of students were failing; widening participation students were disproportionally represented in this group. This enhanced performance in the summative assessment at the end of the course can be attributed to the formative feedback students received within lessons. The high performance also allowed us to introduce further material into the course for future years, thus using culinary analogies and the formative assessment method to increase the material students encountered and to challenge them to increase their quantitative skills.

Indeed, 'a spoonful of sugar' does help the 'medicine go down' if that 'spoonful' allows students to relate seemingly frightening concepts to ones with which they are more familiar and comfortable. There are potential benefits for *all* students but particularly for those students from non-traditional backgrounds who may have greater anxieties about approaching topics or concepts which are alien to them. Using analogies that students are familiar with, are carefully thought through and are linked to the teaching and learning in question can 'level' some of the inequalities that are present in the higher education environment and facilitate learning.

Reference

Rogers, C. (1994) *Freedom to Learn*. New York: Merrill.

Leveraging student engagement with assessment: collecting intelligence to support teaching, student progress and retention

Mark Russell

The situation

I think it was Darwin who first offered the notion that *survival is ultimately dependent on the ability to change and evolve*. This relates not only to the flora and fauna that surround us but also to me, as a teacher of fluid mechanics and thermodynamics. In fact, much of the teaching profession is steeped in ideals of constant reflection and adaptation for the betterment of students and their learning. Hence Darwin's notion of *adapt or die* underpins much of what we should do. Sometimes this reflection and adaptation process manifests itself as minor curricular adjustments, whereas in other instances it leads to significant change.

This chapter presents a case in the latter category. Further, the innovation presented here was not established from some general end–of-year reflections on 'what worked and what didn't', but rather from the stark evidence that far too many of our first-year engineering undergraduates were failing a core engineering module; Fluid Mechanics and Thermodynamics. This innovation, like so many others, was borne out of necessity rather than out of a sense of adjusting for its own sake.

There can be little doubt that fluid mechanics and thermodynamics are two of the most important subjects taught at universities today. Aircraft fly and cars don't because of our understanding of fluid mechanics; power plants are becoming more environmentally benign because of our knowledge of thermodynamics; and the thermal comfort of many of the world's citizens, in both hot and cold climates, is being helped because of our understanding of the various forms of heat transfer. Such is the importance of this subject that our students can often be heard reciting the laws of thermodynamics as they skip to class.

Perhaps the above exaggerates a little too much, but it does convey the importance of the discipline and indicate how it genuinely touches the modern world. While it was hoped that our students would thrive in a discipline area that has demonstrable importance, it is very disappointing to report the performance of a first-year cohort (2000/01). Although these students were reasonably typical in entry profile, the grades from their end-of-year examination were so poor, over 50 per cent of the students scored less than 35 per cent in the module's final exam, that it simply demanded the teaching team take a really close inspection of the curriculum and its attendant teaching, learning and assessment methods.

It is worth noting that the teaching team were highly committed to their teaching and learning activities and were leading in the development of e-learning resources (for this module), such that it was often seen as an exemplar of Blended Learning. That is, the systematic integration of e-learning with conventional teaching and learning settings.

Quite simply, a look at the evidence, both real and anecdotal, of student behaviours and study patterns suggested a fairly disengaged cohort. Tutorial sheets remained unanswered, postings were made to the module's discussion forum at week seven that related to the material taught at week two, and students appeared a little too unprepared for the upcoming lectures. The culmination of this was a disconnection between where the teaching team expected the students to be with their studies and understanding, and where they actually were.

Although these inappropriate study behaviours were the students' and not the teaching teams', they were probably encouraged, or not positively discouraged enough, by the prevailing curriculum and associated teaching, learning and assessment activities. Indeed the main failing, which led to the innovation, was the in-module phase test. This phase test was set towards the end of the module and hence did little to encourage reading around, the importance of regular study, or provide teachers with real evidence of what the students knew and what they didn't.

And so while the subject was core, and in many respects a traditional engineering subject, traditional teaching and assessment settings were not best suited to the growing number of non-traditional students. These included first-generation higher education students/students from families without a higher education background, changing secondary-school curricula and an attendant shift in emphasis from formal examinations to a more coursework-based assessment programme.

While for us it was the students' own performance that forced our re-think, the changing context alone presents a real and exciting opportunity for colleagues to rethink their curricula. An opportunity that, if seized, will enrich the teaching and learning experience for many of the students by drawing on the diversity and the changing student demographic, rather than shying away from it.

The approaches implemented

The innovation primarily set out to re-engage the students via regular assessment tasks. The underpinning principle was: *need to change student behaviour – then change the assessment*. The tasks used here were Weekly Assessed Tutorial Sheets (WATS) which were numerically based, problem-solving, tasks. These can be thought of as consolidating exercises that previously the more engaged students would have attempted as part of their guided learning and general reading.

The content of the weekly tasks was aligned with that of the weekly lecture. Being assessed *forced student activity*, whereas being weekly *distributed the students' effort* across the semester, rather than just focusing their minds around revision time. Revision, for the 2000/01 cohort, was probably more akin to first-vision.

Setting weekly tasks for around 150 students is not trivial. This is particularly true since the intention was also to discourage 'answer sharing'. Indeed, each student's sheet came embedded with their own unique data – see Figure 10.1. Hence, while they were free to discuss and share their thoughts on problem-solving, sharing answers in this assessment made no sense whatsoever.

The assessment regime became feasible because of the development of ICT tools and bespoke computer programs to:

* Create the students' unique data
* Set-up the individualised problem sheets
* Collect the students' numerical submissions
* Collect free text from the students
* Mark the students' numerical submissions
* Provide a personalised feedback e-mail
* Provide evidence to the teacher on the comparative performance of the students:
  * Against each other
  * As a cohort, on each task.

Fluid Mechanics and Thermodynamics

Weekly Assessed Tutorial Sheet 9.

Student Number		160	
Print your name		Mark Russell	
Hand out date	21 Feb 2006	Hand in date	1 March 2006

Q1a). A fluid of relative density 0.98 flows through a pipe of diameter 149 mm at 0.44 m/s. After passing through a gradual reducer the fluid leaves a 72mm diameter pipe and discharges onto a stationary surface. Assuming that the surface slopes at an angle of 'A' degrees from the horizontal plane, as shown below, and that the surface somehow acts as a vane in that the fluid is deflected along its surface - calculate the forces **acting on the surface** for the angles shown in the answer boxes. You may assume that friction effects are negligible.

Figure Q1a. Definition of angle 'A' for the inclined surface.

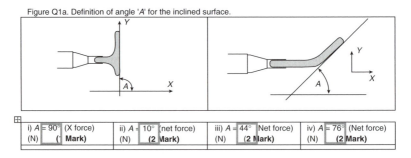

i) $A = 90°$ (X force)		ii) $A = 10°$ (net force)		iii) $A = 44°$ (Net force)		iv) $A = 76°$ (Net force)	
(N)	(Mark)	(N)	(2 Mark)	(N)	(2 Mark)	(N)	(2 Mark)

Figure 10.1 An example of part of a Weekly Assessed Tutorial Sheet (student unique data is highlighted)

Alignment of the assessment with recognised good principles of teaching, learning and assessment at the outset indicated its likely effectiveness. This, coupled with the fact that the technology makes the assessment extremely efficient (all of the above happens at the click of a couple of buttons), now provides an exemplar of an effective and efficient assessment regime that has opportunity for transportation into cognate disciplines.

One example of the effectiveness and efficiency is demonstrated with one button click. This subsequently constructs and delivers a personalised feedback e-mail to every one of the module's students. This allows me to provide the highly prized 'prompt feedback', a few hours after the submission deadline, and provide some personalised diagnostics on their responses. Failure to provide prompt feedback is often a feature of much of today's assessment and was recently rated as an issue by many of the UK students in the National Student Survey.

This work, however, was not simply focused on feeding back to students. It also sought to feed back to me. And so the technology also created a league table of student performance on a week-by-week basis, see Figures 10.2a, b and c. Another button click made this happen. And so, in addition to stimulating a little social competition, and hence a need in the students to be seen to be learning, the league table also provided invaluable data for me. Slicing the table *row-by-row* allows me to compare and contrast the students' performance and hence to identify early which students are likely to be at risk of failure, and which ones are not (see Figure 10.2b). A *column-by-column* slice of the table (see Figure 10.2c) gives an insight into the whole group's understanding of that week's material. Notice how the task set at week 5 (WATS5) failed to differentiate the students. That is, they all demonstrated a good understanding, whereas a wider differentiation was observed with the task set at week 9 (WATS9). Not only do I get to see, at an appropriate time, who is struggling, but I am also presented with real information on what material or topic area might need revisiting. This type of information is essential if we are truly to tackle issues such as progression and retention.

The intelligence community have a notion of using all available data to plan their next move. This data includes information from the field which they refer to as 'ground truth'. This ground truth, or perhaps better still in this example, *class-truth*, now allows me to plan my next actions based on real and all available data. No longer do I have to wait until the examination to see where students X and Y are struggling, nor how many students understood the material at week 6. I get to see this information immediately such that I can better support my students.

In addition to collecting the students' numerical responses, the technology includes the ability to collect free-text responses. Hence, when the students submit their responses to the tasks, they are also asked to respond to questions inviting them to conceptualise their understanding in a free-text format. Sample questions include:

- Describe in your own words the meaning of Bernoulli's equation.
- Often in manometry we ignore the density of the fluid in one of the limbs; why is this?

	1	2	3	4	5	6	7	8	9	10	11	12	13	14	15	16
LBN	56	100	100	100	83	92	63	100	45	81	83	82	22	25	down 2 place(s)
CYM	78	71	86	73	100	92	87	86	27	88	100	81	33	26	up 7 place(s)
COL	78	71	86	92	100	75	97	86	10	31	67	80	27	27	up 0 place(s)
JOR	86	86	100	100	83	100	73	93	45	58	67	80	28	28	up 0 place(s)
BGR	100	100	71	54	100	58	100	100	27	62	100	79	34	29	up 5 place(s)
MDA	56	100	100	100	100	92	80	43	1	100	100	79	35	30	up 5 place(s)
LAO	44	86	57	46	50	33	0	0	1	0	0	29	130	131	down 1 place(s)
BOL	44	57	0	1	100	50	7	1	1	31	0	27	132	132	up 0 place(s)
CAF	44	0	14	1	33	75	13	1	1	54	0	22	133	133	up 0 place(s)
COM	33	57	0	0	67	42	0	14	0	15	0	21	134	134	up 0 place(s)

(a)

	1	2	3	4	5	6	7	8	9	10	11	12	13	14	15	16
LBN	56	100	100	100	83	92	63	100	45	81	83	82	23	25	down 2 place(s)
CYM	78	71	86	73	100	92	87	86	27	88	100	81	33	26	up 7 place(s)
COL	78	71	86	92	100	75	97	86	100	31	67	80	27	27	up 0 place(s)
JOR	78	86	100	100	83	100	73	93	45	58	67	80	28	28	up 0 place(s)
BGR	100	100	71	54	100	58	100	100	27	62	100	79	34	29	up 5 place(s)
MDA	56	100	100	100	100	92	80	43	1	100	100	79	35	30	up 5 place(s)
LAO	44	86	57	46	50	33	0	0	1	0	0	29	130	131	down 1 place(s)
BOL	44	57	0	1	100	50	7	1	1	31	0	27	132	132	up 0 place(s)
CAF	44	0	14	1	33	75	13	1	1	54	0	22	133	133	up 0 place(s)
COM	33	57	0	0	67	42	0	14	0	15	0	21	134	134	up 0 place(s)

(b)

	1	2	3	4	5	6	7	8	9	10	11	12	13	14	15	16
LBN	56	100	100	100	83	92	63	100	45	81	83	82	23	25	down 2 place(s)
CYM	78	71	86	73	100	92	87	86	27	88	100	81	33	26	up 7 place(s)
COL	78	71	86	92	100	75	97	86	100	31	67	80	27	27	up 0 place(s)
JOR	78	86	100	100	83	100	73	93	45	58	67	80	28	28	up 0 place(s)
BGR	100	100	71	54	100	58	100	100	27	62	100	79	34	29	up 5 place(s)
MDA	56	100	100	100	100	92	80	43	1	100	100	79	35	30	up 5 place(s)
LAO	44	86	57	46	50	33	0	0	1	0	0	29	130	131	down 1 place(s)
BOL	44	57	0	1	100	50	7	1	1	31	0	27	132	132	up 0 place(s)
CAF	44	0	14	1	33	75	13	1	1	54	0	22	133	133	up 0 place(s)
COM	33	57	0	0	67	42	0	14	0	15	0	21	134	134	up 0 place(s)

(c)

Figure 10.2 a League table of student performance, *b* League table comparing student performance against each other, *c* League table comparing performance on each WATS

Note: In figures 2a–2c:

Column 1 is a three-letter country code which keeps the data anonymous

Col 1–11 is the student's individual performance at each week task (%)

Col 12 is the student's ongoing average

Col 13 is the student's position in the league table

Col 14 indicates the student's position in the league table last week

Col 15 indicates the student's position in the league table this week

Col 16 indicates the student's movement in the league table over the last week

- Describe turbulence and give an example of its impact in your own engineering discipline.

Other questions, invaluable for teachers too, include:

- What were the three most important things to come out of today's lecture?
- What areas of the module are you finding the most difficult and why?

This addition is important for three reasons:

1   it encourages the students to articulate their knowledge and their understanding of the subject, and not just respond to numerical tasks;
2   their responses, along with the students' performance on the WATS, help shape the lecture such that learning is truly seen as an iterative dialogue between student and teacher. This data helps construct a *learning conversation* where the students' own conceptions and current understandings are seen as an integral part of the current lecture series. Just-in-time teaching, intelligence-led teaching, using class-truth, call it what you will, what is important is the centralising of the students and their knowledge, in the teaching and learning sessions, rather than the information on a module descriptor, and
3   it opens up another line of communication between the student and their teacher.

Discussion

Did it work?

While innovations can be fun and extremely rewarding for their creator, this was not an invention for its own sake. Like so many other inventions, this was borne out of necessity rather than simple curiosity.

Four years on and I am swamped with data. These data include:

- Performance figures in exams
- Correlations between exam scores and WATS scores
- Students' responses to questions oriented around the WATS approach to assessment
- Students' responses to questionnaires aimed at establishing their approaches to learning.

The first three years saw a marked improvement in examination performance – a step change in its first year of use which was maintained though the subsequent years. This enhanced performance at examination, arising from an improved understanding of the subject, was also mirrored with other improvements. The students were now asking the 'right questions at the right time', they appeared better prepared at lectures and at the small group tutorials sessions – a real re-engagement with their subject was observed. Hence there is much teacher evidence to suggest the success of this approach.

But rather than just focus on my own perception or the students performance, it is instructive also to hear the student view – sample quotes below received from students include:

> I think WATS was a good thing as it has made us all review our notes and revise throughout the semester instead of throwing on the floor and not looking at them until the exam.

Yes, I believe the WATS definitely have been proved to be helpful. It was well structured because [it] not only let the student study constantly but also it showed (by publishing the correct solution for each WATS) where eventually the student went wrong. Plus they have been very useful in order to revise the entire module. All the modules should involve WATS.

WATS is a good idea, basically it means we can check our understanding week by week.

Really good idea, helps to understand the lectures.

I think it's a good idea as it makes sure you understand and can apply the work that we have learnt, and encourages you to do well.

No doubt at all that the WATS got me through the exam. The solutions for the WATS were the main factor and made brilliant revision material. It even made some of the complicated stuff look relatively simple. Why is that?

I think the WATS is a brilliant idea!! It's fun, it's flexible, reasonable amount of time to do the questions.

This whole programme was a real help to our process of studying. I know I have not had an excellent track record at it but would just like to thank you.

The WATS was great in encouraging me to do more study and research on a regular basis after each class.

I think it is a good approach to learning because it enables or rather 'forces' us to work on the module every week, and this kind of helps sometimes.

WATS is very good and I now feel confident in my coming exams.

WATS is good and helps in revision and I would recommend it to be used to other modules.

According to me it is an excellent way of teaching both for teachers as well as students. Hope it should be introduced in other subjects as well. Well done – that's what I will say at the end.

Notice how many of the above quotes mention the same values that were intended.

Clearly, it is hoped that the lessons learnt from participating in this overtly assessment-led module will be taken, by the students, to other modules and subsequent years of their study. These include:

- The need to study regularly
- The importance of tackling regular tasks
- Sharing problem-solving methodologies without sharing answers
- Using feedback to help this developmental understanding.

Four years on and the technology has already been applied to cognate, numerically based, subjects including business and pharmacy. They too are reaping the benefits previously observed by the thermodynamists. The challenge for others, and indeed you, lies in taking forward the messages into the more discursive subjects. For here you immediately lose the ability to automatically mark the students' numerical submissions. That said, simply having the facility to ask the students short, one-minute-paper-type questions and collect their responses and present them in a format that helps manual marking/review will, in itself, prove to be an extremely valuable asset. For instance, ask your students at the end of the class to write down *what they understood from today's lecture*, or *in their own words describe theory X* and you will be tasked with collecting scraps of paper, some authored by Mickey Mouse, and a need to decipher a range of handwriting styles. This simple component on the main assessment programme stops that at source.

The key lessons are not linked to thermodynamics and fluid mechanics, but are aligned with many of the recognised good principles in teaching, learning and assessment and hence are transportable across the disciplines. These include:

- Establishing a regular study pattern
- Seeking and articulating high expectations.
- Gathering student understandings on a regular basis
- Using students' own conceptions to inform the teaching
- Proving prompt feedback
- Encouraging collaboration among students without prizing answer sharing
- Seeing learning as a dialogic activity
- Encouraging contact between students and teachers.

None of these ideals is specific to teachers of thermodynamics. They are also yours, to help guide and shape your work and your teaching philosophy. I wish you well with your own endeavours.

Section Three

Disciplines of study

Chapter 4

Facilitating student success

Disciplines and curriculum development

Glenda Crosling

Introduction

Students are more likely to continue in higher education if they are active, interactive and engaged in their learning. These factors also position students to study with understanding and to make meaning, rather than merely accumulating information (Biggs, 1999). A responsive and student-centred approach structures teaching and learning to facilitate this outcome. As the curriculum offers a constant in the student experience, it provides a forum for student-centred, responsive teaching and learning.

While the notion of curriculum in higher education is often used broadly, without a shared understanding of its meaning (Fraser & Bosanquet 2006), our interpretation as discussed in Chapter 1 involves aspects of curriculum such as the content, teaching and learning approaches and assessment practices. It also implies the disciplines of study which embody particular academic cultures of values and ways of advancing knowledge, and in which students must engage for study success. The disciplinary cultures embody particular teaching and learning approaches.

The natures of the disciplines and their teaching and learning preferences can be drawn on to assist students to engage in their learning. At the same time, traditional disciplinary practices can be expanded to facilitate students' engagement. Students need to develop understandings and skills to operate competently within the existing disciplinary practices and responsive and student-centred practices assist all students to do this. In a complementary way, the discipline's traditional teaching and learning practices can be developed in ways that are innovative to the discipline. There are challenges in this venture, but innovative and inclusive practices create situations where the richness of the diverse student body can be accommodated and drawn on, to enhance learning for *all* students. The cases in the final section of this chapter reflect both these approaches to curriculum development, demonstrating how challenges can become the impetus for change, from which students can benefit in their learning.

Students and disciplinary learning and teaching

Student diversity is acknowledged in the view that students hold learning preferences (Wolf & Kolb 1984) and that students can feel alienated from their studies smatch occurs between their preferred learning style, and that embedded in the discipline. The seriousness of this situation is expressed by Kolb (1981: 233): a clash 'between personal learning styles and the learning demands of different disciplines' (Kolb 1981: 247) may 'undermine their [students'] feelings of belonging to the university community and ... lead them to consider dropping out of their studies'. Past life experiences impact on ways that students go about their learning, and therefore on what some students from diverse backgrounds expect of their educational experience. For instance, Kember (2001: 217) explains that, on the basis of past experiences, students may initially prefer teacher-directed and didactic teaching and learning, when what is required for success is a greater sense of independence in study.

The characteristic disciplinary ways of teaching and learning as discussed later in this chapter can be extended to assist students to engage. As Gibbs (2000: 44) explains, 'conventions and pedagogic processes within discourses differ more widely than one might imagine, given the supposed centrality of their epistemology and form of discourse'. For instance, Gibbs (2000: 44) provides the example of nursing education in the UK. It was recognized that nursing students in general had good abilities to cope with a range of teaching and learning modes. Thus, Gibbs (2000) explains that nursing curricula have changed markedly to include new teaching and assessment methods. This means that the needs of students from diverse backgrounds and situations are catered for. The challenge in the disciplines is to change in ways that accord with the students, their situations and needs, but also in ways that extend students' learning repertoires.

At the same time, students' ways of learning are flexible and context-dependent, and as explained by Gibbs (2000: 46), effective learners have flexibility in using a range of learning styles and approaches. In the face of students learning in ways that may result in a clash with that of the discipline and perhaps failure, teachers should attempt to widen their students' learning preferences and expectations. Kember's (2001: 218) comments on higher education teaching in general also apply to the disciplines: the student experience includes 'exposure to alternative forms of teaching, and to accompany them with strategies to ease the transition from one belief set to another' (Kember 2001). Even if students' current learning styles that align with those of the discipline, the introduction of new teaching and learning approaches assists students to broaden their learning repertoire, positioning them to cope in future and yet unknown learning environments.

A significant factor in students' success or otherwise in their learning in higher education and in the disciplines is the intention with which they approach their studies (Marton & Saljo 1984). This affects the degree to which the students engage with their subjects. If they study with a 'deep' approach, they are seeking understanding and meaning. Alternatively, with a 'surface' approach, students have the intention to rote-learn information, without linking knowledge and understandings. A strategic or achieving approach is where the intention is to obtain a high grade (Biggs 1987). Arguably, students who are engaged, deriving meaning and understanding from their studies and therefore demonstrating a deep approach to learning, are more likely to continue. Furthermore, as Fry, Ketteridge and Marshall (2003) point out, while many commencing higher education students believe that their study success depends on learning large amounts of information, the students' approaches to learning can be shaped by the teaching and learning context (Biggs 1999).

Curriculum and the disciplines

Studies in higher education are, generally speaking, broken up along disciplinary lines. Generic skills such as critical and analytical approaches are characteristic of higher education, but the disciplines define the course content, or the body of knowledge. Their academic cultures shape the typical teaching and learning practices, so that different disciplines 'combine generic aspects of teaching in ways quite specific to the discourse' (Neumann 2001: 136). Even though students may study in 'modular' mode and take subjects across the disciplines, their success in these subjects relies on their adaptation to the disciplinary discourse of the subject. However, the cultures which embody the disciplinary values are often implicit and conveyed subtly. In a climate of diversity, some students are not immediately able to access tacit meanings. For instance, the culture reflected in the organization of ideas in lectures, tutorials and texts may be difficult to access for students whose first language is not English (Crosling 1996).

Meyer and Land (2005: 377) discuss students' adaptation to a discipline's ways of operating as a transformation. Students learn to understand a discipline's 'threshold concepts' and these shape the way they then perceive the disciplinary content. Meyer and Land (2005) state that the transformation may be problematic, but removing 'epistemological obstacles' through curriculum interventions can assist students. This includes redesigning activities and sequences, scaffolding, recursiveness, support programs, and so on. These activities aim to make the disciplinary values explicit for students, and to 'induct' them into the modes of teaching and learning. The outcome is that students are assisted to make the transformation. Boud's (2004: 59) view about higher education teaching and learning in general also applies to the disciplines. Responding to student diversity involves recognizing that many learners may require help to cope with the academic demands. An example of an intervention that helped students adapt to the economics discipline is a 'transition tutorial program' in an Australian university. Even at this early stage of their studies, the tutorial held in orientation week helped students to get to know other students in their course, raised students' awareness and laid the groundwork for them to begin to understand the culture of economics and its values (Ward, Crosling & Marangos 2000).

Different teaching and learning practices can draw on and extend the typical disciplinary teaching and learning patterns, so as to engage students, include them in their studies, and foster their intention to study with meaning and understanding. This type of responsive, student- rather than a teacher-centred approach means that the teachers are facilitating and supporting rather than driving their students' conceptual change and development. The emphasis is on what *students* do, constructing their own knowledge and understandings (Lindblom-Ylanne, Trigwell, Nevgi & Ashwin 2006: 285). This contrasts with a teacher-centred approach where the course content, transmission of knowledge and what the *teacher* does in their teaching is the focus (Lindblom-Ylanne *et al.* 2006).

As we have already discussed in Chapter 1, teachers do change their approaches when they are confronted with new situations (Prosser & Trigwell 2002; Lindblom-Ylanne *et al.* 2006). The diversity of the student body provides a stimulus for curricula change to more student-centred approaches. In the disciplines, change such as this in the teaching and learning practices can also contribute positively to the progress of the discipline (Healey 2000: 173). However, it may involve the teachers' changing their 'disciplinary allegiances, ... conceptions of what constitutes teaching, of what a course should be, or what students and our views about what a course should be or what students should do' (Boud 2004: 62).

Disciplinary cultures

Just as there is student diversity in higher education, there is also diversity across the disciplines of study. This is seen in the disciplines' different 'language, norms, and values', and these operate side by side in a university setting (Kolb 1981: 233). Thus, there are differing disciplinary notions of 'the nature of truth and how it is sought', 'patterns of power and authority', and modes of expression, which have meaning for the members (Kolb 1981: 233). Kolb (*ibid.* 242) classifies the approaches to knowledge and learning of established members of the disciplinary communities from concrete to abstract, and from active to reflective. More specifically, disciplinary variation includes the way that knowledge is reported, whether principally in words, images, numerical or logical symbols; inquiry methods, whether case studies, experiments, or logical analysis, predominate; and criteria for evaluation, whether it is practical, or if, for instance, statistical significance is important. For instance, the scientific professions and basic disciplines are principally analytical and endeavour to understand wholes by identifying their component parts and relationships, employing quantitative models and building in inquiry. Students in the science discipline who take a more holistic approach to their studies would benefit from teaching and learning activities that assist them to understand and to use a more analytical approach.

On the other hand, Kolb (1981) maintained that socio-humanistic fields tend to be synergistic, seeking coherence and integration of phenomena because the belief is that the world is not explained by its component parts. In social professions, the dominant philosophy is pragmatism, and truth as defined by how actions shape events. Some fields such as medicine, management and architecture are multidisciplinary: where medicine's concern is for human service and scientific knowledge, architecture's is artistic. Characteristics such as these can be utilized to provide a range of ways of introducing concepts and ideas.

For instance, the artistic preference in architecture can be drawn on, and images increasingly used in teaching and learning. These would be of benefit to students of English as a second language, as well as students who are more visually oriented in their learning.

Becher's later work (1989) on academic disciplinary communities, drawing on Clifford Geertz's (1973) anthropological work (Becher 1989: xi), also maps the 'variegated territory of academic knowledge' and explains that the nature of knowledge is intertwined with the discipline's academic culture. That is, there are 'identifiable patterns ... within the relationship between knowledge forms and their associated knowledge communities' (*ibid*.: 150). For success in their disciplinary studies, students need to adjust their general understandings of academic literacy to those of their disciplines (Candlin, Bhatia & Hyland, cited in Candlin, Gollin, Plum, Spinks & Stuart-Smith 1998).

The disciplinary cultures thus emphasize particular learning and teaching practices and forms. As Gibbs (2000: 43) states, the way a discipline is taught 'is linked inextricably to the way knowledge is generated within the discipline and how the discourse of the discipline functions'. For example, variation in epistemologies and theory means that it may be presented as a 'law of nature' developed from agreed definitions, as occurs in science-based disciplines. Alternatively, it may involve 'disputed meanings' (*ibid*.) as in social science-oriented disciplines, and therefore function in an interpretative way. Some students may not readily pick up these ways of operating, and adjustments to teaching and learning can help them to do so.

While these alternative perspectives impact on the type and balance of teaching methods used in particular disciplines, the challenge is to develop teaching and learning as student-centred and therefore engaging for students. This involves, for instance, approaches that facilitate active and collaborative learning, that enable formative communication with teachers and fellow students, are motivating in that they relate knowledge to real-life situations and issues, and classroom environments that are inclusive rather than alienating. While approaches such as these may already be present in the traditional teaching practices, they can be further emphasized, or included if not present. The case examples following this chapter provide examples of ways that this has been done.

Teaching and learning and disciplinary contexts

Across the disciplines, there is an array of teaching and learning forms that can be drawn on in the student-centred development of disciplinary curriculum. The main forms are lectures, tutorials and seminars, laboratory practicals and field trips (Neumann 2001: 136). The lecture that is used across the disciplines (*ibid*.) to outline the subject and the learning system and to enthuse students is usually one-way transmission of information. However, students can be actively involved if the form deviates from the traditional (Scott 2005). Tutorials are important in the humanities, and laboratory experimentation in science. Furthermore, disciplinary differences are reflected in curriculum and assessment approaches, and in conceptual structure and knowledge validation methods (Neumann 2001: 138). For instance, Neumann (*ibid.*: 139) explains that 'in ... classroom teaching practice, a hard field such as science places stronger emphasis on student research experience in teaching undergraduates, while soft fields focus on student growth and development, oral and written communication skills'. However, these disciplinary forms and preferences are not fixed in concrete and can be adapted and applied to teaching and learning across the disciplines.

The range is also evident across particular disciplines:

- For Engineering and Science, Overton (2003) explains that lectures and small group teaching are important. Lectures appear to be changing in recent years as lecturers have increasingly introduced activities for student interaction and participation. Other common teaching and learning modes are problem-based learning, industry work experience and practical work.
- For Information and Computing Technology, McAllister and Alexander (2003) discuss how regular assessment and feedback is a means used to motivate students and 'improve their overall performance' (*ibid.*: 289). In this discipline, technologically supported learning also assists with the large groups of students, helping to improve communication between students and staff.
- In science-related disciplines, Scott (2005) reports that students in Australia appreciated team and group projects, assignments, field study, hands-on practice, lecture class exercises, laboratory and practical work.
- For Arts, Humanities and Social Science, Martin (2003) explains that students function as active learners, and that successful students are not able to be passive or merely consumers of knowledge. Scott (2005) in Australia found that assignments, class exercises, lecture tutorials, group projects, class discussion, hands-on practice, and seminars with individual presentations were valued by students.
- For Accounting, Business and Management, Lucas and Milford (2003) put forward the view that these are fields subject to many pressures and tensions, of which an important one is whether education in the discipline is *about*, or *for* business. Characterized by great student diversity, another pressure is the need to avoid the 'silo' effect of the fields that make up the discipline, and to strive for integration so that students can understand how the whole of the field in which they study contributes to business activities. Themes can be identified around which to focus student learning, such as the environment and ethics (Lucas & Milford 2003: 403). Assessment may be used as a curricular means to encourage students to make links between subjects studied independently, and this can be fostered through the use of case studies as learning and teaching devices. These also support the development of employment-related skills such as communication and teamwork. As these authors perceive that it is important to educate students *about* business, the development of critical reflection is 'critically important, considering diversity of tensions in business education' (*ibid.*: 404), and students require opportunities to link

'ever-expanding theory with their practice'. Scott (2005) found that management and commerce students appreciate team/group projects, assignments, lectures, class exercises, seminars with individual presentations, tutorials, discussion, case studies, real-world problems and work experience.

*   In health fields, students valued clinical placement, practical experience, lectures, hands-on practice, while for education, teaching practicum, practical experience, completing assignments and hands-on practice were valued learning methods (Scott 2005).

For all disciplines, however, 'a key challenge in seeking to engage students in productive learning' is to identify the combination of learning methods that is the most suitable for each situation and field of education (*ibid*.: 45).

In the context of the diverse student population, students may become disillusioned and drop out if they do not engage with the teaching and learning in their disciplines. The variety within and across disciplines indicates many teaching and learning forms through which the curricula can be shaped to respond to students. For instance, in undergraduate nursing curricula, Butell, O'Donovan and Taylor (2004) discuss the way that the reading and discussion of literature in the form of novels was included in the course. This approach seems strange in the context of the traditional, science-based nursing curricula, but it may develop affinity with some students for whom stories are important in their lives. As well as this, however, through reading and discussing the lives of the characters in the stories, students can develop a deeper understanding of a range of people, and of the experience of illness.

Suggestions for student-centred curriculum development

Evident in the previous discussion in this chapter is a range of teaching and learning activities across the disciplines. While some activities are typically used in one discipline and not others, disciplinary curricula can be adapted, developed or adjusted through the implementation of new teaching and learning activities and approaches. In aligning their curriculum with a student-centred approach, lecturers may consider the following suggestions:

To assist students to engage with their studies by understanding the discipline's key/'threshold' concepts:

*   Scaffold, or 'break down' the key concepts into constituent parts, and sequence their introduction in the teaching program. Make explicit for students and provide a range of examples of the ways that these key concepts shape thought practices in the discipline.
*   Provide support programs that assist students to understand these key concepts and disciplinary thought practices. These can be integrated into the mainstream teaching program, or operate as an adjunct and attended

voluntarily by students. An example of an academic support program for a business law subject can be seen in Crosling (1997)

To encourage students' engagement with the subject and therefore their productive study which seeks meaning and understanding:

* In large lectures, use small group activities and exercises. Thses provide the opportunity for students to clarify progressive understandings with their fellow students, to gain feedback from the lecturer, and to apply the understandings to small problems posed in the lecture.
* Provide problem-based learning and case studies, based on 'real-world' problems. These enable students to perceive the relevance of their study content to everyday and their own personal lives, enhancing the chances of their seeking meaning and understanding in their studies. Smaller problems may also be used in a traditional lecture, applying the subject content at relevant points.
* Include regular assessment and feedback in their learning, and in lectures and tutorials. This serves as a framework for students in their cognitive development, impacting on the affective learning aspects through encouragement and positive feedback which provides guidance for future cognitive development.
* Include computer-assisted learning activities that students can access and utilize in their own time. This encourages the development of students' independence in learning and enables students to apply the subject content to differing situations and scenarios, and gain feedback on their efforts.
* Use team and group work projects, so that students can learn from each other and also develop friendship groups or networks. This approach breaks their isolation, engaging them more in their learning and positioning them for study with meaning and understanding.
* Provide activities for hands-on practice with theoretical concepts.
* Use class presentations to develop students' communication skills and sense of involvement in the teaching and learning process.

The cases

The cases that follow present a range of ways that the curriculum, through the teaching approach, content or assessment, has been developed and adjusted to assist students to relate and engage more readily with their studies in specific discipline areas. The cases also include examples of ways that the curriculum has functioned as a forum to assist students to develop their expectations of teaching and learning and their understandings of the discourse and its processes, so that there is greater affinity between these and those of their subject community. Their perspectives are transformed as the teaching and learning activities require them to interact with the disciplinary discourse.

Veronica Cahyadi, writing of her experiences in teaching physics in an engineering course in a university in Indonesia, explains how the traditional form of teaching – lectures – was developed to include an active student approach. Rather than the students passively taking notes, activities were introduced that required students to interact with the material of their study and their class mates, and to actively participate in their learning. Through the use of a control and an experimental group, Veronica demonstrated that the understanding of physics concepts among the experimental group of students improved, as reflected in the examination results. An interesting point is that, rather than the teachers expressing concern over changes in teaching approaches, this was the reaction of a large number of the students who were expecting the traditional form of teaching. Their conception of teaching and their learning was that they would learn the physics 'laws of nature' through a range of formulae. The students thus rated the dialogue with the instructor as the most unimportant activity. This suggests that as the curriculum is developed to include student-centred approaches, students need to be inducted, or scaffolded, into these alternative ways of learning.

Janette Ryan contributes a case that explains how the changes in the education curriculum were initiated so that the education students in a small rural university in Australia, many of whom were the first in their family to attend higher education, would connect their theoretical studies with practical teaching, and therefore perceive their studies as relevant, and continue. However, the curricular changes had far deeper manifestations than students' engagement. As the students initiated and implemented school community-based projects, their conceptions of the role of the teacher changed, aligning increasingly with the epistemological underpinning of their course. Thus, the students began to see their roles as teachers as facilitating the learning of their students, rather than as the teacher in charge who needs to 'control' the class. In effect, the development in the curriculum enabled students to be subtly and effectively inducted into the discipline and its expectations.

Pamela Garlick and Gavin Brown present a case in which they explore the development of their students' academic and personal skills within the existing course curriculum. At King's College in London in the Medicine degree which now admits students through assessment of their academic potential rather than solely their academic achievements, many students from working class and various ethnic backgrounds are enrolled. The curriculum development was not only an extension of the traditional teaching mode, but also assisted students to adjust better on a personal level to the discipline, and therefore to their future roles as medical doctors. The module that was introduced (PANDA) develops students' written and oral communication skills, as well as their interpersonal skills. It assists students to develop conceptions of themselves as doctors, and at the same time, to be able to engage more fully in the discipline through improved communication skills. Pamela and Gavin provide graphic portraits of the way that some students' self-confidence developed, not only in themselves as students, but also as future doctors.

Kate Kirk's case study of non-traditional students at Manchester Metropolitan University in the UK explains the inclusive and participatory approach taken to establish the support valued by students as they adjust to their higher education studies in the BA Honours Social Work and Youth and Community Work course. As well as providing feedback to assist the lecturers to shape their course as engaging and student-centred, a student-centred and inclusive approach was taken to the gathering of the information. From the outset, this approach not only validates and legitimates the students and their needs and perspectives, but provides information for support approaches that can be built into the course to address students' needs. At the same time, the approach reflects and draws on what may be seen as integral to the discipline of social and community work: that people are valued and can be empowered to function as independent and self-confident individuals. Again, through subtle as well as explicit means, students are inducted into the disciplinary discourse and its values and processes.

Judith Tennant writes about her program in a Business and Economics faculty at a rural Australian campus with a diverse student population. To encourage her economics students to place their studies in a business setting, to appreciate the integrated nature of their disciplines of study in business operations, and to study with meaning and understanding, Judith took her students on an excursion to a local industry. The students had the opportunity to network with other students outside of the classroom on the visit, and if they wished, to taste, the product (beer) around which the business operations were focussed. This experience provided a practical context for the students in their study, and authenticated their classroom teaching and learning. It assisted them to appreciate the discipline's values and operations so that their studies were seen as more relevant to their business studies and everyday lives. Judith found that this experience helped her students to study with greater meaning and understand and extract more from their studies.

Conclusion

Disciplines have distinctive ways of developing knowledge, out of which have emerged 'traditional' modes of teaching and learning. Students need to adapt to these ways of developing and using knowledge for success in their study. Curriculum developments can make these explicit for students so that they can function successfully. In the diverse student population of today's universities, teachers also need to function with flexibility. Student-centred approaches need to be built into disciplinary teaching, so that students can experience a sense of relevance and engagement in their studies. These factors underpin and enhance the opportunity for students to seek understanding in their studies, and hopefully, continue rather than dropping out. The cases in the next section give varying examples of disciplinary teaching being developed in student-centred ways.

References

Becher, T (1989) *Academic Tribes and Territories*. Milton Keynes: The Society for Research into Higher Education and Open University Press.
Biggs, J. (1987) *Student Approaches to Learning and Studying*. Hawthorn, Victoria: Australian Council for Educational Research.

Biggs, J. (1999) *Teaching for Quality Learning at University* Buckingham: Society for Research into Higher Education and Open University Press.

Boud, D. (2004) 'Discourses of access: Changing views in a changing world', in M. Osborne, J. Gallacher and B. Crossan (eds.), *Researching Widening Access to Lifelong Learning.* Abingdon: Routledge Falmer.

Butell, S., O'Donovan, P. and Taylor, J. (2004) 'Instilling the value of reading literature through student-led book discussion groups', *Journal of Nursing Education*, 43, 9.

Candlin, C., Gollin, S., Plum, G., Spinks, S. and Stuart-Smith, V. (1998) *Researching Academic Literacies.* Australia: National Centre for Language Teaching and Research, Macquarie University.

Crosling, G. (1996) 'Multi level structure of meaning in a business law tutorial', *Australian Review of Applied Linguistics*, 19, 1: 91–111.

Crosling, G. (1997) 'Legal language for Commercial Law adjunct program', *Ultibase*, RMIT, Melbourne. Online. Available: http://ultibase.rmit.edu.au.

Fraser, P. and Bosanquet, A. (2006) 'The curriculum? That's just a unit outline, isn't it?', *Studies in Higher Education*, 31, 3: 269–284.

Fry, H., Ketteridge, S. and Marshall, S. (2003) *Teaching and Learning in Higher Education.* London: Routledge Falmer.

Geertz, C. (1973) *The Interpretation of Cultures: Selected Essays by Clifford Geertz.* New York: Basic Books.

Gibbs, G. (2000) 'Are the pedagogies of the disciplines really different?, in Gibbs, *Improving Student Learning: Improving Student Learning through the Disciplines.* Oxford: Oxford Brookes University, Oxford Centre for Staff and Learning Development.

Healey, M. (2000) 'Developing the scholarship of teaching in higher education: A discipline-based approach', *Higher Education Research and Development*, 19, 2: 169–189.

Kember, D. (2001) 'Beliefs about knowledge and the process of teaching and learning as a factor in adjusting to study in higher education', *Studies in Higher Education*, 26, 2: 206–221.

Kolb, D. (1981) 'Learning styles and disciplinary differences', in A. Chickering and Associates (eds.), *The Modern American College.* San Francisco: Jossey-Bass.

Lindblom-Ylanne, S. Trigwell, K., Nevgi, A. and Ashwin, P. (2006) 'How approaches to teaching are affected by discipline and teaching context', *Studies in Higher Education*, 31, 3: 285–298.

Lucas, V. and Milford, P. (2003) 'Key aspects of teaching and learning in accounting, business and management', in H. Fry, S. Ketteridge and S. Marshall (eds.), *A Handbook of Teaching and Learning in Higher Education.* London: Routledge Falmer.

Martin, P. (2003) 'Key aspects of teaching and learning in arts, humanities and social sciences', in Fry, H., Ketteridge, S., and Marshall, S. (eds.) (2003) *A Handbook for Teaching and Learning in Higher Education.* London: Kogan Page.

McAllister, G., Alexander, S. (2003) 'Key aspects of teaching and learning in information and computer sciences', in H. Fry, S. Ketteridge and S. Marshal (eds.), *A Handbook of Teaching and Learning in Higher Education.* London: Routledge Falmer.

Marton, F. and Saljo, R. (1984) 'Approaches to learning', in F. Marton *et al.* (eds.), *The Experience of Learning.* Edinburgh: Scottish Academic Press.

Meyer, J. and Land, R. (2005) 'Threshold concepts and troublesome knowledge (2): Epistemological considerations and a conceptual framework for teaching and learning', *Higher Education*, 49: 373–388.

Neumann, R. (2001) 'Disciplinary differences and university teaching', *Studies in Higher Education*, 26, 2: 135–146.

Overton, T. (2003) 'Key aspects of teaching and learning in experimental sciences and engineering', in H. Fry, S. Ketteridge and S. Marshall (eds.), *A Handbook of Teaching and Learning in Higher Education*. London, Routledge Falmer.

Prosser, M. and Trigwell, K. (2002) *Understanding Learning and Teaching: The Experience in Higher Education*. Buckingham: The Society for Research into Higher Education.

Scott, G. (2005) *Accessing the Student Voice*, Higher Education Innovation Program and the Collaboration and Structural Reform Fund. Commonwealth of Australia: Department of Education, Science and Training.

Ward, I., Crosling, G. and Marangos, J. (2000) 'Encouraging positive perceptions of economics: The effectiveness of the orientation tutorial', *Economic Papers*, 19, 3: 76–86.

Wolf, D. and Kolb, D. (1984) 'Career development, personal growth and experiential approach', in D. Kolb, I. Rubin and J. McIntyre (eds.), *Organisational Psychology: Readings on Organisational Behaviour*. Englewood Cliffs, NJ: Prentice-Hall.

No more 'plug and chug'

Veronica Cahyadi

The situation

'Look at this! It's like they have never been taught about this stuff before. Haven't they grasped any single word that I blurted out in the lecture? Haven't they got any sense of physics at all?' These complaints were all too common from my colleagues marking stage one physics exams. What followed afterwards was an average failure rate of more than 50 per cent! The lecturers involved were devastated, the university managers were unhappy and the students were resentful. This had been happening since I started my teaching career in a large Indonesian private university. Two physics courses, Physics 1 in the first semester and Physics 2 in the second semester, were compulsory for all engineering students in their first year of study.

Physics was regarded as the most difficult of the first-year subjects. A large number of students had to repeat the subject, in some cases five or six times, to pass with a minimum of 48 per cent grade. The courses were run in approximately 10 classes of 50 to 100 students. The teaching had been conducted in a fairly traditional approach: a lecturer stood in front of the class, trying his or her best to convey the information, and to model problem solving. The students just sat there, faithfully copying everything written or said by the lecturer into their notes. They were not asked questions in the class, nor given any homework. There were no teaching assistants to help students with their concepts or problem solving. The assessment was in the form of two quizzes and two exams per semester.

This traditional teaching approach contributed to a number of student difficulties, as has been reported in the last three decades in the physics education community. Students often confuse the concepts they are taught in their studies with real-life experiences, which results in misconceptions. They sometimes try to solve physics problems using their own concepts of physics acquired from everyday experiences and lessons from school. When they seem to be capable of performing the problem-solving procedure, what they do is actually imitate the process modelled by the lecturer. They reveal their poor comprehension of the underlying concepts when they are asked to explain what they do.

The common perception of the term 'physics' among students is well known: physics consists of a vast number of formulae and definitions, or 'laws of nature' to be memorized. Students perceive that solving physics problems is done by matching the variables in the problems with the 'likely' formulae. They do not feel the need to understand the situation in the problem, the concepts involved, possible strategies to attack the problem, or the meaning of the calculation result they obtain. All they tend to do is substitute information from a large collection of formulae to 'plug' the most seemingly correct formula and then use maths to 'chug' out an answer. In other words, they 'plug and chug'! Of course, this 'plug–and-chug' tactic does not always work in the exam, especially when reasoning and explanations are required, or even when the format of the problem is slightly altered from the examples students have been used to seeing. The inevitable result is that a great number of students fail the courses and are left frustrated with a feeling that physics is notoriously complicated.

The lecturers tended to blame the faculty managers for lowering the standard for the university entrance test. The managers, in turn, criticized the lecturers for the high failure rates. The students resented their lecturers for not explaining the material very well, or for giving them hard exam questions. I was among a few academic staff in the institution to suspect that the students' troubles meant more than just ineffective teaching practice or the students' weak physics backgrounds. I did not see any point in throwing accusations at one another in the hope of improving the situation. I understand that the process of teaching and learning involves two parties interacting in two-way communication. It is important for the teacher to impart the knowledge in a way favourable to the learning process, but it is more important for the learner to construct the knowledge and make sense out of it. A lecturer preaching in front of an audience of seemingly attentive students who are writing notes does not suggest an environment conducive to effective teaching and learning. I believe that copying notes has little to do with digesting the information or making sense of it. Most students just do not have the capability of thoroughly comprehending the incessant flow of information for a lecture of 100 minutes, which is the norm in our institution.

I came to the conclusion that the knowledge construction process was missing during the lecture. Of course, students could still read their notes, study the textbook, or practise problem solving at home to enable construction of the knowledge. However, lecturers provided little strong encouragement to do so, and as we are all painfully aware, students often spend the least possible effort to get the best possible outcome, that is, grades. Therefore, I was sceptical that students were able to construct the knowledge if they were left to make efforts on their own.

The approaches implemented

I had just resumed my teaching duties after a couple of years pursuing study overseas, and I found that there was no improvement in the situation. Students still did as badly as ever, or even worse in some cases. The lecturers did nothing significant to solve the problems, except making the exam questions a little easier. None of the lecturers had any background in education, or attended intensive educational workshops or seminars. I decided it was time for considerable effort to do something. Being recently exposed to current literature on physics education and having conducted small educational research projects during my study, I was at the peak of enthusiasm to make a change.

In our institution, first-year students were grouped according to their engineering majors and randomly distributed into several classes of 50–100 students. In the first semester, there were four classes for industrial engineering (ID), four classes for informatics engineering (IF), and fewer classes for other engineering majors. I was assigned to one ID class and one IF class. These two types of engineering students provided an excellent subject for investigation: ID students are a group with a wide range of ability and IF students are less able, and consequently less motivated in physics. There were about 80 students in each of my classes, which became my 'experimental' classes, where the students did not know that they would experience a new teaching approach. Students in other classes were regarded as 'control' subjects.

The control and experimental classes had the same number of contact hours per week: two 100-minutes for ID and one 150-minute for IF. All students received the same amount of material, used the same hand-out and the same exam. All lecturers involved had experience, teaching in the institution for at least seven years. They were very familiar with the subject matter, student characteristics and problems in the classroom. The difference in the two types of classes lay in the teaching approach. The control classes were taught in the traditional manner where the main component was a lecturer explaining the concepts and problem-solving examples. The lecturer would transmit the material using OHP slides or by writing on the board. The students would copy into their notes almost everything they saw or heard. Some lecturers occasionally administered reading quizzes and gave homework, but those activities were not routine.

The experimental classes had a different teaching method, containing a variety of activities. Besides receiving concepts and problem-solving examples, students in the experimental classes had five new activities in the modified teaching approach. I wanted the students to see that physics is not just a long list of formulae, and that doing physics is not 'plug and chug'. Physics is about making sense of our everyday experiences and the real world using established concepts. Doing physics involves understanding the concepts and applying these to explain the phenomena around us. I also tried to show the students that learning physics requires assessing their preconceptions, confronting these preconceptions with the reality, and then assimilating the correct concepts into their knowledge framework. Learning should involve active participation of the learner to construct the knowledge, and this should begin in the classroom. The five activities to achieve these purposes follow.

Reading quizzes

As there would be less time for the usual concept and problem explanation due to other activities, I required the students to be well prepared. To make sure that students read the assigned sections of the hand-out, I gave reading quizzes at the beginning of each lecture. These consisted of three to five simple multiple choice questions which usually took ten minutes to administer. I provided three sets of questions to prevent the students from cheating.

Active learning problem sets (ALPS) (Van Heuvelen 1991)

I set out to lessen the students' tendency to apply the 'plug–and-chug' approach in problem solving. I used selected sheets of ALPS, which are a set of worksheets providing step-by-step guidance for students to systematically solve physics problems. The procedure in attacking problems involves visual, physical and mathematical representations, as well as evaluations on units and the magnitude of the answers. Students are expected to understand the physical phenomena in the problems before writing any mathematical formulations. There were about five sheets for the students to complete in each lecture.

Constructivist classroom dialogue

In this discourse, an instructor is a facilitator rather than a transmitter of knowledge. During the concept explanation, I asked numerous qualitative questions to probe students' understanding. In this way, students' preconceptions were revealed. I then helped them see the discrepancies between their preconceptions and the target concepts. Learning takes place when students can resolve the discrepancies, thus assimilating the new knowledge to their intellectual resources.

Demonstration

I wanted to show the students that physics is about the phenomena they experience in everyday life, rather than a bunch of meaningless formulae. The only practical activities that students encountered were physics experiments in the laboratory. These hands-on exercises had hardly any connection with the concepts taught in the lecture. Consequently, I created a number of demonstration modules that were closely linked to important concepts that I taught. I used materials which were easy to find, such as cardboard, styrofoam and plywood. I often included everyday objects such as toy cars, balls of different size, plastic cups, and so on. In the class, I first described how the demonstration would be done. Students were asked to predict the outcome individually. They were then engaged in a discussion with their neighbours, recorded their final predictions and handed in the prediction sheets. Afterwards, I scanned the predictions and carried out the demonstration.

Peer instruction (Mazur 1997)

The aims of this method are to encourage students' interaction in the lecture and to focus their attention on underlying concepts. I believe that students will understand better what they learn if they can explain it in their own words to others. Peer instruction always accompanied the demonstrations. I posed two or three multiple choice questions on the outcome of a demonstration, and asked the students to think about the answers. Then, they were encouraged to persuade their neighbours that they had the correct answers by putting forward appropriate reasons. I was able to assess the students' understanding by briefly looking at their answers. I could decide accordingly how to proceed with the lecture material.

Discussion

Three aspects of learning were selected to evaluate the effectiveness of the modified teaching method.

Conceptual understanding

All students in both control and experimental classes were given the Force Concept Inventory, or FCI (Hestenes, Wells & Swackhamer 1992), which is a qualitative multiple choice test to probe their understanding of mechanics topics. The FCI was administered twice: the first time (the pre-test) was on the first day of the semester, and the second (the post-test) was in the fourth or fifth week when the topic of mechanics was completed. Below is Table 11.1 summarizing the average scores for the control and experimental classes.

The pre-test scores indicated that the control and experimental classes for both majors did not differ in their background understanding of the topics evaluated by FCI. As indicated by <g>, it is apparent that the two experimental classes fall in the medium-g region (<g> is between 0.3 and 0.7) and the control classes exceeded the control classes in conceptual understanding improvement by at least a factor of 2.5. It is inferred, therefore, that the modified teaching package was more effective than the traditional approach in improving students' understanding of Newtonian mechanics concepts.

Table 11.1 Average FCI scores in percentage

Engineering major	Type of class	FCI pre-test	FCI post-test	Gain <g>*
ID	Control	20.7	30.8	0.12
	Experimental	19.7	44.7	0.31
IF	Control	21.9	26.2	0.06
	Experimental	23.6	41.7	0.24

*The gain is defined as $<g> = \dfrac{[\%<S_f> - \%<S_i>]}{[100 - \%<S_i>]}$

where $<S_f>$ and $<S_i>$ are, respectively, the class average post-test and pre-tet scores.

Problem-solving skills

The problem-solving skills were measured by the student performance on the final exam. The exam was constructed by all lecturers involved, and others who taught other classes outside the experimental and control classes. Each lecturer contributed one problem and graded the answers to his or her problem for all students. The intention was to obtain objectivity and consistency in grading the exam. Below is Table 11.2 summarizing the average exam scores for the control and experimental classes.

To investigate whether the exam scores of the experimental classes are significantly higher than those of the control classes, an independent sample t-test was performed. The total exam score of the two control ID classes is 43.2 (SD = 21.2) which is significantly lower than that of the experimental class [$t(187) = 2.28$, $p < 0.025$]. The effect size of the treatment is 0.34. The statistical calculation also shows that the exam score of IF experimental class is significantly higher than that of the control class [$t(148) = 3.91$, $p < 0.005$]. The effect size is 0.64 which is twice as large as that of the ID classes. It can be concluded that the students in the experimental classes performed better in problem solving than those in the control classes.

Students' attitudes towards the modified teaching method

On casual observation, I noticed that the students in my classes were quite interested in the new activities. Instead of chatting indolently outside the classroom before the lecture, most students attended to their hand-out to prepare for the reading quizzes. The demonstrations never failed to grab the students' attention and hush the restless noise which was usual when they were overwhelmed by the information. A few weeks into the semester, they became more animated in discussions with their peers. They also grew more comfortable in responding to my questions during the lecture.

I asked the students to complete an anonymous questionnaire to establish their responses to the teaching method. Most students (72, or 85 per cent) felt that the activities had a positive effect on them. They stated that the activities were useful, motivating, interesting and stimulating. About 50 per cent of the students mentioned, however, that the lecturer did not thoroughly and clearly explain the concepts and problem solving. This was an inevitable consequence of conducting

Table 11.2 Average exam scores in percentage

Engineering major	Type of class	Average ± standard deviation SD
ID	Control	42.02 (21.02)
	Experimental	50.3 (19.9)
IF	Control	46.7 (19.0)
	Experimental	59.2 (20.0)

many activities in a fixed time period. Lecturing on concepts and problem solving, which is the activity of the traditional classroom, was cut back in the proportion of time spent. The students' responses indicated that they still held the traditional teaching paradigm, which they had experienced for many years.

I also wanted to find out how the students perceived the importance of the various activities. According to 54, or 61 per cent of the students, lecturing on concepts and problem solving was the most important activity. The traditional learning attitude and insufficient time for explanation of concepts and problem solving apparently caused this response. The two reasons may also explain why 36, or 46 per cent of the students rated constructivist dialogue as the most unimportant activity. Most students may not be aware of the dialogue or they may feel uncomfortable in being directly confronted with verbal questions on their understanding. Other activities were rated in between these two extremes.

Overall, I felt that the modified teaching technique succeeded in improving the students' conceptual understanding. A significant number of students from the experimental classes abandoned the 'plug–and-chug' method in the exam. Their answers showed that they had made efforts to understand the situation in the problems by first sketching appropriate diagrams, or writing explanations in words. Physics was no longer perceived by most students as formula crunching as they could see the importance of concepts and their applications.

There were some challenges in implementing the teaching innovation in this institution where the traditional system had operated for a long time. The materials needed to be created from scratch: the questions for reading quizzes and lectures set up, the worksheets translated and retyped, and the demonstration modules constructed. The lecture schedule needed to be very well organized to cater for the various activities in a limited amount of time, and also because it was easy to be side-tracked when students were actively involved. Marking the reading quizzes took time outside the lecture hours. I had to remind the students from time to time of the rationale for the activities. The demand I placed upon the students might have seemed quite daunting, especially when their peers in the traditional classes were not expected to do the same. The biggest challenge, however, was encouraging other lecturers to reflect on their own teaching and to think about improvements. Any attempt to change is always painful; the lecturers as well as the students had been comfortable with the teaching and learning system they had used for so long.

The implementation of this teaching innovation in the future, therefore, requires serious commitment for all involved. The lecturers should explain the rationale and purposes of the interactive engagement activities at the beginning and throughout the semester. As the class schedule is busy with numerous activities, additional hours are required to deal with the problem solving and unanswered questions. Tutorial classes supervised by teaching assistants may be the best solution to this problem. The interactive engagement activities should be reflected in the test or exam, and this will encourage the students to participate seriously. Grading the test or exam should also reflect how much understanding students are expected to achieve. Process-oriented is certainly more preferable than result-oriented!

References

Hestenes, D., Wells, M. and Swackhamer, G. (1992) Force concept inventory, *Physics Teacher*, 30: 141–158.

Mazur, E. (1997) *Peer Instruction: A User's Manual*. Upper Saddle River, NJ: Prentice-Hall.

Van Heuvelen, A. (1991) Overview, case study physics, *American Journal of Physics*, 59: 898–907.

Making a difference

Janette Ryan

The situation

'The classroom just isn't for me.' This was a common lament among third-year students as they withdrew from their Education degree at the University of Ballarat, a small regional university in Australia. But by then, they had amassed a substantial fee debt as well as feelings of failure.

The University of Ballarat mainly serves the rural and regional populations of Western Victoria. It is commonly known as a 'second chance' university. This is because many of its students come from areas with lower educational advantages (small country towns, for example, with few educational resources) and therefore lower entry scores than their city counterparts have been able to achieve. The university also attracts more mature-aged students than most universities. Most students attending the university are among the first in their families ever to attend university. Many of these students face a number of difficulties due to factors such as a lack of economic support and these can increase pressures on their rates of retention and success.

The previous Bachelor of Education course at the university for many students was too 'theoretical' and the students often felt that they didn't have the necessary academic skills required for university study. In addition, they didn't start their teaching placements in schools until the third year of their study, so many felt that the course didn't connect well with their own needs and that they didn't get the chance to 'get their hands dirty'.

Students talked about not getting the 'practical' experiences they thought they would get during their degree. They had initially been nervous about teaching and about being able to 'control' students. These fears only grew as their course progressed. They complained about the course being too theoretical and 'academic', and when they did finally get to spend time in schools, about their teachers at university being 'out of touch' with schools. As they progressed into their degree, they started to doubt their ability to manage a class and indeed their choice of career. By year three, when they entered the classroom to finally 'take charge' rather than just sit and observe, many got a rude shock when they did not manage as well as they thought they would. By then, they no longer saw themselves in 'learner' mode, ready and willing to take risks and make mistakes. They felt that they should be able to operate like the professionals they had been observing. Their disappointment often led to their making harsh judgments of themselves, and feelings of inadequacy. In many cases, this led to a decision to leave the course.

The approaches implemented

To address this 'spike' in attrition, and the loss of potentially excellent teachers, we decided to introduce a new unit into the second semester of the second year of the course. It was clear that in order to redress the students' feelings about of the lack of connectedness with the 'real' work of schools, students needed to have some 'real-life' experiences in schools. The new unit was designed to give students the first-hand experience in schools they craved, while making sure that it was framed by sound theoretical and conceptual underpinnings. Our challenge was to provide a safe environment for students to take risks without loss of confidence. This was done through the inclusion in the unit of a 'real' project for a school, which students develop during their fieldwork placement.

In the unit, students are required to develop projects of benefit to schools and children. Students undertake observation in schools one day a week in the first semester of the year and so are comfortable with the school environment and personnel. They conduct a needs analysis of the school and its community, to ensure that the work they do is useful for the school and the children, as well as for their own learning. They must consult with school staff, the children and members of the school community in developing their project. Before a project can commence, we require that all aspects of the project be demonstrated, via an interim project report (the first assessment task), for the project to be well researched and planned. For example, for any outdoor activities, students must demonstrate the precautions they will take to prevent sunburn or injury, and that students with physical or other disabilities are included. Students take full responsibility for the planning and carrying out of their project, under the guidance of their teacher supervisor.

The project must fit in with the school's curriculum, so the students need to consult closely with teachers. They cannot just copy what they have seen others in the school do, but must come up with their own ideas. Progress on projects is discussed and any problems or issues work-shopped in tutorials. Students must also demonstrate that their projects draw on theories covered in the unit lectures, such as constructivist, experiential and inquiry learning.

The project must be a real project. For example, if the project involves the study of why frogs are disappearing from the local environment, it must encompass fieldwork. One team of students built a frog bog (with the school's year three and year four students). Students work in teams of between two and twelve, depending on how many students are allocated to each school. This gives students further support and the opportunity to share ideas and workload.

Projects must be innovative and creative. Students design projects during the first six weeks of the semester and then present their project report. Projects are carried out over the rest of the semester. This usually involves a series of class activities that culminates in a final activity of some kind. The topics of projects have been wide-ranging and have included tree plantings, wetlands projects, murals, walkathons, recycling programs, concerts in nursing homes or community centres, a school radio station, vegetable gardens, breakfast clubs, a mentoring programme, an astronomy club, playground renovations, school walking bus programs (groups of primary school children, joined by other children along the way as they walk to school under adult supervision), and theme days such as cultural days.

Projects must respond to local needs. In one of the tree-planting projects, for example, students noticed that the grounds of their school were very bare and there was no shade for the children in the summer months. Working with the children in the younger grade levels, they designed plantings of native trees to ring the grounds. The trees were chosen by pairs of children who planted the trees and 'adopted' them while they were at the school, taking responsibility for their watering and care. The tree-planting day occurred after a series of lessons on water conservation and local environmental conditions. Students as well as the children who planted the trees can watch the trees grow for years to come. Another project involved two groups of students at two schools located a few kilometres apart along a creek. The children at each school conducted a series of activities along each end of the creek, such as measuring salinity and undertak-ing native plantings. Each school group worked progressively along the creek over three or four weeks and, in the final activity, met in the middle for a joint picnic and celebration.

Students take enormous pride in their projects, and many have lasting benefits for the schools and the students. Students often return to see how their project is developing, especially where there has been some kind of physical component (such as a playground renovation or school garden).

Students are also encouraged to learn from the experiences of other students. Each year, a number of students from the previous year showcase their projects to the new second year. They often give invaluable advice such as 'make sure you check the venue before the excursion'. One year, a group of students introduced a whole-school mentoring programme adapted from an existing small-group pro-gramme that had been developed for primary schools. The students had noticed that there was a bullying problem in the playground. The teachers told them that despite their best efforts to stop this, it was becoming a real problem. The school was a large one, with dedicated teachers, but the playgrounds were large and spread out, making it hard to monitor children's behaviour during break times. The team of eight students embarked on an ambitious project where they first underwent training in the existing programme and then trained a number of year five and year six children as mentors/leaders. Over the next seven weeks, they trained the child leaders/mentors to take responsibility progressively for the programme in the playground. The child leaders spoke with any child displaying bullying behaviour and were available to assist any child being bullied, with the aim that eventually all children at the school would learn how to prevent bullying. The school wrote to the university to express its appreciation. When the group presented their project to the following year's students, the group leader started with a caution:

> Hot tip, guys. If you're going to introduce somebody else's programme, make sure you fully understand it. We jumped in too quickly and had to learn a lot along the way.

This was invaluable advice for the other students' future careers as well as their projects, as teachers routinely have to introduce new programs. It had much more impact than if teaching staff had tried to give the same advice.

Not all projects are successful. One group built a school vegetable garden, but forgot it would need watering over the summer break. They went back to the school the following year and organised a watering roster for the school holidays among the school families.

Often students are too ambitious and need to curtail their plans, but they are encouraged to learn from their mistakes. Projects do not necessarily need to be successful, as this would discourage risk taking. Instead, they are assessed on the process of the project (not merely its outcome) through a final presentation of their project (the second and final assessment task), and students must demonstrate how they have learnt from their failures as well as successes. The final presentations are assessed by panels including representatives from schools or community groups. These members often make comments or give feedback that would not occur to academic staff and so enrich the feedback given to students.

Discussion

Overall, the introduction of the project system has been highly successful, from the perspectives of both the students and the university. However, it needs to be noted that not all projects progress smoothly. Sometimes students do not pull their weight, but the stakes are high. As well as their university lecturers, the school will be judging them. This means that, generally, the group itself will put pressure on team members to perform. The final presentation requires all team members to explain their own contribution as well as what they have learnt from the project.

As unit staff, we have been constantly impressed at the amount of work that students put into projects. As the projects have become better known, several community groups have asked for students to undertake projects for them. This has included playground audits and safe play programs for a child safety organisation and a mentoring programme for children at risk for a charity that works with children from lower socio-economic backgrounds. Schools increasingly also ask students to undertake particular projects, where the teachers do not have the time or expertise. This often requires good negotiation skills on the part of the students, however, to ensure that they have some say in the project, and are not just used as free labour.

One problem that needed to be overcome was that schools were initially skeptical about the projects. They were nervous that they may not succeed, or that students would require a lot of supervision. However, they have been surprised at how much work students put into the projects and schools now sometimes complain to unit assessors when they think that the students at their school have not received the marks they deserve.

Students themselves continue to be initially skeptical. The project seems very daunting and unlike anything they have done before. Many baulk at the level of work and commitment that might be required, although they are reassured when they hear the previous year's students' presentations.

One major advantage of the programme has been the large 'spin offs' for students and their learning in the unit. They report they feel more engaged with their learning at university, more a part of a school community and that they have indeed made the correct choice of vocation. They feel they can 'make a difference' in their chosen profession. They entered the course feeling like 'neophytes', that they had no knowledge or expertise and needed to observe passively and learn from the 'experts' when they went on teaching rounds in schools. They now are more aware that they bring a range of new perspectives and fresh expertise to schools that teachers often don't have. They feel much closer to being equal partners in the relationship and not an unwelcome burden on their busy supervising teachers.

Strong positive endorsement of the programme is that students report that the project gives them an opportunity to find their 'place' in the school. It gives them an opportunity to display their expertise, rather than just shadowing the class teacher and trying to mimic their practice. They also report that it is the first time that they feel that they have some status and value in the school. Previously students were very much aware of the uneven nature of their relationships with their university lecturers and the classroom teachers with whom they were working. By giving them the space to develop their own ideas and projects in schools and within the unit, this new approach helps to legitimise not only their role and ideas in the school, and in the course, but to give them explicitly status as professionals with worthy knowledge, ideas and expertise.

Several student quotes from research conducted into the unit illustrate the impact on students' motivation and engagement:

> One of the turning points in regards to my learning in this unit was the initial discussion of the project assignment. Initially I was anxious about this assignment ... but now think that it has been one of (if not the most) meaningful work(s) I have completed at uni.

> The project turned out to be an excellent idea and as soon as a topic was decided everyone seemed eager to implement this into their field experience schools as soon as possible.

> Once I began working on the project I found I was much more engaged with the lectures.

Much more than this, and heartening for the staff working in the unit, has been the change in students' philosophies of learning and teaching. In the first year of study, students often write in their fieldwork reflections that they 'can't wait to be the one up the front' and to have their own class. This generally changes after the project to a shift in the focus from them as teacher in charge, to them as facilitator of the learning of others. Their reflections at the end of the unit on their philosophies of teaching and learning demonstrate this shift. When asked what kind of teacher they would like to be, they have replied:

> To be flexible, approachable, compassionate ... Teaching and learning encompasses all aspects of life, so the classroom is only part of the equation and learning can be lifelong and lifewide.

> To be seen as a person who knows some of the answers but not all.

> To inspire not only learning but also life-skills, to equip my charges ... to successfully continue beyond my direct influence.

Another positive aspect is the pride that students feel when they succeed in such a major endeavour. For students, the biggest outcome is when they come to apply for positions at the end of their degree. Graduates often have trouble demonstrating their expertise as opposed to teachers who have been working in schools for some time. The project gives them an opportunity to prove their skills in planning, organisation, project management and teaching. Principals often report to university staff how impressed they have been with the work that students have shown them during interviews, and frequently this has swayed their decision to employ students.

For students, the most significant outcome is that that they feel that they have done something worthwhile, that they have 'made a difference', often their original motivation in choosing teaching as a career. Even if they still do not feel completely comfortable about their ability to teach, they feel more comfortable about taking risks knowing that what they are doing will have a lasting impact on the children. They are less preoccupied with how they will control a class, and more concerned about engaging and motivating students.

The spike in attrition in third year has disappeared, although this is also the result of other changes introduced as part of an overhaul of the programme. Although the description here is about one particular initiative, it was one of several introduced by the course team. When the first cohort of students to undertake the new degree programme graduated, their course evaluation questionnaires rated it the highest of any education degree across Australia. The real test of the initiatives in the programme though will be the lasting impact that the students' learning experiences have on their future teaching, and therefore on their students.

Presentation skills for non-traditional medical students

Pamela Garlick and Gavin Brown

The situation

King's College, London is a large, multi-faculty, research-led university. Increasingly the College is consolidating its expertise as a health-related university, with nearly 70 per cent of the College now consisting of departments involved in teaching and research in medicine, professions allied to medicine and related biomedical and life sciences. The College's medical school is one of the largest in Europe.

Over the last 25 years, the demographics of who trains to be a doctor in the UK have changed significantly. What was once a predominantly white, male profession is rapidly becoming feminised and more ethnically diverse. At King's, more than half of the current medical students are young women and a similar proportion are from minority ethnic communities, predominantly young people of Indian heritage. However, despite these changes in gender and ethnicity, the majority of medical students still come from professional middle-class families and most have attended high-achieving, selective schools.

In an attempt to broaden its student population further, the School of Medicine launched the Access to Medicine Project in May 2001 to help raise the aspirations and achievements of young people attending state schools in ten inner London boroughs, with a view to enabling them to train as doctors. As part of the project, the School created a six-year Extended Medical Degree Programme (EMDP) to enable it to recruit these local students, even if they had not obtained the high A level grades normally required for admission to a medical degree course.

The conventional medical curriculum is divided into three phases. During their first semester at medical school, students study Phase 1. This intensive period of study is designed to equip them with both the basic language of science and medicine and the study skills they will need for the remainder of their degree. Phase 2 is studied over the next 18 months with the aim of preparing students for the final three-year clinical phase of their studies. Phase 2 is structured around a series of week-long patient scenarios, which integrate the teaching and learning of basic medical sciences, psychology and medical sociology and basic clinical skills in the context of a range of common medical conditions.

Students on the EMDP complete Phase 1 and 2 in three years rather than the standard two. Essentially, they take most of the conventional first year of study over a two-year period and do not have a major summative assessment until the end of their second year.

Given that the EMDP students are recruited from state schools in inner London, compared to their peers on the conventional five-year medical degree, most of the EMDP students are from working-class families. The majority come from minority ethnic communities, with a far broader diversity of backgrounds than our conventional students. A significant minority were born outside the UK and have English as a second or additional language. Few of them come from families with any significant prior experience of higher education (certainly in a UK context).

In large part, the selection of students to the EMDP is based on an assessment of their future academic potential rather than their current academic achievements. This is in recognition of the fact that (although in some cases they are improving rapidly) the academic performance of many schools in the areas of inner London where we work are poor in comparison to the national average. In some cases, students on the EMDP have succeeded in obtaining a place at medical school despite attending secondary schools where pupils attain average exam scores that are four times lower than the national average for their age cohort. These are schools with little history of student progression to higher education, let alone prestigious degrees like medicine.

Although these young people are intellectually very capable of excelling on a demanding medical degree (and their exam results at medical school over the last five years certainly prove this), they arrive at medical school without much of the social and cultural capital with which their more middle-class peers have grown up.

In the early years of running the EMDP, one of the most apparent areas of 'deficit' (a concept we're not entirely comfortable with) among these students was the quality of their academic English and the paucity of their formal presentation skills. Interestingly, however, one of their greatest assets as a group (and this has been commented upon by many of our clinical and academic colleagues) is their highly developed communication and interpersonal skills, especially when dealing with patients. This is perhaps not surprising given their backgrounds, as these are young people who have had to learn from an early age how to negotiate and perform multiple, contextual identities and ways of presenting themselves. Nevertheless, their poor grasp of academic English and their hesitant (or sometimes inappropriate) tutorial presentations meant that a large number of these students were not obtaining the assessment grades that truly reflected their intellectual ability and their understanding of scientific topics.

The approaches implemented

The EMDP was designed so that there was space in the curriculum to offer these students additional academic tutorial support around those topics that we knew many students found conceptually difficult. Within this 'white space' in the timetable, EMDP students were also offered some basic additional study skills support. However, it is probably fair to say that we underestimated the amount of study skills support that these students would need.

In response to our growing awareness of our students' need for academic English support, in the Spring Term of 2003/4 we introduced the 'PANDA' module for students on the second year of the EMDP. PANDA was named with a knowing wink towards the pun on pandas in Lynn Truss's polemic book on the deteriorating standard of English usage, *Eats, Shoots & Leaves*.

Clearly, beyond offering the students practical assistance in maximising their academic potential, the PANDA module was conceived as an important aspect of their broader professional development as future doctors – after all, we all want to know with some confidence that the notes our doctors write about us during treatment are clear and unambiguous. Indeed, this was an important 'hook' for getting the students on board with a series of classes that they might otherwise have found uninteresting and a little pointless – when we pointed out that we might be saving them from unnecessary future malpractice suits, the attention levels in the classes improved dramatically!

This short, four-week, module included sessions on syntax, punctuation, spelling, comprehension and précis, as well as presentation skills. The aims of the written part of the module were that students should, by the end of it, be able to: understand the way in which sentences are constructed; avoid ambiguity of meaning; punctuate a sentence appropriately and spell 'problem' words correctly. However, it is the sessions on presentation skills that we wish to concentrate on in this case study.

In the presentation skills strand of the PANDA module, the students were expected to make three separate presentations to their peers. In the first session, students were asked initially to stand up and give a three-minute presentation about themselves. In the light of the feedback they received on this initial off-the-cuff talk, they were asked to speak later on in the session for a further five minutes on a topic of their choice. In most cases, the students spoke about a hobby of theirs or a topic that was close to their hearts. Further feedback was given. For the second session, each student had to prepare a five-minute presentation with visual aids on a scientific topic that had been selected for them; this more formal presentation was recorded on video. Extensive commentary from both their peers and the tutor was given to them at this point and recorded on a flipchart (for subsequent transcription and feedback to the individual). In the final session in the series, the video presentations were reviewed and students were given a brief opportunity to have another attempt at presenting material without the distracting 'tics' or interjected 'ums' that they now saw dominated their original effort.

Discussion

Before deciding on how to deliver the PANDA module, we considered several options. The 'do nothing' approach was not viable, as we believed it would have resulted in the students under-achieving in assessments and being at greater risk of leaving their course. We could have brought in the College's centrally provided English language sessions for international students, but we believed this would not have been appropriate to the needs of our students, as most of them have grown up speaking English. Our students do not need to learn English from scratch, but do need to develop more formal use of syntax and grammar. Finally, we considered the development of self-directed delivery through a virtual learning environment. Although this approach had some merit, an immediate response was needed and there was no time available in which to develop these resources. Furthermore, it would have been difficult to deliver all aspects of the PANDA module through the internet.

One of the best ways of assessing the strengths of the presentation skills strand of the PANDA programme is to consider the positive impact it had on a couple of our students.

When she was first asked to stand up and speak about herself, Debbie was mortified and throughout the first session she kept refusing to volunteer to talk. Consequently, she was the final student to present both of the first two talks, which exaggerated her existing embarrassment. At the end of this session, one of us took her aside and had a quiet chat about her fears and concerns. We discovered, after some coaxing, that she was very self-conscious about being overweight. Together, we devised a strategy for her to approach the presentation in the following session, which was to be videoed, much to Debbie's horror. We encouraged her to shed the baggy jeans and T-shirt that she was wearing and to turn up to the following session wearing clothes that she felt good and confident in. She took this advice and arrived for the second session in clothes that she felt less self-conscious wearing. Indeed, with this light-touch 'make-over' her appearance changed from scruffy, overweight schoolgirl to confident young doctor of the future. The quality of her final presentation improved dramatically, as well. Debbie's work across the course has also improved dramatically – having barely scraped through her first year, her exam results in subsequent years have placed here in the top third of her class.

Reshma is a young Bangladeshi Muslim woman. At the start of the PANDA programme, she too was extremely embarrassed at the prospect of standing up and talking about herself to the class. In response to her initial attempt at making a presentation, she was encouraged by the tutors to speak up and project her voice. She was also offered advice about her posture and body language. We encouraged her to stand tall, rather than literally trying to minimise the physical space she took up in front of her peers. Again, these tactics seemed to have a positive impact on how she presented herself subsequently. For her scientific presentation, Reshma (like several of her classmates) was asked to give a five-minute talk about prostate cancer. This was a deliberate test of 'professionalism'. Despite being reminded that, as medical students, they would have to discuss potentially embarrassing conditions in an appropriate and professional manner with their patients in the near future, several of the class seemed to be incapable of talking about this serious condition without giggling uncontrollably. This was not a problem for Reshma, who gave a very clear and competent description of the causes, diagnosis and treatment of prostate cancer. Indeed, she found the presentation skills so useful for her personal development that she persuaded one of our colleagues to provide her with a number of additional sessions after the PANDA module ended. Although these presentation skills sessions do not appear to have made any significant impact on Reshma's academic performance, she has 'gelled' far more with her peers since then and become more engaged with the life of the medical school, including acting as a student ambassador working with a younger generation of students from widening participation backgrounds.

We assessed the success of the spelling and punctuation part of the PANDA programme by means of a dictation test. A very 'dense' piece of prose (500 words) was constructed, containing all possible punctuation marks and at least thirty of the most commonly mis-spelt words. One of us then recorded a spoken version of it – first straight through, and then in small (memorable) sections, and then straight through again. We were thus able to give the students an identical dictation test before and after the PANDA programme. All the students obtained higher marks the second time round, with the largest improvement being found among the students for whom English was not the first language.

Two of the main weaknesses of the PANDA intervention, as we originally developed it, are that, first, it comes too late in the students' time here and secondly, that it is a 'one-off' module. Our future plan, therefore, is to offer PANDA to students in their first year and to increase its impact by having some follow-up sessions (probably web-based) in their subsequent years.

Since we first implemented the PANDA programme, the size of the annual student intake to the Extended Medical Degree Programme has grown from 20 to 50 students. It is not possible to offer the practical presentation skills classes to a single group of 50 students. For it to continue to be effective, this aspect of the PANDA programme now needs to be run with three parallel groups of students. Clearly, this makes the delivery of an already teaching-intensive short module even harder. We also, increasingly, realise that it is not just the students on the EMDP who stand to benefit from this intervention. Ideally, it needs to be offered to all new first-year students. With an annual intake of nearly 400 students to our medical degrees, that poses some serious logistical problems. In future, we hope to deliver the punctuation, spelling and syntax aspects of the module through a virtual learning environment. Once this development has been implemented, we intend to have the EMDP students completing some revision tasks in each year of their studies, in order to sustain and improve the quality of their academic English. At present, we are still working on timetabling all the presentation skills sessions.

Diversity and achievement: developing the learning of non-traditional HE students

Kate Kirk

The situation

With a diverse student body and a high proportion of students entering higher education (HE) through 'non-traditional' routes on the Applied Social Studies Programme at Manchester Metropolitan University, we recognised the importance of providing support for learning in the first-year curriculum. A participatory research project with a cohort of our students provided more than feedback on our approach. It also revealed much about the 'student experience' of first-year non-traditional entry students, their hopes and aspirations. We wanted to be able to 'see ourselves through our students' eyes' and to gain insight into the *different* ways that our students experience the first year at university. As Brookfield (1995: 92) explains:

> Seeing Ourselves Through Our Students' Eyes – Of all the pedagogic tasks teachers face, getting inside students' heads is one of the trickiest. It is also one of the most crucial. When we start to see ourselves through our students' eyes, we become aware of what Perry (1988) calls the different worlds in the same classroom. We learn that students perceive the same activities in vastly different ways.

In order to 'get inside our students' heads' and understand how they experienced our approach to supporting and developing their learning, we carried out an in-depth evaluation of their experience in the first undergraduate year on the BA Honours Social Work and Youth and Community Work courses. Our teaching and learning strategy was designed to enable our students to develop as independent and self-confident adult learners. This was important for both their academic progress and for their development as confident and competent social work and youth and community work practitioners. As the majority of our students had come into university through 'non-traditional entry' routes, we wanted to be sure that the foundation provided best enabled their transition into higher education (HE), the development of their learning in the first year and their progression to Level Two.

In the UK, students are described as 'non-traditional' either because they are from families, backgrounds and/or communities traditionally underrepresented in HE or, because they have taken a pathway to university that is not the 'normal' sixth form school-leaver's 'A' level route. Underrepresented groups in HE in the UK include students from low socio-economic backgrounds, members of black and 'minority ethnic' communities, mature and older people returning to learn, students for whom English is not their first language and disabled people. On our programme, the majority of students can be described as non-traditional in that they come from a diverse range of backgrounds, cultures and communities, with a significantly high number who are disabled and/or dyslexic. They include mature students returning to learn and an increasing number for whom English is not their first language.

Due in part to past educational experiences, many of our students perceived themselves to be inadequately prepared for study at university; they lacked confidence and often perceived themselves as 'undeserving' of a university place. While it is true that some students struggle and some leave in their first year due to difficulties in meeting the required standards, more often than not, drop-out is due to pressures that arise in managing university life together with, perhaps, parenting demands and financial commitments. Most, if not all, of our students have to work to support themselves while studying and many are the breadwinner in the family.

We wanted to make sure that we provided the right kind of support to enable our students to succeed in their studies. At the same time, though, it was important for us not to adopt a 'spoon-feeding' approach as this would mitigate against our goal of creating independent and autonomous learners. So, we knew that we needed to learn more about how our students were experiencing their first year at university. We wanted to understand factors that contribute to the support, development of their learning, progression and retention, and to ensure that our support for learning strategy continued to be developed as appropriate and meaningful.

This need prompted us to carry out an in-depth evaluation exercise with a recent cohort of students towards the end of their first year of undergraduate study. Support and funding from the Social Policy and Social Work Learning and Teaching Support Network (SWAP LTSN) enabled us to expand on the usual, less detailed, end-of-year evaluation exercise.

The approach that underpinned our work reflected Rowland's attitude to research on students' perceptions of learning:

> This research attitude demands that we consider the role of teaching to be one of listening as much as one of speaking: that teaching is a two way process of communication, and that what students have to say about their learning is always most significant. Such an approach is to be contrasted with the normal student feedback questionnaires that have now become an integral part of the quality control machinery'.
>
> (Rowland 2000: 32)

We anticipated that the evaluation exercise would provide us with an understanding of the student experience that would guide us in developing our provision and making appropriate changes where required. This case study shows how we took account of the student voice to further develop an inclusive support-for-learning strategy.

The approaches implemented

The evaluation

Our approach to the evaluation was student-centred and participatory right from the beginning. Students participated in adapting the standard end–of-year questionnaire and in designing the questions for the group interviews that followed. These provided scope for an illuminative and expanded study of key issues arising from the questionnaire. Students also made decisions regarding the gathering of information on identity, and ensured that the composition of the focus groups represented the diversity of the student body. It was agreed that the interviews would be taped and that students would have the opportunity to approve transcripts. A 'working agreement' was facilitated at the start of each group. Students were free to choose which focus group they attended and six groups were formed.

Carrying out the evaluation

The questionnaire asked students to score elements of support-for-learning provided both on the programme and by the central university services. It also contained an open question asking them to identify external sources of support.

Over 70 per cent of the cohort completed the questionnaire. Results showed that the *highly* valued elements of programme provision were: lectures, e-learning, the use of the internet for learning, the Approaches to Learning unit, the induction programme, seminars and small group work, and the university library. What is remarkable is that while there were a number of varied responses and some significant qualifying comments, no elements were rated to be of little, or no value, overall.

The group interviews, with over one third of the cohort, were mainly concerned with further investigation of the elements that gained varied responses in the questionnaire, that is, where at least 50 per cent placed high value on these, but where a significant proportion gave a lower score. Clarification of comments and qualifying statements regarding highly valued elements was also sought, and the questionnaires also revealed the need to further explore feedback on support resources for particular learning requirements. These included, for example, the needs of disabled or dyslexic students and those for whom English is not their first language.

The focus groups provided rich information and further detail that we built into the support for learning strategy, as follows.

Pre-course preparation

The original approach included web- and paper-based information, suggestions for pre-course reading, opportunities to visit the university for course-specific 'taster' days and the opportunity to submit a short piece of writing on a relevant topic for diagnostic feedback from a programme tutor. The evaluation exercise showed that although this was highly valued by over 50 per cent of the cohort, a significant number, nearly half, had been unable to access this support as they had applied late or obtained a place on the course through 'clearing' – that is, at the last minute! On the basis of this finding, we ensured that paper-based information was provided to late applicants. The opportunities for visit and taster days were also extended until late in the summer vacation period.

Discussion in the focus groups on pre-course provision revealed much about students' willingness to be prepared and ready for study. Students expressed a strong desire for pre-course reading lists and information on assessment. We found this to be an interesting finding, as it contradicted the common notions that non-traditional entry students are reluctant to prepare and take responsibility for their learning.

Induction

While the focus group discussion revealed that the start-of-year induction programme was a highly valued element, a significant number of qualifying statements provided evidence that many students felt 'bombarded' and 'overwhelmed' by this process. Consequently, we reorganised induction week, and some induction activities were phased in later in the term. For example, in consultation with library staff, the library induction became directly related to the construction of the first assignment. This made the introduction to the library more relevant and meaningful for students.

While feedback indicated that the provision of e-learning course units was highly valued, it also revealed much about the variation in students' prior experience in use of the internet and in their access to computers for learning. This led us to ensure a more inclusive and thorough approach was taken in our induction to e-learning sessions and led us to create specific timetabled slots for students to access the university's computer labs.

Peer learning

In the focus groups, it was apparent that students valued collaborative work highly. Seminars and small group discussions following the large lectures were identified as particularly important for dyslexic students, some disabled students, and those for whom English is not their first language. In the face of a declining resource in staffing and increased student numbers, the team, in order to preserve small group work, adopted a strategic approach, prioritising some course units for intensive staffing resources over others. When unable to provide staff-led seminar groups, we managed time and space and designed guidelines and exercises for student-led discussion groups to take place.

In discussing the peer mentoring scheme where students are encouraged to work in pairs, strong evidence emerged that students had independently set up small study groups. These collaborative groups extended beyond friendship groups, as students spoke about sharing materials and resources and creating opportunities to clarify and discuss aspects of the curriculum, assignments and the construction of their portfolios. Indeed, 'other students' featured as one of the top five elements identified by students as being outside university or programme provision and having made a significant contribution to learning. It was therefore important for the programme team to recognise student autonomy and increase scope for choice when managing peer learning activities.

Portfolio and assessment

Students create a portfolio of learning and professional development in each of the three undergraduate years. The process of portfolio construction requires them to develop as reflective learners and reflective practitioners. They amass evidence and provide a reflective 'critical commentary' on their learning and professional development. It is used to encourage students to take responsibility for their learning and professional development and it is a mechanism for planning and identifying future goals and targets for continuing professional development and learning.

There was significant difference between students about the value of portfolio construction. The portfolio is assessed and carries academic credits. Over 50 per cent of the students surveyed provided positive feedback, acknowledging the contribution that the portfolio made to learning and professional development. This contrasted with comments from a significant minority of students who felt that the portfolio was an additional task on top of a heavy assessment load; it was a 'burden', a 'waste of time'. This feedback led the programme team to re-examine the entire Year One assessment package, including the portfolio, and to develop an imaginative assessment scheme that incrementally builds and develops knowledge and key skills through creative diagnostic and formative assessment procedures, integrating these into the production of the portfolio.

The tutorial system

In previous years, the individual tutorial relationship and the value of tutorials (which are work-focussed rather than 'pastoral') have been rated as the most highly valued contribution to learning and development in Year One. Again, this was the view of 50 per cent of this student cohort. However, while some students gave examples of excellent support offered by temporary, part-time staff, others felt that they had suffered because part-time staff were not familiar with procedures and were often not as accessible as full-timers. The staff team was aware that a combination of the expansion of student numbers and the loss of full-time experienced staff who had not been replaced had a detrimental effect on the tutorial system. The team tackled this issue head-on by ensuring that a full-time member of staff took a coordinating role and this, together with a system for induction and mentoring new colleagues and guidelines for the focus of each tutorial, led to an overall improvement in the provision of tutorial support.

Support for particular learning requirements

While the programme team felt confident that care had been taken to meet the needs of students with particular learning requirements, feedback indicated that, while the majority of students had had positive experiences, a significant minority still felt that their needs had not been met. This was particularly the case for some dyslexic and hearing-impaired students who reported that some lecturers did not take a proactive stance to ensure an inclusive experience. Subsequently, the team revisited guidelines and procedures for good practice in working with dyslexic and hearing-impaired students and renewed their commitment to ensuring that all staff, including visiting lecturers, were made aware of, and followed good practice protocol.

The evaluation also provided information on central university learning support services. Although a majority of students were positive about this, a number felt that support was inadequate, or had not matched expectations. The team's response to this was to work more closely with central services and to involve individual staff from the learning support team to collaborate in the delivery of the Approaches to Learning unit.

About half of our students for whom English is not their first language reported that they were satisfied, but nearly half again felt that they had not received adequate support. This was investigated further in the focus groups, and it became apparent that procedures and criteria for referral needed to be clarified. This led to an improvement in communication between central services and the programme team and in better provision for students.

External sources of support for learning

The second part of the evaluation exercise was to determine other sources of support that students independently accessed and made use of, outside university provision. The responses gave a clear indication of student autonomy and independence. For example, feedback showed that students regularly independently accessed public libraries and placed great value on the resources that they found available in external agencies in their communities. Other evidence of students' self-reliance also shone through. For example, the fact that students identify other students as significant sources of support and that many have established mentoring relationships with work colleagues in external agencies, indicates the extent to which students themselves take a proactive approach to their learning.

Strong identification of the family as a source of support emerged. Students made the distinction between 'moral' and practical support with their studies. While some students had both forms of support, most felt that the family was mainly a source of personal or material support. Consideration was also given to the fact that some students do not have family support, so this area was treated with sensitivity. This is a good example of attention to 'minority voice'. Even though the family was deemed to be the most popular source of external support, it must not be assumed this is the case for all students. A small number identified themselves as 'care leavers', having been fostered or 'looked after' in other ways. They emphasised their own self-determination and autonomy in terms of their success in gaining entry to, and succeeding, in the first year of HE.

Some students gave examples of how their own children were supportive in that they showed understanding and helped in the house when 'mum has to do her homework too'. Some spoke of the fact that their studying had encouraged their children to work harder themselves, as they now have positive role models. Several parents spoke of their desire to succeed being linked to their own educational aspirations for their children.

Several students revealed that their entry to HE had a negative effect on partners, some of whom felt insecure, or afraid they were 'being left behind'. Several mature women students spoke of the negative attitudes of partners and/or in-laws who criticised them for neglecting their family duties because they had 'abandoned' the traditional mothering role. They were deemed to be 'selfish' and 'uncaring'. So the family, as ever, proved to be a potential source of support and also a source of conflict for women.

Independence, motivation, resilience and drive!

The focus groups rounded up with the question: 'Has the provision made to support your learning in Year One prepared you for Year Two?' The quotes below exemplify the responses:

- 'Provision was a happy medium – less support than at college, but this is a good thing as we will need to be independent when we go out to work.'
- 'It makes me be mature, you're not followed around, you gradually learn to manage your own time, I enjoy that'.
- 'I appreciate not being mollycoddled'!
- 'My confidence has grown'.
- 'I can see how I have developed – I used to get angry when I didn't agree with someone, now I ask questions, say can you explain'?

In addition, students were keen to receive as much information about Year Two as possible, including assessment criteria -'stepping up a level', and reading lists – 'so as we can buy books and read before the children finish school for the summer'.

- 'Everyone wants to better themselves, to prepare for Year Two'.

And when students were asked if they were more independent than when they started Year One, agreement was mixed with indignation:

- 'I have always been independent – you have to be with children and a job to manage, as well as your studies!'
- 'I left my family overseas to come here, so I have always been independent!'

Information began to emerge of students who had increased in confidence over the year, who had a strong desire to play an active part in managing their learning and who were resilient and able to manage complex situations in their own lives while succeeding in their studies. This picture contrasts with a commonly held image of non-traditional entry students as lacking in motivation, low in aspiration and as passive and dependent learners.

Discussion

A 'holistic' approach

The evaluation exercise helped us to make considerable improvements to our support-for-learning strategy. It also confirmed that we were on the right track in providing a strategy that is based on a rejection of a 'deficit model'. We positively recognise that students bring richly diverse *resources* as well as needs to the classroom. This was evidenced by students' appreciation of small group work and collaborative learning opportunities, and they provided examples of ways in which they had learned from each others' different experiences and perspectives.

Student feedback also indicated that a universal approach with support–for-learning offered to all students was preferable to a remedial one or a 'study skills' model. While feedback led to greater cooperation with central learning support services, it also helped us to strengthen the 'holistic' approach and to further integrate support for learning into the design and delivery of the curriculum and assessment processes.

Discussion in the focus groups demonstrated that students were keenly aware that the philosophy, values and principles that underpin professional practice in social work and youth and community work were reflected in our provision of inclusive and equitable learning opportunities. The desire to promote inclusive and equitable opportunities for adult students from a diverse range of backgrounds, cultures and communities was appreciated. The strategy had been designed to meet the requirements of a diverse student body, including disabled and dyslexic students, those for whom English is not their first language and mature students returning to learning. While our approach was inclusive from the beginning, we learned more about the different and sometimes specific, requirements of our students.

Feedback obtained enabled us to further *integrate* support for learning into the design and delivery of the curriculum – it became an integral aspect of the learning and teaching strategy. Further refinements led to more care in managing and coordinating the system as successful implementation relies on a whole team approach. An example of this is evident in the way that we developed the Approaches to Learning unit that is delivered throughout the first term. This unit provides important induction and an introduction to studying at university. The curriculum extends beyond a 'study skills' model as students are introduced to reflective learning theories and there is an emphasis on a critical and analytical approach to the use of evidence and sources to support both the construction of assignments and the development of students as reflective learners and professional practitioners. Positive feedback and constructive criticism on this unit led us to give it a pivotal role in our 'holistic' system in that we synchronised the tutorial system, the construction of a portfolio of learning and the weekly professional development group with the delivery of sessions in the core Approaches to Learning unit.

In addition, the integrated approach was further strengthened through increased opportunities for peer learning, both through our peer mentoring scheme and through an increased emphasis on independent study and collaborative experiential and participatory learning. Guidance on the above ensured that outcomes from student-led activities could be directly fed into the construction of the portfolio of learning that provides the basis for personal development planning.

New developments

The evaluation exercise revealed much about the experiences of non-traditional entry students, and has prompted a more in-depth research project. This new project involves a series of longitudinal studies, the first with a group of students from the cohort that took part in the evaluation, another with students of African and African Caribbean heritage (in partnership with Cariocca, an independent educational trust that provides support to members of the African Caribbean community in Manchester). The third is a comparative study with colleagues and students from Monash University in Australia.

The aim of these studies is to trace non-traditional pathways into HE and to follow participants through their undergraduate years. The purpose is to document ways in which students from a diverse range of backgrounds, communities and experiences manage a multiplicity of challenges as they pursue academic achievement.

Case study material illustrating the achievements of participants will provide positive role models to inspire and encourage future non-traditional entry students. The publication of findings will contribute to widening participation in higher education and to progressive and inclusive learning and teaching and support-for-learning strategies.

Acknowledgement

Thank you to all student participants from Year One (2002–3) on the Applied Social Studies Programme. This work could not have been carried out without your participation, commitment and enthusiasm.

References

Brookfield, S. D. (1995) *Becoming a Critically Reflective Teacher*. San Francisco: Jossey-Bass.

Perry, W. G. (1988) 'Different worlds in the same classroom', in P. Ramsden (ed.), *Improving Learning: New Perspectives*. East Brunswick, NJ: Nichols.

Rowland, S. (2000) *The Enquiring University Teacher*. Buckingham: Open University Press.

The business involved in making beer

Judith Tennant

The situation

As unit coordinator for the Introductory Microeconomics and Macroeconomics units at the regional campus of a large Australian university, I am continually looking for ways to enhance my students' learning by making the units more relevant to the students. In addition, I am also the Chair of the Orientation Committee for my faculty at the campus. As part of this role, I developed the BusEco (shortened form of 'Faculty of Business and Economics') Student Club which aims to bring first-year students together in a 'learning community', providing academic assistance and guidance throughout the year. I came up with the idea of stimulating student interest in their business degree overall by taking students on a visit to the local brewery. This 'on site' visit also provided a focal discussion point of microeconomics 'in action' for my economics students, as introductory microeconomics is a core unit in the Bachelor of Business and Commerce. Introductory macroeconomics is also required for students completing the accounting major and wishing to meet the requirements of the Certified Practising Accountants (CPA), the professional accreditation body.

Not all students are equally enthusiastic about undertaking these economics units. University study can be challenging enough for students without the obligation of undertaking units in which they have little immediate interest. Our students come from a variety of backgrounds; some are entering the unit straight from secondary school, and some are mature-age students returning to study after a period in the workforce. In addition, students come from a variety of countries to study on our campus. For instance, the cohort for the year 2004 included students from Australia, China, Germany, Malaysia, Norway and Singapore. With such a diverse group of students, it is a major challenge to find ways to stimulate the students' interest in their studies in the business and economics faculty.

The students entering university straight from secondary school do not always have a clear vision of where they see their future careers. Some have preconceived notions, but change their minds during the course of their studies. Students have differing levels of prior knowledge of the business world. Some will have undertaken a variety of business units at secondary school such as business management, economics or accounting, others will have no previous experience of studying these areas. In addition, the way in which business is conducted in various countries can differ widely. This means that an example used in teaching that is relevant to Australian students will not necessarily be familiar to international students. For example, a discussion of the operation of 'Woolworths', a major Australian supermarket chain, may not have much relevance to students from China without a more detailed explanation of the nature of the industry and a comparison with similar industries in China.

In the classroom situation, I always encourage students to discuss the relevance of various economic theories to particular industries, or to the actions of individuals, groups or governments. Students are able to share ideas and compare experiences from their own countries. This adds richness to the discussion and certainly provides a context for, and to some extent makes real, the various economic theories under discussion. However, while these experiences are shared through discussion, they are not shared experiences in the physical sense and can never generate the same depth of discussion and understanding as can an experience that is shared physically. On a microeconomic level for example, students can share experiences of the operation and cost of public transport in their own countries. This is something most students would have experienced, but the experience is still different and the resulting discussion can often be quite superficial.

The lack of shared experience in relation to macroeconomic issues can be more extreme, with students often having no relevant experience to draw upon. For example, this often applies to the macroeconomic concept of why central banks around the world are concerned with keeping inflation at low levels, while at the same time keeping unemployment low. Many of our younger students have lived most of their adult lives in a low inflation environment in Australia, or have never been personally affected by struggling to pay off a mortgage with interest rates running above 15 per cent. Nor have many of them personally experienced the effects of long-term unemployment. This lack of personal experience is good from a personal viewpoint; however, it also means that the problems of high inflation and high unemployment have less relevance to them.

The approaches implemented

I perceived that taking students to visit a local brewery was one way to provide students with a common shared experience of a local industry and the way in which theories learnt in class could be applied to that industry. It was a way of 'anchoring' their studies in real activities. This would provide a more relevant and enriching experience for students, with an element of fun.

My fellow teachers asked why I chose a brewery. There are several reasons for this. Young people in Australia typically drink beer. Beer is a widely advertised product in the media and is often available at many of the social activities run by the Student Union on campus. Beer is also a drink familiar to students from many different countries. Sampling the 'local brew' is a popular leisure activity among many students. Even if students don't drink beer, or any other form of alcohol, they are still aware of beer as a popular product and are interested in its production. My choice of industry turned out to be a good one. The students were genuinely attracted to the chance to visit a brewery and to learn how beer is made. The opportunity to be able to taste the end product was seen in a very positive light by some students, especially as there was no cost borne by students.

Organising the brewery visit seemed simple on paper, but required a great deal of planning. The main obstacle concerned the timing of the visit. The brewery was quite happy to have a small group of students visit, but could not cater for any more than twenty students in their facility. This is because the brewery is a small business and not particularly geared for tours and tasting sessions, hence the visit had to coincide with a time when the chief brewer, John, would be available to speak to our students. Timing also had to coincide with my availability to accompany the students. I had other teaching and administrative commitments that had to be worked around. University regulations also required the presence of a staff member with appropriate first-aid qualifications. This added another variable to the timing equation.

To further complicate the issue, we planned to take students by bus to the brewery. The local bus company offers reasonably priced bus hire if you hire a bus for use in between school bus 'pickups'. A number of their buses are dedicated to the picking up and taking home of primary and secondary school students, but are relatively idle between 10:00am and 2:30pm. Timing our visit to the brewery (a 30-minute drive from the campus) between these hours achieved a considerable cost saving. This also overcame the problem of those students who held probationary driving licences not being able to taste the beer. In Victoria, drivers who have not held their licence for three years are required to have a zero blood alcohol content while driving. If caught driving with a positive blood alcohol content, their licences are cancelled.

A final timing complication related to the students themselves. The brewery visit was entirely optional for students and had to be scheduled at a time when most students could attend. This effectively restricted the trip to a Friday when none of the students involved had classes to attend. The trip could not be undertaken during the lecture period scheduled for either the microeconomics or macroeconomics classes as this timing did not fit in with other restrictions. A drawback of scheduling the visit on a Friday was that a number of students had outside work commitments on Fridays – as they had no scheduled classes on that day. After the date for the visit was finally determined, we ended up with twelve students and four staff members attending the visit. I decided to allow students from my second- and third-year economics classes also to attend if they wished. The final group included first-year students from Australia, Singapore and Hong Kong, a second-year student from Malaysia and a third-year student from Norway. Although I was disappointed not to have a greater number of students attending, I was heartened by the number of students who expressed regret at not being able to attend due to other commitments. Having such a mix of students was also rewarding, however. In hindsight, it was also better to have a small group like this due to space restrictions at the brewery.

The only costs involved in the brewery visit were those relating to the bus hire, plus lunch for the students. The restaurant located on the same premises as the brewery provided a lunch for the students at a reduced cost. Students were not required to contribute to the cost of the visit. This was absorbed by the BusEco Student Club.

On arrival at the brewery, students were welcomed by the chief brewer, John, who explained the beer-making process and how it included the various sections and functions of the business. The business produces a number of varieties of beer for both domestic and international markets. In itself, this was an extremely valuable exercise in that John's discussion covered the range of business functions which form the units that students study for their degrees. The discussion helped the students develop a broader and more integrated view of their business studies, making it more meaningful and relevant for them.

Students asked how various aspects of the subjects studied in their degree related to this small business. For instance, in relation to economics, one student asked how the business went about gaining an export licence. This question was of particular relevance for the student, who had actually bought some of the beer made by the brewery from an outlet in Singapore. The process of gaining access to markets in Singapore was of great interest to him. This then led to an animated discussion among the students and John relating to other export markets, as well as a lively comparison of Australian beer versus beer from Singapore, and Norway.

The production environment and diversity of markets for the products provided a rich context for discussions of pricing policies in different markets, taxation policies relating to the excise taxes that must be paid in Australia on alcohol, sourcing of raw materials and associated comparative costs of inputs, the relative labour/capital-intensity of various production processes and cost savings related to automating various production processes, reasons for brand proliferation and policies adopted to increase market share. In addition, students were able to explore the relevance of other areas of their core studies – accounting, law, management and marketing – to the operations of this small business. For example, students were able to see the importance of keeping accurate records of all business transactions, from both an efficiency and a legal perspective. They were able to appreciate how an understanding of concepts studied in business law, such as 'contract law', were relevant to this business. The importance of product design, product labelling and selection of target markets are all areas that are discussed in their core marketing unit, and students observed these first-hand at the brewery.

The discussion was lively, and I could see how interested the students had become in the whole production process. In fact, one student commented to me that they had no idea how complicated the whole process was. 'Could the type of water added to the recipe really make that much difference to the end product?', she asked.

Students then toured the brewery before lunching in the restaurant. Over lunch, the students discussed the merits of various beers they had tasted, and were very excited at the prospect of the beer tasting to come. After lunch, the students were given the opportunity to sample the range of beers produced on the premises. At this time discussion continued to relate the reasons for the development of the various styles of beer, the rationale for packaging and labelling designs, and targeted markets. After a visit lasting around three hours, the group thanked John for his time. The thanks were genuine and wholehearted, with all those attending agreeing that the experience was worthwhile from an educational viewpoint. It was also highly enjoyable.

Discussion

No formal evaluation was taken of student responses to the brewery visit. This was deemed unnecessary given the students' overwhelmingly positive reaction to the visit. The return bus trip to the campus was filled with animated discussions of various aspects of the visit, including, but not limited to, an evaluation of the various products sampled at the brewery and a comparison of samples purchased by staff and students alike.

Back at campus, word quickly spread about the enjoyment of the visit, with a number of students asking if I could arrange a second visit for those who were unable to attend the first trip. Unfortunately, this was not possible due to time and other constraints. Word also spread to students new to the campus in 2005, with students in the BusEco Student Club asking me on a number of occasions when I would be able to arrange a visit to the brewery for them. Certainly, the notion of 'free beer tastings' was part of the attraction, but there was also a large element of genuine attraction to the idea of seeing a small business such as this in operation.

In classes held following the brewery visit – both lectures and tutorials – students shared their experiences with those in the class who were unable to visit the brewery. Apart from inciting the envy of those students who 'missed out', the visit provided an actual experience shared by some that could be further shared via discussion with others.

Throughout the rest of the semester, students' experiences at the brewery were frequently expressed. In my introductory microeconomics class, we incorporated a discussion of the way in which the brewery had entered the export market into the topic on international trade. We incorporated a discussion of the various types of beer produced at the brewery into a discussion of competitive strategies. The brewery was also used as an example when discussing the nature of fixed and variable costs associated with production. This incorporated the visit to the brewery more formally into the learning experience of students. The visit also was confidence-building for some students. Two of the students who attended were very quiet students, who did not offer much to class discussion. However, these students were able to draw upon their experiences and began to contribute more confidently to class discussions. Even though only a small number of students had attended the visit, others in the class had sufficient familiarity with beer as a product to be able to contribute to the discussion and ask questions of those who did attend. This had the effect of bringing the class together in a more united discussion than if I had chosen a product with which fewer students were familiar. It enabled students to be more engaged with their studies and provided a richer learning experience for all concerned.

The major problem with the brewery visit was an organisational one. Due to various factors discussed above, not all students could attend the visit. Even if the visit was made compulsory, size constraints alone would necessitate making at least three separate visits to the brewery. This would not have been possible given staff availability issues at the time.

While the brewery provided an ideal venue in terms of allowing students to see the direct application of a wide variety of economic theories as well as relating directly to other core areas of study and thus business operations, the inability to take a large student group limited its effectiveness. This can be overcome in the future with forward planning – the whole trip was conceived, planned and undertaken within a three-week period.

Although 'beer' is not relevant to all students in terms of consumption, it is a product of which most students have heard. There was no pressure placed on students to consume or purchase the beer by staff at the brewery, or by other students. It was made clear to students when the visit was first mentioned that the purpose was to see how a small business operated and to examine the way in which the theory they were learning in their units was relevant to a small business. There may or may not be an opportunity to taste/purchase beer, but this was not to be expected. It was not until we actually arrived at the brewery that we found that we would be given the opportunity to taste the beer. Not all staff (including myself, as personally I dislike the taste of beer) and students tasted the beer; however, this did not detract from the visit. The object of the visit was not to expose students to 'beer'. Rather, the visit was designed to allow students to view a small business in operation. I would suggest that it is impossible to select a small business that everyone is equally enthusiastic about visiting. Apart from the actual product, I had to choose a business that was reasonably accessible from a transport point of view, that was able to have us as visitors from a security and occupational health and safety point of view and that would be interesting for most students. On the basis of these criteria the brewery was ideal.

In all, the educational outcomes from the visit were very positive. The students developed deeper understandings of their studies and their relevance, as well as networks with their fellow students. On both levels, the trip enabled them to engage more readily with their studies, which can only operate for the benefit of the students themselves, as well as for their teachers.

Chapter 5

Conclusions and curriculum-based retention approaches

Some suggestions for future action

Glenda Crosling, Liz Thomas and Margaret Heagney

Introduction

This book has presented and discussed curriculum-based approaches as the optimum and most feasible way to improve the retention of students in higher education. Students dropping out before completion of their studies has personal and economic implications for the individuals and their families, as well as for institutions and society in general. Students and their families are increasingly responsible for financing higher learning, including the payment of fees and covering living costs – internationally, sufficient mandatory student grants are a thing of the past. Institutions are motivated to improve student retention, in part as they recognise the significance of the financial and psychological burdens of withdrawing for individual students, but more pertinently because of the negative consequences for themselves. Institutions are penalised financially by student withdrawal, as there is a reduction in student-related income, and in some instances governments may fine poorly performing HEIs. In addition, the publication of indicators, league tables and harmful media coverage provide a further incentive for universities and colleges to improve student retention and success (Yorke & Longden 2004). Economically and socially, people with higher-level skills developed through HE are increasingly valued. Developed, knowledge economies require a highly skilled workforce, and third-level education is seen to be essential for societies to manage within a rapidly changing and globalised world.

Governments are increasingly concerned with the quality of higher education, and greater accountability with regard to student retention and attrition are significant indicators of this. Evidence of this is the Australian Commonwealth Government-commissioned national attrition survey of students who commenced first-year courses in 2004, to establish the degree to which students continued with their studies, changed university and left university study altogether by 2005 (Long, Ferrier & Heagney 2006). Furthermore, in England the National Audit Office is undertaking another review of student withdrawal and retention – this follows a similar review (NAO 2002), and consideration of the same issue by a House of Commons Select Committee on Education and Employment (2001).

As the diversity of the student population is increasing and patterns of engagement are changing, the quality of the learning experience, student retention and success become evermore challenging issues. In particular, traditional modes of teaching and learning may not be as effective now as they were in previous times when the student population was more homogenous, and less engaged in other non-university-related activities, particularly part-time employment.

In Chapter 1, we have discussed the importance of students' experiences of university and their engagement, the impact on their decisions to continue or withdraw, and also in relation to quality educational outcomes and students' productive learning. Both the academic and social dimensions of engagement are implicated in student retention. Students need to engage and identify on a personal level with their university, and opportunities to develop friendships and networks with their fellow students assist in this process. Academically, active and interactive learning can assist students to develop networks, and also to engage with their subjects so that they are interested and study for meaning and understanding, rather than merely to remember enough information to pass their assessments. We have also discussed the role of the curriculum as a constant in the student experience and therefore a place where students' academic and social engagement can be encouraged and enacted. While in previous times students may have engaged through activities outside the curriculum on their campus, with today's pressures, many students spend little time on campus or participating in activities that assist their engagement. The curriculum, interpreted broadly in this book as teaching and learning approaches that are student-centred and responsive, encourages students to feel included, to engage and to approach their studies with the intention to seek meaning and understanding. This approach underpins their success in their studies, and encourages them to continue rather than withdraw early. The cases in this book present a plethora of curricula development that are responsive to and seek to engage students.

In this final chapter, we draw together and review our exploration of curriculum-based student retention approaches. First, we examine some general approaches that arise from the cases under the particular themes – student diversity, alternative modes of teaching and learning and disciplines of study. We then look at the cases in relation to three aspects of curriculum-based retention, which we identified in Chapter 1. These are:

- curriculum development that is responsive to the particular student cohort,
- academic and social engagement,
- active learning.

Drawing from the cases, we identify ways that these strategies above can be realised in curriculum development. Finally, we present some reflective questions that we have extracted from our pedagogical discussions and analysis of the cases which aim to assist our readers to consider and develop their own practice.

Curriculum approaches to improving student retention

Under the major themes of this book, in this section we summarise the key ways presented in the cases that curriculum approaches have been used to improve student retention and success.

Student diversity and the cases

The student diversity cases show how students from non-traditional backgrounds can be transformed into active and engaged learners when curricula are changed to incorporate learning styles which reflect their diversity, interests and life experiences. For example, working in small groups had positive outcomes for mature-age students in Case 5, 'Maximising educational potential in HE: a curriculum response to student diversity', as it did for students from minority ethnic backgrounds in Case 3, 'Educational innovation: an unexpected diversity tool?'. The students felt they could better manage their learning by working in small groups which also gave them the chance to develop the confidence to speak out and interact with their teachers and their peers. Australian students in the cultural awareness programme described in Case 2, 'How much is enuff rope?' experienced a non-traditional style of small group learning when they met with their teachers who were two Indigenous leaders. Sitting around a campfire under a starlit night sky, students had the opportunities to ask questions and discuss difficult and contentious issues such as land rights and deaths in custody with their teachers in an immediacy that no lecturer in a large metropolitan lecture theatre could achieve.

Modes of teaching and learning and the cases

The modes of teaching and learning cases illustrate ways in which induction, learning, teaching, curricular contents and assessment can be reshaped to be more relevant to students' needs, interests, and previous experiences. The approaches adopted in these cases stress greater student engagement and the use of more active learning strategies. For example, in Case 7, 'Thinking and writing history: an integrated approach to learning development', learning about study skills is integrated into an introductory history module, thus making it relevant to students and developing their identity as historians. In Case 8, 'Internationalisation of the curriculum in an interconnected world', project-based active learning strategies are used effectively to promote intercultural learning in different discipline areas among all students. In Case 10, 'Leveraging student engagement with assessments: collecting intelligence to support teaching, student progress and retention', Mark Russell demonstrates how technology can be used to develop problem-based learning, and give students feedback about their assessments, while also alerting teaching staff to topics with which students are struggling.

Disciplines of study and the cases

The discipline-specific cases demonstrate ways that the curricula, in responding to students, have deviated from traditional disciplinary forms of teaching and learning. These changes aim to mesh students with the teaching and learning and therefore enhance their understandings of and appropriate functioning within the disciplinary cultures; students will not be successful in their disciplinary studies if they are not able to align their approach to study with disciplinary values and ways of operating. For instance, in Case 12, 'Making a difference', through assessing needs and designing and implementing projects, students not only operate successfully within, but *enact* the educational epistemology as they operate as 'facilitators' of development, rather than as the founts of information. In Case 14, 'Diversity and achievement: developing the learning of non-traditional HE students', a similar situation of enactment occurs as the students articulate their transition needs and those of their fellow students; they are empowered as their responses are used to shape the ensuing academic support programme. An excursion to a business organisation is included in the curriculum in an economics subject in Case 15, 'The business involved in making beer'. By participating in the business processes of a product that is meaningful in their lives, students witness the relevance of economics to the finished product, and to the other disciplines they study in their business degree. This allows them to actually see and experience their disciplines of study more realistically than is possible in the classroom.

Key aspects of curriculum-based retention

Extracted from an analysis of the cases, we present key ways that the curriculum-based retention strategies outlined in this book are realised. To reiterate, these strategies are: student-responsive curriculum development; social and academic engagement; active learning. The key ways identified from the cases under these strategies constitute a resource base for future action for our readers as they undertake curriculum development activities.

Student responsive curriculum development

This section considers student-responsive curriculum development. Developing the curriculum so that it is responsive to students requires understanding of the backgrounds, needs and expectations of the student cohort. Teaching and learning is then adapted or changed so that a closer meshing is encouraged between the students and their university experience and learning. Through the cases presented in this book, we have identified a number of ways in which the curriculum is being developed in response to student need. These are:

- Introduction of alternative learning, teaching and assessment approaches
- Development of more relevant curricular contents and tasks to make it more related to students' lives and future plans

- More effective induction process to increase transparency and fill gaps that students have in their knowledge
- Integration of study skills into the core teaching.

Introduction of alternative learning, teaching and assessment approaches

A number of cases describe ways in which alternative learning, teaching and assessment approaches have been utilised to better suit the needs of students. For example, in Case 3 outlined by Wolff, Severiens and de Crom, retention rates were improved for non-traditional students from ethnic minority backgrounds in the Netherlands. This was achieved through breaking down the curriculum from large lectures into small learning blocks and introducing new settings for learning such as working in small groups. In Case 11, 'No more plug and chug', Veronica Cahyadi explains how the very high failure rate for the physics subject demonstrated the need for rethinking the teaching and learning approach. The purpose of the resultant changes was for the students to understand and therefore be able to apply the physics principles, rather than simply rote-learning them. The form of the lecture was altered, moving the focus from the teacher to the students, and engaging the students actively and interactively with the subject content and with each other. The development of students' communication skills through interactive activities was integral to these changes, and students received feedback on their academic development from both the teacher through the reading quizzes and problem-solving activities, and from their peers through discussions and explanations. A similar situation arose in a core engineering module in fluid mechanics and thermodynamics at the University of Hertfordshire (see Case 10). Too many students were failing the end-of-course assessment, and thus the course needed to become more engaging and to provide on-going feedback about students' progress. The case describes the way in which the teaching, learning and assessment strategy was changed. This included the introduction of regular problem-based assessments and the provision of formative feedback. The changes described resulted in students having an improved understanding of the issues and higher achievements in the summative assessment.

Development of more relevant curricular contents and tasks for increased relevance to students' lives and future plans

An important way to improve the relevance of the curriculum to the student cohort is to re-evaluate the curricular contents and tasks, and to make them more immediate to students' past experiences and what they intend to do in the future.

For example, in Case 5 by John Bamber, curricular changes responded to the needs of mature age students, who were studying part-time and also engaged in the work force. The curriculum was redesigned to include group work which centred on solving practical professional problems from a range of perspectives.

This encouraged the students to think for themselves and engage in critical analysis of sources of information. Lectures were replaced by special exercises and essays; small groups or learning clusters were set up to work through action-learning exercises based on issues drawn from students' professional practice and experience. These changes helped students to develop confidence in their abilities – something many mature-age students lack, particularly when they have been absent from formal education for a long period.

In Case 9, McMillan and Solomon describe the ways in which they changed the presentation of the quantitative methods course to utilise common understandings about cooking so as to communicate statistical concepts. This made alien concepts feel and seem familiar, and has helped to overcome the fear of numbers held by many mature students, as well as other social science undergraduates. In Case 12 by Janette Ryan, the changes were instigated by the rural students' perceptions of the course. These students, who had entered the university with low scores, perceived the course as too abstract and theoretical, not practical, and with little relevance to their futures as teachers. The new subject discussed in the case addressed these concerns by taking the students out of the classroom and away from the teacher focus, to the community primary schools where they conceived, designed and implemented projects. This 'hands on' approach meant that the subject content was relevant and real for the students, and the activities subtly developed the students as facilitators of development, rather than as directors of it. In Case 15 by Judith Tennant, where the students perceived economics as abstract and where they could not readily perceive it as relevant to their business studies or business operations, a curricular addition was the excursion to the beer manufacturing company. This excursion provided the students with the opportunity to perceive and understand the relevance of their economics study to, first, a product with which they were familiar, and to business operations. In so doing, the relevance of the study of economics to the students themselves and to the other disciplines that make up business studies was exemplified and amplified.

More effective induction procedures

Some cases have sought to improve the effectiveness of the induction process, and in particular to prepare students, make explicit the expectations and perhaps fill the gaps in knowledge that many have about studying in higher education.

In Case 6, 'Students getting down to work before they start at university: a model for improving retention' at Bournemouth University, staff have tried to support students from as early a time as possible to develop their understanding of studying and learning in higher education. They provide information electronically to enable students to prepare for the transition into higher education. This has proved particularly valuable to students from non-traditional backgrounds, as it helps to reduce their fears about studying at HE, it provides an opportunity for them to ask questions if they are unsure, and it enables them to start engaging with discipline-specific material at an earlier date.

Another approach to improving the transparency of the learning experience is demonstrated in Case 1, 'Turning apartheid around'. This focuses on black students in post-apartheid South Africa, who came to higher education from under-resourced secondary schools; they had not been well prepared for higher education and their retention rates were low. In order to demystify English literature for these students a senior academic (the chair of the faculty) taught a new curriculum which explored the discipline's aims, purpose and techniques, giving students a better understanding of lecturers' expectations and helping them to develop critical reading skills. As a result their failure rates were reduced and they no longer needed supplementary tuition support.

Integration of study skills

Many of the cases show the positive outcomes which result from changing the curriculum to include additional academic support tailored to the needs of students from diverse backgrounds. As noted above, many students enter higher education with underdeveloped study skills. However, supplementary study skills are rejected by many students if they are offered on a voluntary basis. Furthermore, generic skills programmes are often thought to be dull and unimportant by students and staff and appear to have limited impact on students' academic performance. Integrating skill development into the discipline context removes barriers to participating in such programmes, allows all students to benefit from improved academic skills and helps to develop a shared understanding of course expectations. Furthermore, in the context of student diversity, integration tends to normalise the process of having difficulties with study and the need for assistance. It also addresses difficulties that may arise for students before they are manifested in poor academic performance.

In Case 7, Digby Warren describes how he developed a new core introductory history module that assisted students to develop their understanding of study skills and develop their identities as historians. Similarly, in Case 13 the local, ethnic minority students, often with English as a second language and lower entry scores than the majority of the cohort, developed confidence as well as skills that underpin academic success through the module that was developed. Deviating from the traditional approach in medical curricula, the students not only developed academic skills that positioned them for success in their studies, but also positive conceptions of themselves as future doctors.

In Case 14 by Kate Kirk, changes were made to the course for the students who had entered through non-traditional pathways. Students 'self reported' their own needs for study success, which were then built into the curriculum. In Case 4, 'My father wants me to study engineering!', language skills were incorporated into the Engineering curriculum to assist the students from non-English-speaking-backgrounds who came from Indonesia, China, Sri Lanka and Iran to study at the Monash Malaysia campus. They gained the confidence necessary to present papers in English and were able to participate more effectively in the course.

Building language support into the curriculum is essential if students are to become active learners. The integration of the study skills in the mainstream curriculum means that they are immediate to students' needs and therefore more likely to be taken on board.

Academic and social engagement

Socially and academically engaged students are more likely to remain in higher education and to be successful. Social engagement involves students making friends and developing peer networks, breaking their isolation and stimulating their identification with their faculty and university. Improved academic engagement means students take a real interest in their studies so that they seek to understand, rather than to merely pass the assessment. They have increased motivation levels and are more likely to ask for assistance if required – from either their peers or teaching staff. Academic engagement is linked with social engagement in that it is more likely that students will engage academically if they feel comfortable and have friends at university and in their course. Academic engagement can also be fostered through the development of links between staff and students, thus encouraging them to enter into debate, undertake additional study, ask for support, and so on.

In the cases presented in this book, academic and social engagement are promoted in a number of ways. Often, they reinforce each other. We have identified the following approaches to promoting increased engagement:

- Early academic engagement through induction and introductory modules
- Developing social and academic engagement through collaborative learning activities
- Including new curricular contents that promote academic and social engagement
- Using assessment to improve academic engagement
- Improving academic skills to enhance engagement
- Increasing communication and understanding between students and staff.

Early academic engagement through induction and introductory modules

Many students withdraw from higher education during the first few weeks of study, and some who have accepted places never enrol. This suggests the importance of starting to build institutional and disciplinary engagement and commitment as early as possible. This can be achieved by helping students to understand the programme they are to participate in, developing a community of learners and encouraging the formation of friendships and social networks.

At the University of Bournemouth as explained in Case 6, they have found that a pre- and post-entry induction programme has assisted students to engage with course material as early as possible and develop their understanding of their subject.

In addition, students are encouraged to communicate by email with staff about anxieties or concerns, and thus they are starting to develop staff–student relations. These two approaches enable students to feel part of a learning community before they attend the university and during those important early days and weeks. Introductory modules that integrate learning skills also assist students to develop understanding about studying at university, and of their disciplines in particular. The development of appropriate learner identities builds commitment and engagement. For example, in Case 7 Digby Warren uses an introductory module to enable students to learn about the discipline of history, to acquire the skills needed to study this subject and to develop their identities as historians.

In Case 14, course-specific 'taster' days were provided before the term began to familiarise students with their course and the university. Students were also able to submit a short piece of writing for diagnostic purposes, and induction activities took place over the term rather than just at the beginning. To ensure the pervasiveness of quality teaching approaches, a mentoring programme was established for new tutors, who were provided with guidelines for the focus of each tutorial.

Developing social and academic engagement through collaborative learning activities

A primary way in which students can engage with their peers and teaching staff – and ultimately with their study – is through collaborative learning activities. For example, in Case 11 students are assisted to engage with their physics discipline through variation from the traditional form of lecturing. Rather than passively listening and taking notes, students take part in activities directed towards knowledge construction individually and with their classmates. These included reading quizzes, active learning sets, and demonstration modules where physics concepts were applied, using everyday materials such as toy cars and plastic cups. Social engagement was facilitated through opportunities in lectures for students to participate in dialogue with the lecturer and through peer instruction, where they discussed solutions to physics problems with their neighbours in the lecture.

Similarly, in Case 5 working in groups countered social isolation which is often the lot of students studying in part-time mode. This was also the case for non-traditional students from minority ethnic backgrounds in Case 3 as it gave them the chance to interact with one another. In Case 8 Betty Leask describes how students work in groups to research and learn about specific aspects of intercultural difference in relation to curriculum areas. Mark Russell also employed a problem-based approach to learning fluid mechanics and thermodynamics in Case 10, thus encouraging peer interaction. Students were set weekly problem-based assessments and were encouraged to discuss how to solve these tasks.

Embedding cultural diversity training into the curriculum was a direct response to the diversity of the student cohort outlined by Teoh Kok Soo in Case 4. As the students in this case came from many ethnic and cultural backgrounds, working in groups would not deliver successful academic and social engagement for them unless cultural diversity issues were addressed and cross-cultural understandings increased. Students were grouped in pairs and asked to find out from each other their country of origin, culture, tradition and way of life. This helped to promote tolerance and acceptance of each others' cultural backgrounds and resulted in an improvement in the group's dynamic. This enabled the students to experience the social and related academic engagement that comes from belonging to a well-functioning study team.

New curricular contents that promote academic and social engagement

In our cases, we find a number of examples where new curricular contents have been introduced that promote both academic and social engagement. Often, but not always, they involve taking students out of the classroom setting.

In Case 12 in education studies in a rural Australian setting, students' academic engagement was encouraged through the introduction of a new subject, so that students could have first-hand and practical experience in applying the theoretical side of their studies through their community projects. Social engagement is assisted as students mentored other students, and as they worked in teams with fellow students and school staff in the project implementation. In a similar way, in Case 15 Judith Tennant explores the inclusion of an excursion in the curriculum, so students could experience first hand not only the contribution of their economics study to the running of a business, but also its role in relation to the other disciplines in which they study in their business degree. Socially, students developed networks as they shared the experience, creating a basis for future relations and collaboration.

The development of a new curriculum in a remote Australian outback setting is described by Ellender and Drysdale in Case 2. Forty medical and nursing students travelled to a remote indigenous community to participate in an immersion-style cultural awareness programme. The remote location threw students together in a unique way, providing them with opportunities to work together and support each other – practical skills that are necessary in their professional practice. The programme also provided unique learning opportunities through meetings with Indigenous people who passed on their specialist knowledge directly to the students via stories and activities. During the trip one of the students became ill. She was strongly supported by the staff, the Indigenous community and by the students themselves who took it in turns to watch over her. The situation presented a practical learning experience, bringing together the importance of teamwork and an understanding of the pressures of dealing with health crises in remote locations; it also challenged students' prior understandings of Indigenous culture.

The theme of academic and social engagement continues in Case 5. The mature-age student cohort was organised to work through complex practical problems in groups so that multiple perspectives would be brought to resolving the problems. As the practical problems were issues raised in the students' work-places they became actively engaged in their own learning.

Using assessment to improve academic engagement

A traditional role of assessment is to check students' understanding of their studies at the end of the module. It can, however, be used in a number of ways to promote student learning, retention and success. In our cases, we find some examples of how more innovative assessment tasks have been used to promote greater peer engagement among the students, and concomitantly, greater academic engagement.

In Case 9, Lesley McMillan and Lucy Solomon integrated weekly formative assessment into their statistics course for sociology students. Groups of students designed approaches to researching specific problems, and these were reviewed by the other students as well as staff. The use of culinary analogies gave the students, many of whom were mature, the confidence to talk about and critique each other's work in this area, and thus increase student interaction and provide useful feedback. In Case 10, Mark Russell used a new assessment strategy to encourage students to engage more with the material, with each other and with staff. Rather than relying on a summative end-of-module assessment, he introduced weekly assessments. These required all students to demonstrate their engagement in and understanding of the course through on-going engagement with the material, rather than just 'cramming' for an end-of-module assessment. The tasks were problem-based and this was intended to encourage discussion between students to solve the questions set – although each student was given a slightly different problem in order to avoid plagiarism. Furthermore, the assignments included open questions which were designed to encourage dialogue with staff about the learning process. This feedback in particular, as well as the performance of the students on the weekly assessments, provided staff with valuable information about the learning process, and enabled them to adjust their teaching accordingly.

In Case 11, Veronica Cahyadi used activities including Active Learning Problem sets and constructivist dialogue in the lectures. This meant that students could get feedback on their current understandings as their course progressed, and the teacher could gain feedback on the students' progress on a regular basis. Importantly, the peer and constructivist dialogue enabled the students to get valuable feedback so that they could align their ways of learning and their understandings with the expectations of the course and the discipline. This worked against students losing confidence and interest because of lack of understanding, encouraging them to continue. Kate Kirk explains in Case 14 how new students were provided with the opportunity to submit a short piece of writing for diagnostic purposes before their course began. This provided students with an indication of the expectations of academic writing in the early stages, positioning them to close any gaps that may have existed between their expectations and those of the university.

Improving academic skills to enhance engagement

Some students lack specific skills that would facilitate their academic and social engagement. Curricular changes can improve these skills and therefore increase engagement. For example, academic skills programmes are included in the curriculum to meet students' academic needs in Cases 13 and 14. In the PANDA case, students are positioned to engage through the development of their academic communication skills, both written and spoken. As the students developed the skills that underpinned their study success, their personal confidence increased, and they began to develop the demeanour and skills necessary for the medical profession on completion of their studies. Social engagement is assisted through the creation of a supportive student climate in the PANDA module, as students evaluate each other's oral presentations and provide advice and guidance.

In Case 14 the shape of the academic support programmes was determined through information obtained from the students themselves concerning their needs and situations. It included pre-course learning, induction, peer learning, and a tutorial system, among others. Socially, students related with each other in small group work and collaborative learning. The initial process of understanding students' experience of the course provided opportunities for social engagement as students participated in focus groups, and most importantly, their views were valued and acted on by their teachers in the ensuing curriculum development.

Increasing communication and understanding
between students and staff

Students often have limited opportunities to communicate with staff, and many students, particularly from non-traditional backgrounds, lack confidence to approach staff for information, advice and guidance. Therefore, mechanisms that increase communication, and thus understanding, between students and staff, can improve engagement.

For example, as noted above, in Case 10 Mark Russell has introduced weekly assessments that offer students a way of communicating with staff about their learning, and for staff, this process provides 'intelligence' about the issues students are struggling with, and areas that have been understood well. In Case 6 Chris Keenan uses the pre-entry work as an opportunity to encourage students to complete and return an on-line self-profiling questionnaire. This questionnaire asks them to report on their previous learning experiences and to reflect on them. This asks the students to reflect on how they feel about going to university, and to provide some examples of what they have enjoyed doing at school, and how they like to learn. One of the benefits of this approach is that students are able to share concerns about making the transition into higher education, and there is an opportunity to ask staff questions about their course, learning in higher education, etc., which helps to develop a rapport between tutor and student. The questionnaire, and the more informal interactions, can identify students who have particularly significant concerns about starting at university. Once identified these students can be offered additional support, which can include monitoring their attendance, or a more proactive approach, such as making personal contact just before the course starts. In Case 15 communication between the teacher and the students was facilitated as both parties saw each other in a situation outside the more hierarchical classroom, thus 'demystifying' the teacher and opening communication lines.

While communication between students and staff can occur on a more individual nature, as in the cases above, mechanisms can be put in place to encourage a 'mass' form of communication. For instance, in Case 14 the survey and focus groups were instruments used to communicate with a large number of students. The ensuing action based on students' responses completed the communication cycle, having the effect of assisting the students to feel that their voices are heard and that they do have some control over their course. In Case 15 the excursion shared by the students with their lecturer enabled both parties to understand each other out of the institutional setting.

Active learning

When students are active learners, they develop understanding and make meaning for themselves. This requires them to participate in activities where they need to analyse and evaluate information, and to apply it in a problem-solving way to new situations. Active learning may be contrasted with passive learning, where the student merely absorbs information from the teacher like an 'empty vessel', and restates it as demonstration of learning. Some of the ways in which the cases promote active learning are:

*   Encouraging students to take responsibility for their learning
*   Using teaching methods that promote collaboration and participation
*   Supporting students to learn from their own experiences
*   Providing formative feedback and feed-forward.

Taking responsibility for learning

Active learners take responsibility for their own learning, rather than being dependent on teaching staff. The extended induction programme at the University of Bournemouth (Case 6) encourages students to take greater responsibility for their learning from when they first accept a place on the programme. As discussed above, some of the preparatory exercises encourage students to reflect on their approaches to learning and enable them to play a more active role in their learning once the course begins.

The recognition that students come to university with different learning styles, some of them culturally specific, is discussed in several cases. For example, some students experienced a 'rote'-learning approach in their primary schooling; they needed to experience other learning styles if they are to be transformed from dependent to independent active learners. This was the challenge facing higher education staff in Case 1 as the students' early schooling in South Africa had been based on rote-learning and regurgitation of facts. Changing the focus of an English literature curriculum to foster critical reading skills (described above) was one of the ways a South African higher education institution responded. In Case 13 students' responsibility for their learning increased as they developed underpinning skills, For instance, oral communication skills were developed in the PANDA programme that would enable students to participate in class discussion and to engage with patients as part of their professional development skills.

Collaborative teaching methods to promote active learning

Many of the ways of promoting active learning are the use of alternative teaching methods that utilise student participation. For example, group work, workshops, games, projects, etc. require students to work together and engage with their studies in a more active way. These can be contrasted by more traditional approaches in which students play passive roles, for example, listening and taking notes.

The redesign of the introductory history module in Case 7 gave Digby Warren the opportunity to introduce a wide range of active learning tools. For example, he introduced task-oriented seminars, a small-group project, an essay-writing workshop and 'feed-forward' tutorials. These approaches encouraged students to work together and learn through collaboration and discussion with each other and staff, and to develop their knowledge incrementally. Similarly, Case 11 involves students in knowledge construction in physics, as the students participate in the activities in their lectures, rather than simply taking notes.

Another active learning opportunity is discussed in Case 4 when learning oral presentation skills in a teamwork setting was introduced. The students, from culturally diverse backgrounds, had to make presentations to each other and peer assessment was instituted. Students reported they were happy with learning these skills in a small group setting and with being assessed by their peers.

In Case 14 peer learning through seminars and small group discussions following lectures were introduced. The portfolio of learning and professional development shows students actively making meaning as they explain the contribution for their personal and academic development of their academic activities.

These are all examples of the use of tools that facilitate active learning in a classroom context, and without the need for major new learning materials. Learning from experience, discussed below, requires more fundamental curricular reform that takes the learning from the classroom to other settings. It is possible to incorporate it into established curriculum through special visits and activities, and these may operate as trials or pilots for more substantial 'outside' learning. For example, Case 15 discusses one such instance. However, a thorough experience-based approach requires significant change, as seen in the following cases.

Learning from experience

Active learning is facilitated by the use of real-world experiences, which require students to be more directly involved in the learning process. In Case 5 John Bamber describes how a focus on active learning facilitated the involvement of a class of part-time mature-age students, many of whom had been absent from education for a considerable period of time. Bamber recognised the power of participatory learning to engage and retain his students. They were empowered to discover elements of course content and knowledge for themselves, thus reshaping the teacher's role from an authority figure and source of knowledge to a facilitator of the students' learning. In achieving this, John explains how the major learning for the course was placed in the workplace, and the classroom was used as a forum for reflection and discussion of workplace issues and their resolution.

Rather than taking notes in a large lecture theatre on a city campus, students in the cultural awareness immersion programme outlined in Case 2 were able to learn about Indigenous perspectives from Australian Indigenous people in a remote outback setting. Furthermore, they were able to discuss their learning directly with their teachers. When one member of the group became ill, they had the opportunity to apply some of that knowledge in a remote location, with all the challenges working in outback Australia presents to practitioners in their professions. In Case 12 Janette Ryan explains how the students apply the theoretical aspect of their education studies in their community projects in local primary schools. Perhaps unwittingly, they use this knowledge as they conduct a needs analysis to identify issues, negotiate with the school community and university staff to set up a project to address the issue, design it, and then implement it. The academic development of the students that occurs as they undertake their projects is reflected in their philosophies of learning and teaching which are recorded in their fieldwork reflections; no longer do they solely perceive themselves as educators as the teacher in charge, but more as the facilitators of the learning of others.

It is not always possible to enable students to learn directly from experience – either their own past experiences, or new experiences that are delivered as part of the learning opportunity. This has resulted in development of 'problem-based' or 'project-based' learning activities, which draw from the real world, but often take place in the classroom. For example, in Case 8 Betty Leask has made use of simple but effective independent and group project-based research activities to create an active learning environment. Students use email and the internet to research and develop their understanding of specific issues from the perspective of people from other countries and cultures.

Feed-forward and feedback

Another way in which the cases are promoting active learning is through feed-forward and feedback. This helps students to gain greater understanding of the learning process, to play a more active part in it, and, in the feed-forward aspect, provides information to the teacher on the students' learning, for incorporation in the teaching approach. In Case 9 the authors utilise peer formative assessment to contribute to their construction of knowledge about quantitative methods. This teaching approach is facilitated by the use of culinary analogies in the teaching of quantitative research methods, as this provides the students with the language and confidence to talk about and critically assess each others' work. In Case 13 the PANDA module students receive feedback from each other to assist them further develop their presentation skills. In his new history module described in Case 7 Digby Warren introduced an essay-writing workshop. This participative approach enabled students to understand what is required of a history essay in higher education – thus this feed-forward gave greater information and control to assist them to be successful in their first essay.

Reflective questions

This penultimate section of the book offers a set of reflective questions to assist readers to review their own teaching practices and to consider ways in which curriculum development might assist students further to be effective, engaged, deep learners, and to remain in higher education and be successful. Some questions are:

- How aware are you of your students' backgrounds, previous educational experiences and other interests? What methods do you use within your teaching to find out about these issues?
- How do these aspects shape your students' expectations of their education?
- In what ways do you support students to be responsible for their own learning?
- Do you include sufficient collaborative and participative learning approaches in your teaching to enable students to get to know each other and become active learners?
- In what ways could you draw on students' own experiences more to help them engage in their learning and to become more active?
- Could you utilise problem-based or project-based learning activities rather than lectures to teach any more aspects of your course?
- Is your induction process engaging, participatory and focused on improving transparency of expectations and norms?
- Are academic skills built into your curriculum?
- How would you describe your relationship with your students? Are there ways in which you could develop more communication channels with them?
- What forms of assessment do you use? Is there scope for a wider range of methods, and to incorporate feed-forward as well as feedback to assist students to have a better understanding of their learning?

Conclusion

Effectively addressing retention issues cannot be achieved through one-off interventions which take place outside of the classroom. The changing context of mass

HE means that students are often no longer able to participate in the co-curriculum in the way they could in the past. An integrated approach which benefits all students is required, and thus curriculum change is essential. In this book we have explored the pedagogical issues that pertain to curriculum change and provide a set of real-world examples to illustrate how others have improved student retention and achievement. In this chapter we have extracted the key issues that need to be considered when developing curriculum-based approaches to improving student retention and success.

What is evident is that changes stimulated or necessitated by a particular group of students benefit all students, and thus have a positive impact on the achievement and retention of the whole cohort. Thus, many, if not all of the curriculum developments discussed in this book would be considered as good learning and teaching practice *per se*, rather than remedial measures. Many of the case authors were prompted to take action because of challenging circumstances (e.g. poor retention rates, high number of assessment failures, etc.), but the learning from their experiences has the potential for much wider application.

We hope that the book is of use to our readers. We hope that it stimulates thinking about student retention and success, and provides a rationale for curriculum-based approaches, examples of changes that other colleagues have made, inspiration and, importantly, encouragement for people to review their own practice in the light of their students and their educational objectives. The authors/editors are very happy to communicate with readers on the issues addressed in this book, and email addresses have been included in the preliminary section.

References

House of Commons Select Committee on Education and Employment (2001) *Sixth Report, Higher Education: Student Retention*. Online. Available www.publications. parliament.uk.

Long, M., Ferrier, F., and Heagney, M. (2006) *Stay, Play or Give it Away? Students Continuing, Changing or Leaving University Study in First Year* (Canberra: Department of Education, Science and Training, Commonwealth of Australia). Available online www.dest.gov.au/sectors/higher_education/publications_resources/profiles/.

NAO (National Audit Office) (2002) *Improving Student Achievement in English Higher Education*. Report by the Comptroller and Auditor General (London: The Stationery Office).

Yorke, M. and Longden, B. (2004) *Retention and Student Success in Higher Education* (Maidenhead, UK: Open University Press).

Index